THE WORLD'S GREATEST
MILITARY AIRCRAFT
AN ILLUSTRATED HISTORY

THE WORLD'S GREATEST
MILITARY AIRCRAFT
AN ILLUSTRATED HISTORY

Thomas Newdick

amber
BOOKS

Published by
Amber Books Ltd
74–77 White Lion Street
London
N1 9PF
United Kingdom
www.amberbooks.co.uk
Appstore: itunes.com/apps/amberbooksltd
Facebook: www.facebook.com/amberbooks
Twitter: @amberbooks

ISBN: 978-1-78274-263-0

Project Editor: Michael Spilling
Picture Research: Terry Forshaw
Design: Andrew Easton

Printed in China

PICTURE CREDITS:
Art-Tech/Aerospace: 8–17 (all), 21 (top), 24–81 (all), 89–105 (all), 119, 155
Dassault: 183, 203
Ukrainian State Archive: 85
U.S. Department of Defense: 21 (bottom), 110, 123–151 (all), 163, 171, 175, 187, 195, 199, 206–219 (all)

All artworks courtesy Art-Tech except for the following:
Military Visualizations, Inc: 216–218 (all)

Contents

Introduction

From the frail, canvas-covered machines that fought over the trenches in World War I, to the sophisticated, high-performance super-fighters of the twenty-first century, military aircraft have come an enormous way in a century of air warfare.

With one exception, all the famous aircraft presented in this book have, to varying degrees, forged their reputations in combat: most recently, the US Air Force's premier air dominance fighter, the F-22 Raptor, which first saw battle over Syria in 2014. The Raptor, which represents the so-called 'fifth generation' of manned fighter, continues an illustrious line that began in World War I, when the first purpose-designed fixed-wing combat aircraft were fielded.

In the first half of the 20th century, the development of the manned fighter was spurred on by two world wars, in the course of which pilots progressed from firing at

World War II saw military aircraft come of age, as they began to take on an increasing range of missions in theatres across the globe. Typical was the B-25 Mitchell, developed as a medium bomber but equally efficient in roles as diverse as maritime patrol and photo-reconnaissance.

each other with hand-held small arms from open cockpits to attacking enemy aircraft in the air, and targets on the ground, with increasingly powerful and sophisticated armament, up to and including the first, primitive rockets and missiles. The fighters described in the following pages represent different design philosophies in the effort to provide the most effective blend of a range of sometimes conflicting requirements: performance, manoeuvrability, strength, handling and firepower. With the F-35 Lightning II, the only aircraft included that is yet to see operational service in a combat environment, the manufacturer and customer air forces aim to provide the ultimate combination of these demands. Only time will tell how successful is this latest bid at providing the 'definitive' all-round fighter.

While fighters remain the most familiar military aircraft, and dominate this type selection, attention is also given to bombers, which also launched their first raids during

The French Rafale is typical of the latest generation of multi-functional warplanes. However, the acquisition and operating costs of such advanced platforms puts them beyond the reach of all but the most wealthy air forces.

World War I. In the course of World War II, the delineation between the strategic bomber – primarily intended for long-range bombing missions against key fixed targets including cities – and the tactical bomber – typically intended for striking objectives close to the front lines or for attacking enemy shipping – became increasingly blurred. At the same time, the expanding potential of the fighter permitted the introduction of a new class of fighter-bomber that could undertake either defensive or offensive missions. Although the fighter-bomber was further developed to yield multi-role fighters, the first true exponents of which appeared in service mid-way through the Cold War, there remains a place in the 21st century for the dedicated long-range bomber, like the B-2 Spirit and the venerable B-52 Stratofortress.

With a few exceptions, however, today's front-line warplanes are typically intended to be flexible in terms of role and application. Multinational projects like the Eurofighter Typhoon bring air defence and offensive capabilities together in a single airframe. While earlier generations of dual-role or multi-role fighters could perhaps only conduct a single function during the course of a mission, advanced fighters like the Typhoon and Dassault Rafale can switch between missions in the course of a single sortie: their respective manufacturers thus describe them as 'swing-role' or 'omni-role'.

The era of military aircraft tailor-made for a single role has almost disappeared. Back in World War II there was still a place for a dedicated night-fighter, such as the P-61 Black Widow, or a heavily armoured close support aircraft like the Il-2 *Shturmovik*. Today, the A-10 Thunderbolt II 'tank-buster' is a rarity, and one whose long-term future has consistently come under threat.

Support Roles

The very first role in which manned aircraft found themselves co-opted by the military was reconnaissance, and this exacting mission has seen the consistent development of a series of innovative specialist designs.

The demands of range, invulnerability and stealth have led to some classic reconnaissance aircraft, ranging from the versatile de Havilland Mosquito to the breathtaking SR-71. More recently, however, the role of intelligence-gathering has increasingly fallen to reconnaissance satellites and unmanned aerial vehicles, or drones.

Today, even military transport aircraft are often expected to possess the versatility to undertake duties in addition to the simple conveyance of personnel or cargo. Since World War II at the latest, the value of transport aircraft to the military has never been in doubt. However, such types lack the glamour and popular appeal of their fighter and bomber cousins, and have tended to be neglected. Just two examples, the long-lived C-47 Skytrain and the record-breaking C-5 Galaxy are present in this book, but their respective contributions to successive military and humanitarian campaigns cannot be overstated.

World War I and World War II

While the military aeroplane came of age during World War I, aircraft design underwent unprecedented progress in the years between the wars. In the process, the primarily wooden and fabric scout and reconnaissance biplanes and triplanes that provided the bulk of the combat aircraft fleets during World War I were superseded by sleek monoplanes with enclosed cockpits, retractable undercarriage, purpose-designed armament and powerful engines offering performance more than doubled compared to their forebears. By the end of World War II, the first jets were also in service, heralding a new era.

Opposite: A British Royal Air Force recovery team examine the fuselage of a *Luftwaffe* Junkers Ju 88 shot down during the Battle of Britain, July 1940.

🇬🇧 Sopwith Camel (1916)

Perhaps the most famous British fighter of World War I, the F.1 Camel typified the increasing aerial dominance enjoyed by the Allies from early 1918, but was a handful to fly, demanding the very finest qualities from those who piloted it.

Apparently (and unofficially) named in recognition of the distinctive 'hump' over the breeches for its twin Vickers machine guns, the Herbert Smith-designed Sopwith Camel appeared in prototype form in December 1916, powered by a Clerget engine. Originally designated as the Biplane F.1, the fighter was schemed with equal dihedral (the upward angle given to the wing) on both upper and lower wings, but this was abandoned in a bid to ease manufacture. Instead, the aircraft featured a flat upper wing, while the dihedral on the lower wing was doubled. The result was a characteristic 'tapered gap' between the wings.

Unlike the Sopwith Pup and Triplane that preceded it, the Camel was notably tricky to fly. It was blessed with

Armament
The two synchronized forward-firing Vickers machine guns could be supplemented by up to four 11kg (25lb) bombs carried externally.

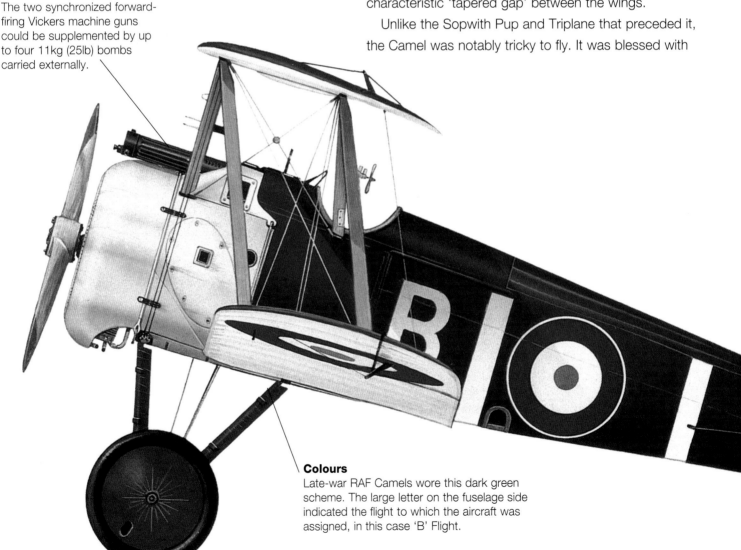

Colours
Late-war RAF Camels wore this dark green scheme. The large letter on the fuselage side indicated the flight to which the aircraft was assigned, in this case 'B' Flight.

Sopwith Camel

Camel F6314 was on strength with No.120 Squadron, part of the newly established Royal Air Force in 1918. The unit saw much action during the German offensive on the Western Front in spring 1918.

Construction

The Camel was built on the basis of a conventional wire-braced wooden box girder structure, with aluminium covering immediately aft of the engine. Further aft, the covering was plywood as far as the rear of the cockpit, while the rear fuselage was covered with fabric.

power in abundance and its agility was manifest in a very tight turning circle. Schemed as a more agile successor to the Pup, the Camel was also more powerful and somewhat heavier.

A key factor in its manoeuvrability was the fact that the power unit, pilot and armament were all concentrated within a limited volume at the front of the fighter, and were combined with enormous engine torque and gyroscopic couple. One particular trait was experienced during a turn to the left: the nose would rise abruptly, while a turn in the opposite direction would see the nose drop. The pilot had to make extensive use of the rudder to counteract these habits, and prevent the fighter entering an uncontrollable spin. In certain scenarios, pilots discovered they could forego a simple one-quarter left-hand turn in favour of a three-quarter right turn, which some argued could be executed faster – and with a useful disorientating effect on a potential foe. In one example of wartime gallows' humour, RFC pilots joked that the Camel offered the choice between 'a wooden cross, the Red Cross or a Victoria Cross'.

If mastered, the Camel could be unbeatable in an aerial duel, but it remained unforgiving. Among the leading Commonwealth aces who flew the Camel were Raymond Collishaw (who scored a total of 60 victories on this and other types), Donald MacClaren (54), William

Sopwith Camel

Barker (53) and Henry Woolett (35, including six in a single day in March 1918), while flying Camels.

Maiden Flight

The first prototype F.1, ordered by the Admiralty, completed its maiden flight in February 1917 and was followed by two more development airframes with

The navalized 2F.1 variant differed from the basic Camel in its armament of a single Vickers gun in the port position, supplemented by a Lewis gun above the wing centre section.

different engines. Initial Camel deliveries were to the Royal Naval Air Service (RNAS) in May 1917. The first Camels into action, albeit without claiming any kills, were RNAS examples stationed at Dunkirk, which scrambled to intercept a formation of German Gotha bombers after the latter had raided the coastal town of Harwich, Essex, in July 1917. In the same month the Camel began to be delivered to the Royal Flying Corps (RFC), equipping No.70 and No.45 Squadrons that month. July saw the Battle of Ypres, in which RFC Camels were involved. By the end of 1917 no fewer than 1325 F.1 Camels had been accepted into service.

The majority of aircraft were delivered with Clerget, Le Rhône, Gnome or Bentley radial engines. Production continued after the end of World War I, and ultimately over 5000 examples were built by nine different contractors.

As well as their service on the Western Front, Camels saw action on the Home Front with RFC night-fighting

Specification

Type:	Fighter
Dimensions:	Length: 5.64m (18ft 6in); Wingspan: 8.53m (28ft 0in); Height: 2.59m (8ft 6in)
Weight:	667kg (1471lb) maximum take-off
Powerplant:	1 x 112kW (150hp) Bentley B.R.1 9-cylinder rotary piston engine
Maximum speed:	187km/h (117mph)
Endurance:	2 hours 30 minutes
Service ceiling:	6095m (20,000ft)
Crew:	1
Armament:	2 x 7.7mm (0.303in) fixed forward-firing Vickers machine guns

units, in Italy, in the Adriatic and Aegean with the RNAS. American-flown Camels served with the 17th Aero Squadron of the U.S. Army Air Service in France, albeit mainly demoted to training duties. Equipped for the night-fighting role, Camels of the Home Defence Squadrons featured a revised cockpit mounted further aft and twin Lewis guns replacing the Vickers weapons. It was in this role that a Camel achieved the first recorded fighter victory over an aircraft at night, downing a Gotha bomber over London in January 1918. Some Camels were also used for ground-attack work, notably at the Battle of Cambrai in March 1918. Indeed, a specialist ground-attack version was developed, as the T.F.1 (Trench Fighter), equipped with downward-firing machine guns, but this did not enter production.

By the end of the conflict, Camels had been credited with downing a greater number of enemy aircraft than any other fighter, the figure – based on official records – exceeding 3000. Contributing to this impressive tally was one remarkable individual aircraft, B6313, flown by Canadian RFC pilot William 'Billy' Barker. The pilot retained this same aircraft as he progressed through the ranks of different squadrons in France and Italy, and even when assigned to a Bristol Fighter squadron. In this time, the combination of Barker and his B6313 accounted for a total of 48 enemy aircraft destroyed – likely to be the highest tally of any single aircraft. Following the war, Camels served with the Royal Air Force in Archangel, Russia, as part of the Slavo-British Aviation Group, which included the ace Alexander Kazakov, who had been most successful Russian flying ace of World War I.

Camels at Sea

With the aim of providing aircraft for launch from light cruisers, Sopwith developed a naval version of the Camel. The prototype for the navalized Camel, the FS.1, was equipped with jettisonable wheeled undercarriage for launch, and floats for landing. The wings were shortened and the rear fuselage could be folded for stowage within a warship. From summer 1917 the Camel began to be flown off the decks of warships, now under the revised designation 2F.1. Beginning the following year, the Clerget-powered aircraft were deployed aboard Royal Navy battleships. In July 1918, seven bomb-armed Camels flying from the deck of HMS *Furious* attacked the Zeppelin sheds at Tondern, destroying *L.54* and *L.60*. However, only two of the Camels returned safely to the ship.

Another maritime use of the Camel involved taking off on skids or wheels from towed lighters. This method was used to good effect in August 1918, when a lighter-launched Camel downed the Zeppelin *L.53* over the North Sea – this was the last German airship claimed in the war. Other naval Camels were used in experiments to provide airships with fighter protection, the fighters being released from *R.23* using a trapeze mechanism.

Fokker Dr.I (1917)

Thanks to the exploits of the legendary 'Red Baron', the Fokker Dr.I has become the archetypal fighter of World War I in terms of the public imagination. Aside from its fame, the Fokker Triplane suffered from a number of operational shortcomings.

The Fokker *Dreidecker* (triplane) was conceived as a response to the British Sopwith Triplane fighting scout. Designed by Reinhold Platz, the Dr.I was intended to counter the feared manoeuvrability and rate of climb enjoyed by the Sopwith machine, which had begun to appear over the Western Front with the Royal Naval Air Service (RNAS) in early 1917. The wreckage of least one Sopwith Triplane ended up at the Fokker factory in Schwerin, where it helped inform the Dr.I, although the first iteration of the Fokker Triplane incorporated three cantilever wings without interplane struts.

First flown in prototype V.4 form in May 1917, the aircraft suffered from severe wing vibration before interplane

Tail
The 'comma' rudder without a separate fin was a classic trademark of Anthony Fokker's early fighter designs. A tailskid was fitted immediately below the rudder.

Fokker Dr.I serial number 152/17 was one of a batch of 30 built early in the production run. Assigned to Jasta 11, the aircraft was one of a number flown (albeit not exclusively) by Manfred von Richthofen and was preserved after the war.

One of a number of Dr.Is flown by the 'Red Baron', it was serial number 425/17 in which von Richthofen met his death. It is uncertain whether he fell victim to a Sopwith Camel flown by Arthur Brown or by ground fire from Australian troops.

Gun Armament
The twin LMG 08/15 'Spandau' guns were arranged side-by-side in the upper part of the forward fuselage. Air-cooled and belt-fed, the weapons were each provided with 500 rounds of ammunition, housed behind the fuel tank.

Lifting Surface
The impressive agility of the Fokker Dr.I was further enhanced by an additional lifting surface (aerofoil) that enclosed the axle of the fixed main undercarriage.

Configuration
In its three-wing layout, the Dr.I was one of a number of contemporary fighting scouts to adopt the proven configuration of the British Sopwith Triplane.

Fokker Dr.I

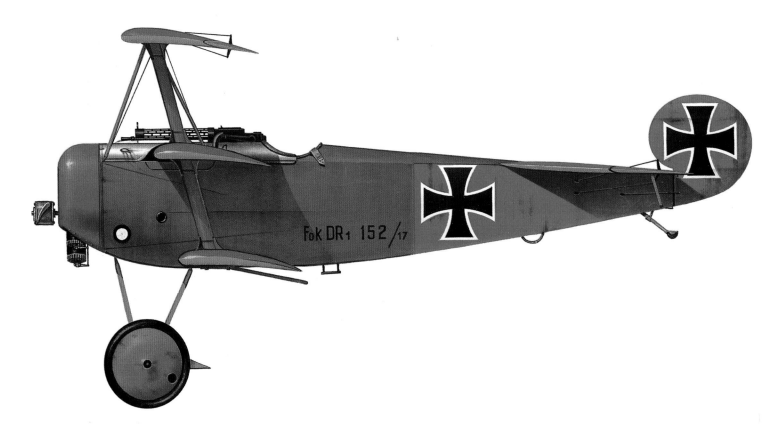

struts were added, linking the wings near their tips and thereby providing strengthening. While the V.4 was originally developed to meet an Imperial Austro-Hungarian requirement, a further V.4 and two revised V.5 prototypes were completed in accordance with a German contract. The V.5 established the pertinent features of the subsequent production machine, including a Thulin licence-built Le Rhône radial engine (or alternatively the unlicensed

A side view of Dr.I 152/17 reveals the characteristic slab-sided fuselage, strut-braced tailplane and fixed landing gear. A key attribute of the *Dreidecker* was its simple, low-cost construction.

Oberursel copy of the same engine) and armament of twin 'Spandau' machine guns firing forward through the propeller arc using synchronizing gear. The 'definitive' V.7 prototype, meanwhile, was used to test different powerplant options and also introduced modified wings, with span increasing from bottom to top.

Production Run

After testing in the hands of the famed ace Werner Voss, the *Dreidecker* was ordered into production (originally as the F.I, soon revised to Dr.I) in summer 1917, and on 21 August the first two prototype examples were taken on charge by Jagdgeschwader 1 based at Courtrai, Flanders. The two aircraft were immediately assigned to leading fighter aces Manfred von Richthofen, and Voss, the commander of Jasta 1. On his very first Triplane mission on 30 August, Voss claimed a victory while von Richthofen repeated the feat two days later, to score his 160th victory. Von Richthofen's first Dr.I was lost in combat with Sopwith Camels of No.10 Squadron, RNAS, while in the hands of another pilot, Kurt Wolff of

Specification

Type:	Fighter
Dimensions:	Length: 5.77m (18ft 11in); Wingspan: 7.19m (23ft 7in); Height: 2.95m (9ft 8in)
Weight:	586kg (1291lb) maximum take-off
Powerplant:	1 x 82kW (110hp) Oberusel Ur.11 8-cylinder rotary piston engine
Maximum speed:	185km/h (115mph)
Range:	300km (185 miles)
Service ceiling:	6100m (20,015ft)
Crew:	1
Armament:	2 x 7.92mm (0.31in) fixed forward-firing LMG 08/15 machine guns

Jasta 11. Voss enjoyed success in his aircraft, claiming 21 enemy aircraft shot down between 30 August and 23 September, when he was killed in battle with SE.5s of No.56 Squadron, Royal Flying Corps.

Despite the early modifications to improve wing stiffness, the initial *Dreidecker* suffered a number of structural failures, typically involving the loss of the upper wing. This was attributed to poor workmanship and deterioration of the wing's fabric covering. The entire Dr.I fleet was grounded as work began to replace the defective upper wings, and the result was a significant delay in deliveries to the front line.

Fearsome Reputation

Once in battle, the Dr.I soon displayed its hoped for agility. By late 1917 operating restrictions placed on the fighter had been lifted, and the Fokker Triplane soon experienced success over the Western Front in the hands of other pilots, including Lothar von Richthofen, Hermann Göring, Ernst Udet and Adolf Ritter von Tutschek. The wing fault, however, continued to have an effect on availability, and as of November 1917 there were only 30 examples of the *Dreidecker* with combat units, from a total of around 170 planned to have been delivered by this date. Ultimately, the Dr.I equipped at least 15 Jastas, although it was relatively quickly eclipsed by more capable Allied fighters. Compared to its rivals, the Dr.I was lacking in straight-line speed, leaving it vulnerable, and its rotary engine was also representative of a previous generation of fighting scouts. On the other hand, expert fliers like Manfred von Richthofen prized the Fokker Triplane for its manoeuvrability and rate of climb, the latter factor aided by the radial powerplant.

Flying Circus

Alongside its undoubted prowess in aerial combat, the notoriety of the Dr.I among Allied pilots was certainly sealed by the activities of Manfred von Richthofen's Jagdgeschwader 1, the 'Flying Circus' (or 'Richthofen's Circus'), in which pilots were encouraged to apply eye-catching personalized colour schemes to their mounts.

While the propaganda value of Jagdgeschwader 1 did serve to exaggerate the capabilities of the Fokker Triplane, the reputation of the Dr.I among German pilots was such that certain leading exponents continued to fly the type even after the arrival of more modern equipment. Although 320 examples were eventually built by the time production ended in May 1918, at no time were there more than 171 Dr.Is in service, making it all the more impressive that it became such a feared foe, and in such a relatively short space of time.

The 'Red Baron'

Born into an aristocratic family in Silesia in 1892, Manfred Freiherr von Richthofen was the leading air ace of World War I, with 80 aerial victories. Commencing flying training in May 1915, he began his career as an observer on the Eastern Front, before training as a fighter pilot. Transferring to the Western Front, and Jasta 2, he scored his first kill near Cambrai on 17 September 1916, his victim an F.E.2b. After 16 victories in Albatros D. IIs, von Richthofen was given command of Jasta 11, where he scored 40 kills in a period of just six months. He was appointed commander of the first Jagdgeschwader in June 1917, and he was leading JG 1 when killed in action on 21 April 1918.

SPAD XIII (1917)

Famed as the colourful mount of the American Expeditionary Air Force's 94th Aero Squadron, the French SPAD XIII was one of the finest Allied fighting scouts of the war, and was also flown by renowned aces Guynemer and Fonck.

First flown in April 1917, the SPAD (Société Pour L'Aviation et ses Dérivés) XIII was designed by Louis Bechereau as a development of the earlier SPAD VII and added a new powerplant in the form of a more powerful, geared Hispano-Suiza 8a that drove a propeller in the opposite direction to that of its predecessor. This power unit was markedly superior to the inline Benz engines that powered German Albatros fighters of the time. Other modifications made to the SPAD XIII compared to the earlier aircraft included inverse tapered-chord ailerons, a slightly increased wingspan and rounded tips to the tailplane and vertical fin. Increased rudder area served to enhance the fighter's

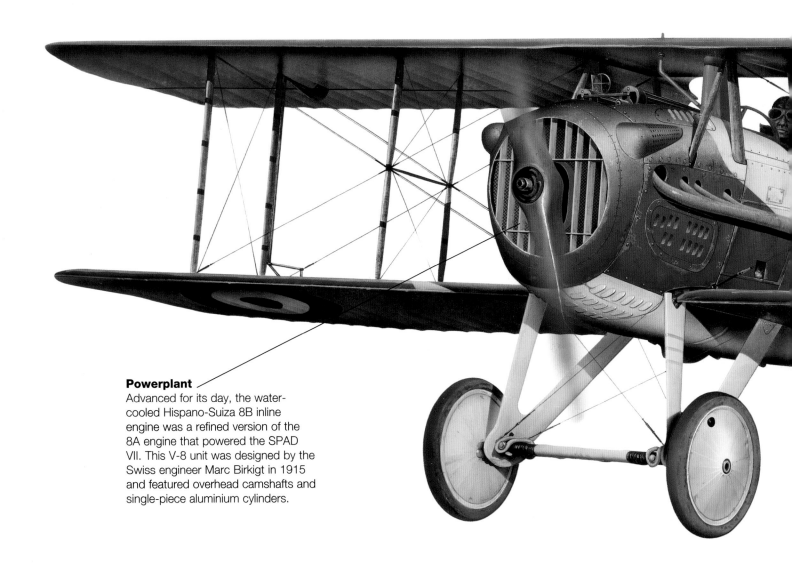

Powerplant
Advanced for its day, the water-cooled Hispano-Suiza 8B inline engine was a refined version of the 8A engine that powered the SPAD VII. This V-8 unit was designed by the Swiss engineer Marc Birkigt in 1915 and featured overhead camshafts and single-piece aluminium cylinders.

manoeuvrability. The revised armament consisted of a pair of Vickers guns, using synchronizing gear to fire through the propeller arc.

Rugged Construction

The SPAD VII was already a potent fighter, heavier and faster than many of its contemporaries and although less agile it was of notably rugged construction. These same qualities were inherited by the SPAD XIII, which offered similarly sparkling performance, a result of the SPAD's heritage in the successful line of Deperdussin racers (SPAD being the successor organization to Deperdussin when the latter declared bankruptcy in 1913). However, the fighters proved trickier to handle during take-off and landing, a result of the considerable torque generated by the engine. In order to counter this, the pilot was required to make

liberal use of left rudder. In contrast to many fighters of its era, the SPAD was also unable to glide, which required full engine power on landing. Once on the ground, the pilot had to be careful to avoid ground-looping.

The first examples of the new SPAD fighter reached the Western Front by the end of May 1917. It was in the cockpit of a SPAD XIII that the French ace Georges Guynemer (53 victories) met his mysterious death over Poelcapelle in September 1917. Shot down seven times prior to his final mission, the exact circumstances of Guynemer's demise have never been fully established, and neither the body of the pilot or the wreckage of his aircraft were ever recovered.

Meanwhile, René Fonck, the leading Allied ace of World War I, scored most of his officially credited 75 victories in the SPAD XIII (Fonck put his personal tally at 127 victories).

Wing
The construction of the wing was based on hollow spruce box bars with plywood ribs. The leading edges and wingtips of thin, shaped wooden strip, while the trailing edges were of stretched fabric.

Construction
Typical for its day, the SPAD XIII was fabric-covered from behind the cockpit, with aluminium panels for the nose and cowling. The fuselage was constructed of four longerons with spruce struts and stringers.

This French SPAD XIII wears the crowing cockerel insignia of Escadrille SPA 48 along the rear fuselage. French squadron numbers were prefixed by the basic type of aircraft flown by the unit, 'SPA' in this case designating the SPAD fighter.

SPAD XIII

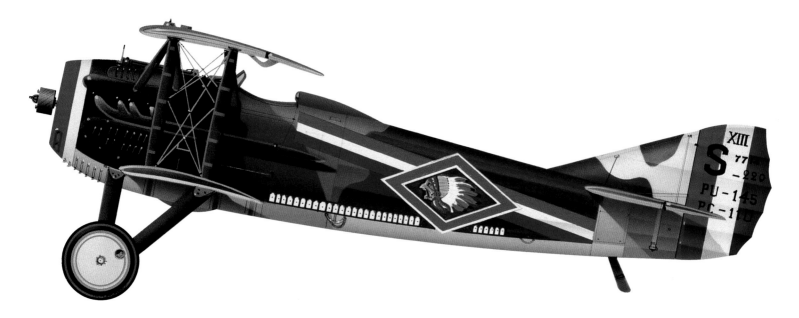

The insignia of the Lafayette Escadrille is worn on the fuselage of SPAD XIII C.1 serial number S7714. Many members of Lafayette joined the 103rd Aero Squadron after the U.S. entered the war.

In one famous incident, Fonck's marksmanship and use of deflection shooting despatched three enemy aircraft with just 27 rounds fired. In a separate incident, Fonck despatched three enemy aircraft and troops on the ground found their wreckage all within a radius of just 400m (1312ft). On two separate occasions, Fonck succeeded in downing six enemy aircraft in a single day. Another leading French ace to fly the type was Charles Nungesser,

who finished the war with 43 victories. The SPAD was not agile enough to take on the Fokker Dr.I on its own terms, but excelled in the dive, lending itself to 'hit and run' tactics, engaging the enemy in a single, high-speed diving manoeuvre.

American Service

The U.S. decision to adopt the SPAD XIII was taken in July 1918, seeking a successor to the problematic Nieuport 28. Of the American pilots to serve in World War I, the most celebrated was Eddie Rickenbacker of the American Expeditionary Force's 94th Aero Squadron 'Hat in the Ring'. Rickenbacker was the much decorated leading ace of the Expeditionary Force, with most of his 26 victories coming in a period of a few weeks at the end of the war.

In the word's of Rickenbacker himself, the SPAD XIII was 'the best ship I flew'. Meanwhile, Frank Luke Jr was the fastest-scoring American pilot, with a tally of 18 achieved flying SPAD XIIIs, including a number of observation balloons.

At the outset, production of the SPAD XIII was somewhat slow. By the time of the last major German offensives of the war, in March 1918, SPAD XIIIs were still outnumbered in service by SPAD VIIs. By this time, the earlier aircraft was outclassed by the German Fokker D.VII. However, during the last 14 months of fighting, a total of 81 French escadrilles were flying the SPAD XIII, and these were joined by two squadrons of the British Royal Flying Corps, as well as additional

Specification

Type:	Fighter
Dimensions:	Length: 6.15m (20ft 2.5in); Wingspan: 7.80m (25ft 7.75in); Height: 2.12m (6ft 11.5in)
Weight:	740kg (1631lb) maximum take-off
Powerplant:	1 x 112kW (150hp) Hispano-Suiza 8Aa V-8 inline piston engine
Maximum speed:	192km/h (119mph)
Endurance:	2 hours 15 minutes
Service ceiling:	5300m (17,390ft)
Crew:	1
Armament:	1 or 2 x 7.7mm (0.303in) fixed forward-firing Vickers machine guns

Belgian and Italian units. In the case of Italy, the SPAD XIII was flown by Francesco Baracca, the leading World War I ace of that country, with 34 aerial victories. By the time of the Armistice a total of 16 American pursuit squadrons were operating SPAD XIIIs.

Post-war Service

Ultimately, an impressive total of over 8000 SPAD XIIIs

Another view of S7714 together with pilot Robert Soubiran of the 103rd Aero Squadron, U.S. Army Air Service. The aircraft was based at Lisle-en-Barrois, northeast France, in November 1918.

were completed. Post-war operators included Japan, Poland and Czechoslovakia, while SPADs remained with the U.S. Army Air Service until the mid-1920s, latterly in the fighter training role.

Eddie Rickenbacker

Born in Columbus, Ohio, Edward Rickenbacker was a famous racing driver before the U.S. entered World War I. Enlisting in the U.S. Army as General Pershing's chauffeur, Rickenbacker transferred to the Air Service soon after arriving in France and learned to fly. Rickenbacker then requested a transfer to the front, where he joined the 94th Aero Squadron, a unit that he went on to command. Rickenbacker emerged as the leading U.S. ace of World War I, with 26 confirmed victories. In one remarkable action in September 1918, Rickenbacker tackled a group of seven enemy aircraft, and successfully launched an attack, downing two of them. Rickenbacker survived the war and received the Medal of Honor in 1930.

Junkers Ju 87 Stuka (1935)

The Stuka is remembered as a symbol of the success of Nazi Germany's Blitzkrieg operations in 1939 and 1940. Although rapidly outclassed in its original dive-bomber role, the Ju 87 saw service with the *Luftwaffe* until the end of the war.

The Sturzkampfflugzeug (dive-bomber, abbreviated to Stuka) concept was tailored to support Nazi Germany's Blitzkrieg combined-arms doctrine. A form of flying artillery support, work on three prototypes commenced in 1934

with the design team headed by Hermann Pohlmann, and the Ju 87 was first flown in September 1935. The earliest prototypes featured twin tailfins and a Rolls-Royce Kestrel engine. However, this aircraft was lost in dive

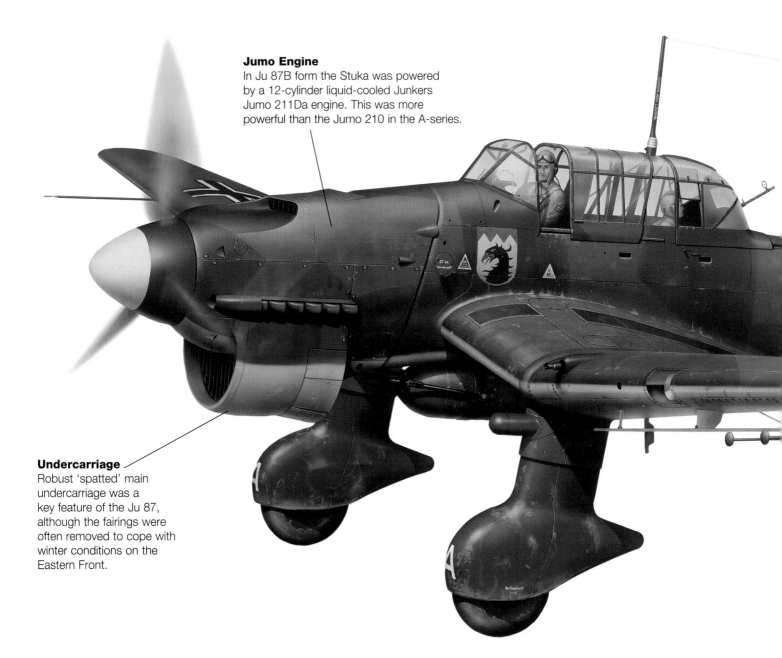

Jumo Engine
In Ju 87B form the Stuka was powered by a 12-cylinder liquid-cooled Junkers Jumo 211Da engine. This was more powerful than the Jumo 210 in the A-series.

Undercarriage
Robust 'spatted' main undercarriage was a key feature of the Ju 87, although the fairings were often removed to cope with winter conditions on the Eastern Front.

tests when the tail unit collapsed. The second prototype employed a single fin and a Junkers V12 Jumo 210A petrol engine. The prototypes were followed by a pre-production batch of Ju 87A-0 aircraft, now with the Jumo 210Ca engine.

When the initial Ju 87A-1 production version entered service in spring 1937, it soon began to replace the Henschel Hs 123 biplane in the close support units of the fledgling *Luftwaffe*. Small numbers of Ju 87A-1s and B-1s were deployed by the Legion Condor for testing under operational conditions in the Spanish Civil War during 1938–39. Here they met little in the way of fighter opposition and did much to convince *Luftwaffe* leaders of the viability of the Stuka concept.

By the time of the invasion of Poland in September 1939, the *Luftwaffe* included nine Stukagruppen, all equipped with Ju 87s, and the dive-bomber developed a notorious reputation as a terror weapon, striking lines of communication, bridges, rail targets and airfields. On occasions, the *Luftwaffe* further exploited the psychological effect of the Stuka attacks by fitting the aircraft with sirens, so-called 'trumpets of Jericho'. However, the Ju 87 relied upon air superiority in order to deliver its tactical blows with the required accuracy, and in the course of the Battle of France it revealed itself vulnerable to fighter interception.

During the Norwegian campaign, when the Stukas enjoyed success in attacks on British shipping, efforts were made to extend the range of the Ju 87, resulting in the

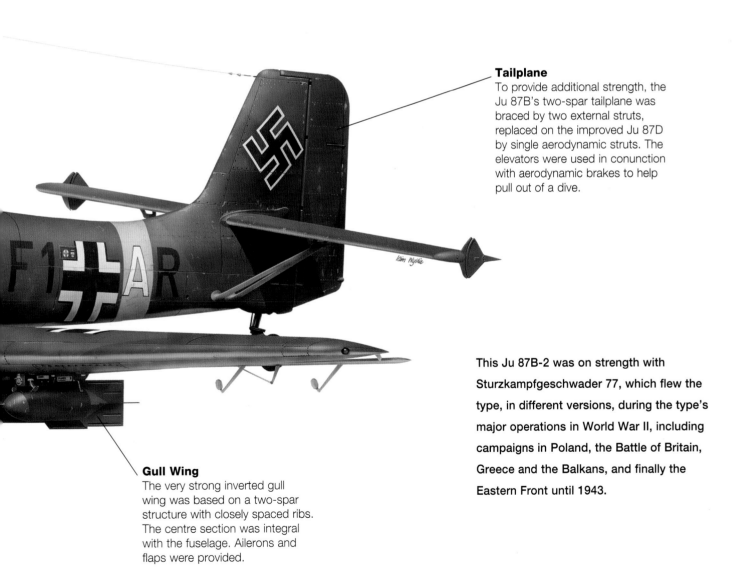

Tailplane
To provide additional strength, the Ju 87B's two-spar tailplane was braced by two external struts, replaced on the improved Ju 87D by single aerodynamic struts. The elevators were used in conunction with aerodynamic brakes to help pull out of a dive.

Gull Wing
The very strong inverted gull wing was based on a two-spar structure with closely spaced ribs. The centre section was integral with the fuselage. Ailerons and flaps were provided.

This Ju 87B-2 was on strength with Sturzkampfgeschwader 77, which flew the type, in different versions, during the type's major operations in World War II, including campaigns in Poland, the Battle of Britain, Greece and the Balkans, and finally the Eastern Front until 1943.

Ju 87R equipped with underwing fuel tanks. The Ju 87R and the Ju 87B were heavily involved in the opening phase of the Battle of Britain, but the type was withdrawn after suffering heavy losses at the hands of Fighter Command in the summer of 1940.

The Battle of Britain saw the *Luftwaffe* fighter arm stretched to the limit in defence of the bomber raids, such that the Ju 87s were often left vulnerable without adequate

Ju 87-Ds wear temporary winter camouflage for operations on the Eastern Front in 1942. The aircraft are armed with AB 500 cluster bomb containers and centreline SC 250 bombs.

cover. During a 10-day period that summer, the Stuka arm lost 66 dive-bombers and crews, including 17 aircraft from Sturzkampfgeschwader 77 that fell in a single day of operations. Nevertheless, before they were withdrawn from the theatre, the Stukas left their mark in heavy raids launched against British airfields along the south coast.

Improved Version

A change of fortunes was presented by the war in the Mediterranean, where Stukas crippled the Royal Navy carrier HMS *Illustrious* in January 1941. A refined version of the crank-winged Stuka appeared in late 1941, in the form of the Ju 87D, with a more powerful Jumo 211 powerplant. This saw battle during the invasion of the Soviet Union and was introduced to the campaign in North Africa in 1942.

It was on the Eastern Front that the Stuka enjoyed its greatest success, albeit in a close support role rather than as the dive-bomber originally envisaged. However, as the tide of the war turned against the *Luftwaffe*, the Ju 87 was found increasingly vulnerable, and by 1943 losses were such that the aircraft was switched to the night assault role.

Specification (Ju 87D-1)

Type:	Dive-bomber and assault aircraft
Dimensions:	Length: 11.50m (37ft 8.75in); Wingspan: 13.80m (45ft 3.3in); Height: 3.90m (12ft 9.5in)
Weight:	6600kg (14,551lb) maximum take-off
Powerplant:	1 x 1044kW (1400hp) Junkers Jumo 211J-1 inverted-Vee piston engine
Maximum speed:	410km/h (255mph)
Range:	1535km (954 miles)
Service ceiling:	6100m (20,015ft)
Crew:	2
Armament:	3 x 7.92mm (0.31in) machine guns plus bombload of up to 1800kg (3968lb)

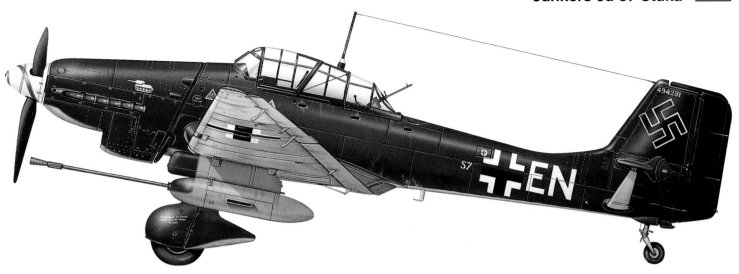

The Ju 87G-1 with its twin underwing pods for Bordkanone BK 3.7 (Flak 18) guns. This particular 'Kanonenvogel' ('gun bird') served with the 5. Staffel of II./Schlachtgeschwader 3 based at Jakobstadt, Latvia, in late 1944.

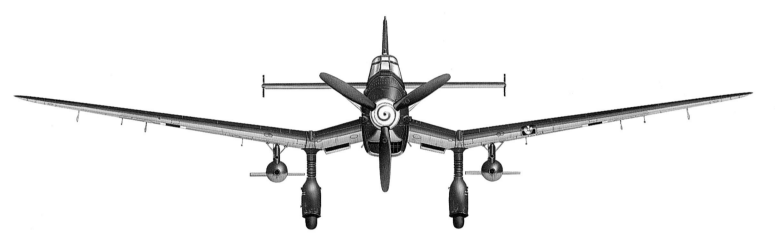

Hans-Ulrich Rudel

On the Eastern Front, the greatest exponent of the tank-busting Stuka was undoubtedly Hans-Ulrich Rudel. Originally an observer/gunner, Rudel had retrained as a pilot by the time the Nazis launched their invasion of the USSR. On the first day of the campaign alone, he flew four combat missions. In spring 1943 Rudel began flying the anti-tank Ju 87G, the development of which he had contributed to. In the first day of operations at the Battle of Kursk, Rudel used his Ju 87G to destroy 12 T-34 tanks. By the time time the war came to an end, Rudel has posted claims for a battleship, cruiser and a destroyer sunk, in addition to 519 tanks destroyed, in the course of around 2530 combat missions. He was himself shot down on 30 occasions. Rudel was described as Hitler's favourite pilot, a fact attested to by his being the sole recipient of the Golden Oak Leaves to his Knight's Cross.

Tank-busting Stuka

The Ju 87G represented a specialist anti-tank aircraft, armed with a pair of 37mm (1.45in) under the wings. This, the final operational version of the Stuka, served with seven Staffeln. The Ju 87G had the dive brakes deleted and although the additional gun armament added considerable weight, the weapons had a muzzle velocity of 850m (2,789ft) per second, making them suitable for penetrating the toughest of armoured targets. As an alternative to the guns, the Ju 87G could carry bomb armament.

Total Ju 87 production amounted to 5709 aircraft. When the conflict came to an end, a total of 125 Stukas were still on strength with the *Luftwaffe*, albeit now replaced in their primary close support role by the Focke-Wulf Fw 190 fighter. As well as service in German hands, the Ju 87 was also employed during the war by Bulgaria, Hungary, Italy and Romania.

Messerschmitt Bf 109 (1935)

The classic *Luftwaffe* fighter of World War II, the Bf 109 served throughout the conflict in a series of increasingly capable variants. On the way, it was the mount for Germany's most celebrated aces, including Hartmann, Barkhorn and Marseille.

The origins of the Bf 109 lie in the creation of the *Luftwaffe* in the mid-1930s and the concurrent demand for a new generation of modern fighters. As the schematic basis for a new fighter design, Willy Messerschmitt took the Bf 108, a low-wing cantilever cabin monoplane with retractable main undercarriage. In fact, preliminary work on a new fighter had begun before the Bf 108 took to the air.

The initial prototype of Messerschmitt's Bf 109 completed its maiden flight in May 1935, powered by a Rolls-Royce Kestrel engine, while the second prototype featured the planned Junkers Jumo 210A. In a fly-off

competition, the Bf 109 saw off competition from the Arado Ar 80 and Focke-Wulf Fw 159, and together with the rival Heinkel He 112 prototype was selected for further development, an initial batch of 10 examples of each being ordered. The Bf 109A pre-production prototypes tested a variety of armament installations, and served to refine the design of the initial production model, the Bf 109B, which received improved Jumo 210B, 210D, 210E or 210G engines.

Deliveries of the fighter commenced in early 1937, and initial machines went to the *Luftwaffe's* premier fighter

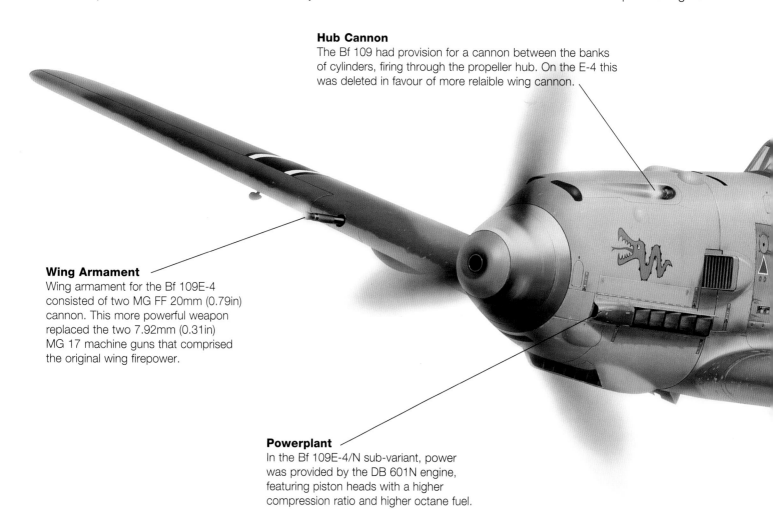

Hub Cannon
The Bf 109 had provision for a cannon between the banks of cylinders, firing through the propeller hub. On the E-4 this was deleted in favour of more relaible wing cannon.

Wing Armament
Wing armament for the Bf 109E-4 consisted of two MG FF 20mm (0.79in) cannon. This more powerful weapon replaced the two 7.92mm (0.31in) MG 17 machine guns that comprised the original wing firepower.

Powerplant
In the Bf 109E-4/N sub-variant, power was provided by the DB 601N engine, featuring piston heads with a higher compression ratio and higher octane fuel.

unit, Jagdgeschwader 132 'Richthofen'. In the summer of 1937 the type was subject to combat trials in Spain, as part of the Legion Condor. Before the end of the year a specially prepared Bf 109 took the world land plane speed record, at 610.55km/h (379.38mph), making use of a boosted DB 601 engine. Next of the production versions was the Bf 109C, with a Jumo 210Ga engine and armament increased from three to four machine guns. By September 1938 almost 600 examples had been completed, using production facilities at Arado,

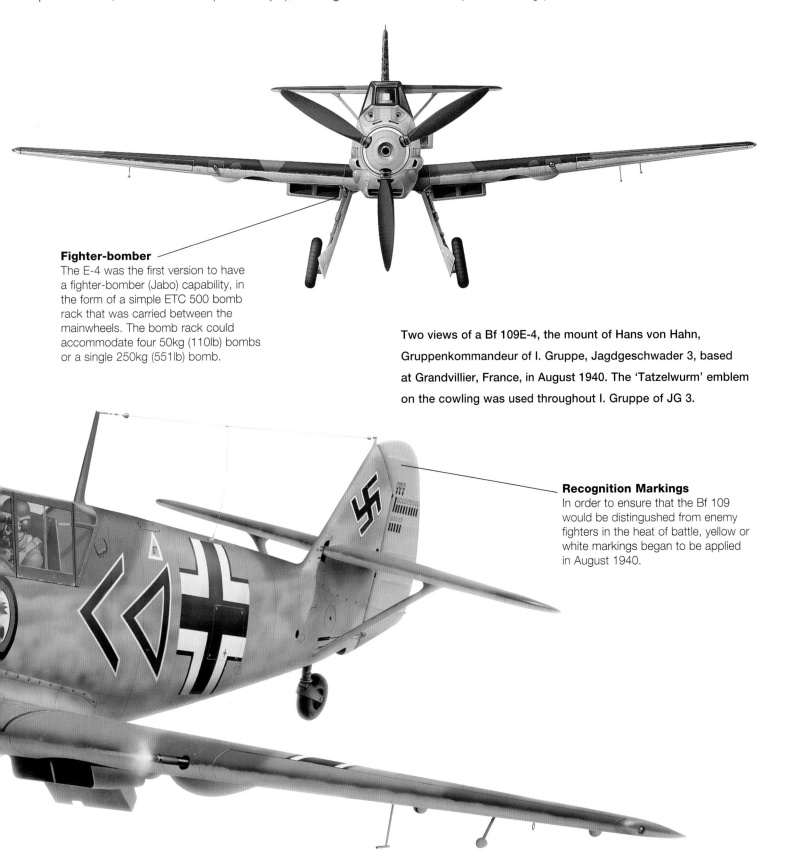

Fighter-bomber
The E-4 was the first version to have a fighter-bomber (Jabo) capability, in the form of a simple ETC 500 bomb rack that was carried between the mainwheels. The bomb rack could accommodate four 50kg (110lb) bombs or a single 250kg (551lb) bomb.

Two views of a Bf 109E-4, the mount of Hans von Hahn, Gruppenkommandeur of I. Gruppe, Jagdgeschwader 3, based at Grandvillier, France, in August 1940. The 'Tatzelwurm' emblem on the cowling was used throughout I. Gruppe of JG 3.

Recognition Markings
In order to ensure that the Bf 109 would be distingushed from enemy fighters in the heat of battle, yellow or white markings began to be applied in August 1940.

Messerschmitt Bf 109E

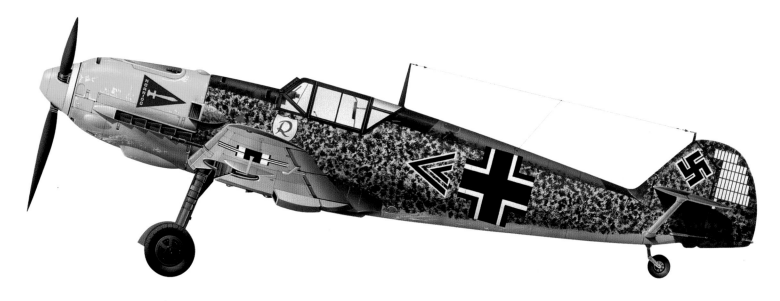

Erla, Focke-Wulf and Fieseler. The Bf 109D featured the Daimler-Benz DB 600 engine and a hub-firing cannon. It was produced in 1938–39. The first of the 109s to be built in significant quantities was the Bf 109E, powered by a DB 601D engine with direct fuel-injection. Armament options for the 'Emil' were based around two machine guns, four machine and a single hub cannon. Representing the versatility of the basic design, the Bf 109E was fielded in specialized fighter-bomber and reconnaissance sub-variants.

By making continual improvements to the basic design, the Bf 109 remained viable right until the end of World War II, and despite the appearance of the more capable

This Battle of Britain Bf 109E-4 was flown by Helmut Wick, Gruppenkommandeur of I./Jagdgeschwader 2 'Richthofen', based at Beaumont-le-Roger, France in October 1940. Wick was the highest-scoring *Luftwaffe* ace at the time of his death.

Fw 109, the Bf 109 remained the backbone of the *Luftwaffe* fighter arm. The Bf 109 remains associated, therefore, with the legendary aces of the Jadgverband.

Top-scoring ace of all time, Erich Hartmann achieved his tally of 352 victories in the space of three and a half years, all while at the controls of a Bf 109. The highest-scoring German ace in North Africa, Hans-Joachim Marseille similarly scored all his 158 victories flying the Messerschmitt fighter.

Specification (Bf 109G-6)

Type:	Fighter
Dimensions:	Length: 9.02m (29ft 7in); Wingspan: 9.92m (32ft 6.5in); Height: 3.40m (11ft 2in)
Weight:	6600kg (14,551lb) maximum take-off
Powerplant:	1 x 1342kW (1800hp) Daimler-Benz DB 605AM inverted V-12 piston engine
Maximum speed:	621km/h (386mph)
Range:	720km (447 miles)
Service ceiling:	11750m (38,550ft)
Crew:	1
Armament:	2 x 13mm (0.51in) MG 131 machine guns and three 20mm MG 151 cannon

Progressive Development

While the Bf 109E was the primary *Luftwaffe* fighter during 1939–40, it was superseded by the Bf 109F, powered initially by the DB 601N and later by the DB 60E, and with nitrous-oxide power boost, faster-firing guns and provision for underwing gun pods. Tropicalized versions of both the Bf 109E and F spearheaded the fighter arm in North Africa during 1941–42. Numerically the most important version was the Bf 109G, built from 1942–45 and active on all fronts. The 'Gustav' featured a DB 605 engine and a variety of armament options, including 30mm (1.18in) cannon. The similar Bf 109K featured boosted versions of the DB 605.

The Bf 109 had also been intended for service aboard the abortive aircraft carriers of the *Kriegsmarine*, and a

Operating from an airfield in Greece, Bf 109G-6s of 7./JG 27 patrol over the Adriatic Sea. The two aircraft to the rear are equipped with tropical filters and underwing cannon gondolas.

Record-breaking Me 209

Officially the world's fastest piston-engined aircraft between 1939 and 1969, the Messerschmitt Me 209 V1 was loosely based on the Bf 109 airframe, with the specific aim of capturing speed records for Nazi Germany. Based around a specially prepared DB 601 engine that had a peak power output of 1715kW (2300hp), the one-off Me 209 was flown by Fritz Wendel on 26 April 1939, when it took the speed record at 755.136km/h (469.22mph). In an effort to increase the propaganda value of the achievement, the German authorities described the record-breaking aircraft as the Me 109R, suggesting a version of the production Bf 109 fighter. Wendel and the Me 209 retained the speed record for piston-engined aircraft until April 1969, when Darryl Greenamyer flew the Grumman Bearcat Conquest I to an average speed of 769.23km/h (477.98mph).

batch of navalized Bf 109T versions were completed with folding wings, arrester gear and tailhook. In the event, these aircraft saw service from land bases.

Production Numbers

By the outbreak of World War II, a total of over 1000 Bf 109s had been delivered, production increasing in 1942 when Messerschmitt completed close to 2700 examples, and additional aircraft began to be completed at production facilities in Hungary the following year. In 1944 German industrial output accounted for almost 14,000 aircraft. Although no comprehensive records survive, it is estimated that around 35,000 Bf 109s were ultimately built, making it the most prolific fighter of all time.

Alongside Germany, the Bf 109 was operated by Bulgaria, Finland, Hungary, Japan, Romania, Slovakia, Spain, Switzerland, the USSR and Yugoslavia. Beginning in 1945 it was also built under licence in Spain as the Hispano HA-1109 and improved HA-1112. Bf 109s were also built post-war in Czechoslovakia, as the Avia S-99 and S-199, and both Czech and Spanish derivatives remained in service into the 1950s.

Hawker Hurricane (1935)

The Royal Air Force's first monoplane fighter began a dynasty of Hawker warplanes. The most successful British fighter during the Battle of Britain subsequently excelled in the ground-attack role in North Africa and the Far East.

The RAF's first modern, 300mph (483km/h) fighter was designed by Sydney Camm and first flew in November 1935. Camm had begun drafting the Hurricane as early as 1933, with the concept being a monoplane version of the successful Fury biplane, initially with the Rolls-Royce Goshawk engine and later the Merlin from the same manufacturer. After official trials in the course of 1936, production deliveries of the Hurricane to the RAF commenced in December 1937, the first aircraft going to No.111 Squadron at Northolt.

The initial Hurricane Mk I production version was powered by a Rolls-Royce Merlin II and was armed with eight machine guns. At the time of the Battle of Britain the Hurricane Mk I was Fighter Command's most important fighter, and was responsible for downing more enemy aircraft during the battle than all other defences – air and

A total of 4711 Mk IICs had been completed when production came to an end in September 1944. Equipped with a four-cannon wing and bomb racks, it was the most widely deployed version.

Powerplant
The Hurricane Mk II introduced the Merlin XX engine with two-stage supercharging, driving a three-bladed Rotol propeller.

Cockpit
The pilot sat under a heavily framed sliding canopy, protected by armour plate to the rear and a bullet-proof windscreen.

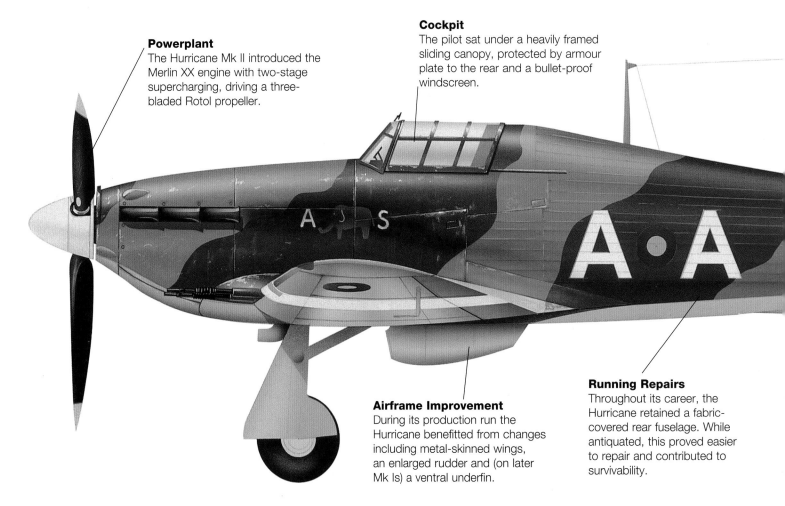

Airframe Improvement
During its production run the Hurricane benefitted from changes including metal-skinned wings, an enlarged rudder and (on later Mk Is) a ventral underfin.

Running Repairs
Throughout its career, the Hurricane retained a fabric-covered rear fuselage. While antiquated, this proved easier to repair and contributed to survivability.

ground – combined. At the height of the battle, on 8 August 1940, Fighter Command strength included no fewer than 32 Hurricane squadrons, compared to 19 of Spitfires. It was at the controls of a Hurricane that James Nicholson won the Victoria Cross, the only such medal awarded to a member of Fighter Command. Despite his Hurricane burning badly, Nicholson successfully pressed home an attack on a Bf 110 heavy fighter. Before the end of 1940 the Mk I had been joined in service by the Mk II powered by an uprated Merlin XX. Sub-variants included the Mk IIB with a 12-machine-gun armament and the Mk IIC of 1941, introducing four 20mm cannon. The Mk IIB/C versions also

brought new flexibility in their capacity to carry two 500lb (227kg) bombs or other stores.

Until 1943 the Hurricane remained a vital component of Fighter Command in all theatres, and had expanded its activities to include fighter-bomber, night-fighter, intruder and photo-reconnaissance missions. As a fighter, the Hurricane lacked straight-line speed compared to its contemporaries, but was always regarded as a manoeuvrable platform that was capable of absorbing battle damage. By the end of the war, however, the Hurricane only remained in front-line Fighter Command service in the Far East. In the night-fighter role, the Hurricane first

Cannon Armament
The Hispano 20mm (0.79in) cannon was selected for use on the Mk IIC after comparative trials against an Oerlikon weapon. The aircraft carried four Hispanos in the wing, although two were sometimes removed to save weight when operating in the Middle East.

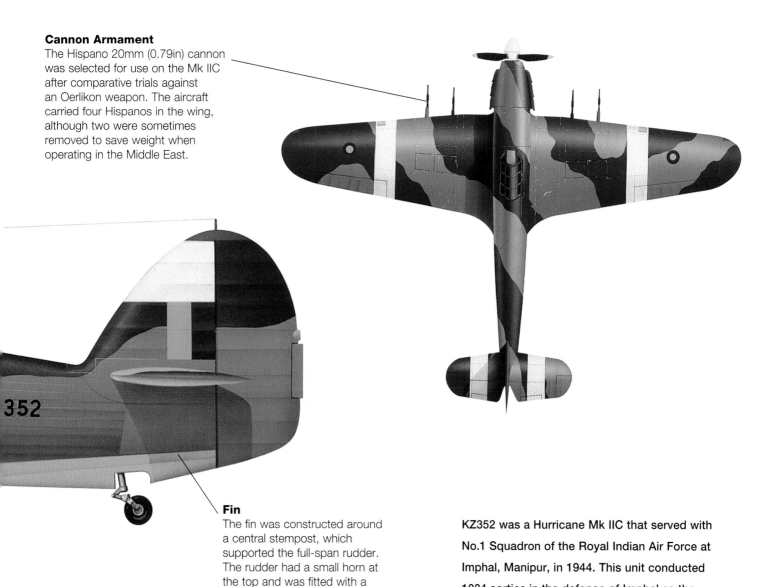

Fin
The fin was constructed around a central stempost, which supported the full-span rudder. The rudder had a small horn at the top and was fitted with a navigation light.

KZ352 was a Hurricane Mk IIC that served with No.1 Squadron of the Royal Indian Air Force at Imphal, Manipur, in 1944. This unit conducted 1034 sorties in the defence of Imphal as the Commonwealth forces inflicted a defeat on the Japanese, marking a turning point in the Burma campaign.

Hawker Hurricane

A Hurricane Mk IID of No.6 Squadron, famed as the leading exponent of the tank-busting art using this type. The Mk IID's effectiveness in the role in the Western Desert saw the squadron adopt the nickname 'The Flying Can-Openers'.

saw service in the Battle of Britain, and by the time the Mk II arrived on the scene, nocturnal work was becoming more important for the type. This also extended to intruder missions over occupied Europe, active during 1941–42. Night-fighter Hurricanes also served in the Middle East, defending the Canal Zone in May 1941, while radar-equipped Mk IICs saw action in India from May 1943.

Specification (Hurricane Mk IIC)

Type:	Night-fighter/intruder
Dimensions:	Length: 9.75m (32ft 0in); Wingspan: 12.19m (40ft 0in); Height: 4.00m (13ft 1.5in)
Weight:	3583kg (7800lb) maximum take-off
Powerplant:	1 x 954kW (1280hp) Rolls-Royce Merlin XX V-12 liquid-cooled piston engine
Maximum speed:	546km/h (339mph)
Range:	740km (460 miles)
Service ceiling:	10,850m (35,600ft)
Crew:	1
Armament:	4 x 20mm (0.78in) cannon plus (intruder) two 500lb (227kg) bombs

Anti-tank Hurricane

A specialist anti-tank version was the Hurricane Mk IID, armed with 40mm (1.57in) cannon under the wings. The Mk IID appeared in service in 1942 and was primarily engaged in North Africa.

A 'universal wing' was the primary feature of the Hurricane Mk IV, and this could mount up to eight rocket projectiles or other external stores. Indeed, the Hurricane Mk IV was the first Allied aircraft to deploy air-to-ground rockets, a capability that did much to extend the operational utility of the basic airframe. Tailored for the ground-attack role, the Mk IV proved to be the final Hurricane production version.

The Hurricane enjoyed a total production run of 14,231, including aircraft built in Canada (the Hurricane Mks X, XI and XII) and Sea Hurricanes. The latter variant was typically produced through

Pilots scramble to their Hurricanes at Hendon. On 15 September 1940 Hurricanes from No.504 Squadron at Hendon destroyed eight enemy aircraft and damaged five more.

'Hurricat'

While it subsequently flew from MAC-ships (Merchant Aircraft Carriers) and conventional carriers, the first Hurricane to go to sea was developed as a stopgap measure to provide protection to convoys in the North Atlantic. This 'Hurricat' was to operate from CAM-ships (Catapult Armed Merchantmen) and as such would launch from a catapult on the ship's bows, before conducting a one-way flight to intercept a marauding Focke-Wulf Fw 200 Condor long-range aircraft. Unless there was land within range, the pilot of the 'Hurricat' was forced to ditch his aircraft as close as possible to the convoy, whereupon he would hope to be rescued. Although this was clearly a desperate solution to the Condors (dubbed 'scourge of the Atlantic' by Churchill), the 'Hurricat' and CAM-ship combination saw some success, destroying six enemy aircraft in 1941. The first victim to fall to the 'Hurricat' was an Fw 200 downed in August that year.

conversion of land-based fighters, and the first carrier-capable iteration was the Sea Hurricane Mk IB, with catapult spools and V-frame arrester gear. Adding the Merlin XX produced the Sea Hurricane Mk IIB, while the Sea Hurricane Mk IC was similar but with cannon armament.

Carrier Hurricanes

The first carrier-based Sea Hurricanes entered service in March 1941 and were involved in the raid on the Arctic port of Petsamo, flying from HMS *Furious*. With the arrival of the smaller escort carriers, the Sea Hurricane established a new niche for itself, and operated in this capacity in the Arctic and Mediterranean – including notable action in support of the Malta convoys – until being replace by more modern equipment in 1943.

The last Hurricanes in active front-line Royal Air Force service were disposed of by No.6 Squadron in January 1947. As well as its service with the RAF and Fleet Air Arm, Hurricanes were employed by wartime operators including Egypt, Finland, India, Ireland, Persia, Turkey and the USSR.

Boeing B-17 Flying Fortress (1935)

Responsible in no small degree for the defeat of the *Luftwaffe* in World War II, the B-17 was a mainstay of the U.S. 8th Air Force, ranging across occupied Europe and experiencing some of the hardest-fought air battles in history. The Flying Fortress also served widely in other theatres and in a variety of different roles.

Today best remembered for its role at the centre of the U.S. Army Air Forces' daylight precision bombing operations over Europe, the four-engine B-17 was one of the pre-eminent high-altitude heavy bombers of World War II, having first flown back in July 1935 as the Model 299, prepared in response to a U.S. Army Air Corps specification of May 1934. At this early stage,

the then USAAC was of the opinion that a high-flying, heavy hitting bomber was the most effective means of destroying strategic targets in daylight raids, a theory that would be put to the test in the bombing offensive of 1942–45.

Top Turret
The power-operated Sperry top turret was operated by the flight engineer, who was also responsible for fuel management and basic in-flight repairs.

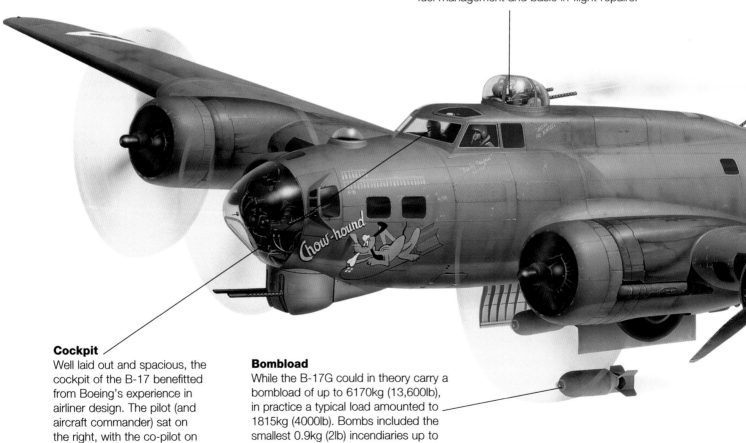

Cockpit
Well laid out and spacious, the cockpit of the B-17 benefitted from Boeing's experience in airliner design. The pilot (and aircraft commander) sat on the right, with the co-pilot on the left.

Bombload
While the B-17G could in theory carry a bombload of up to 6170kg (13,600lb), in practice a typical load amounted to 1815kg (4000lb). Bombs included the smallest 0.9kg (2lb) incendiaries up to the heaviest 907kg (2000lb) demolition bombs. Only one of the latter could be carried, due to the dimensions of the bomb bay.

The Boeing Model 299 (unofficially XB-17) was followed by a pre-production series of Y1B-17 (later designated YB-17) and Y1B-17A (B-17A) aircraft that were subjected to rigorous testing during 1936–38. An evaluation of the new bomber involved small batches of B-17B, B-17C and B-17D aircraft in the period 1939–41. At the time of the B-17B's limited service entry in 1939, the Flying Fortress was the fastest and highest-flying bomber in the world.

It was the B-17E that represented the first true service version of the Flying Fortress, and a total of 512 of this

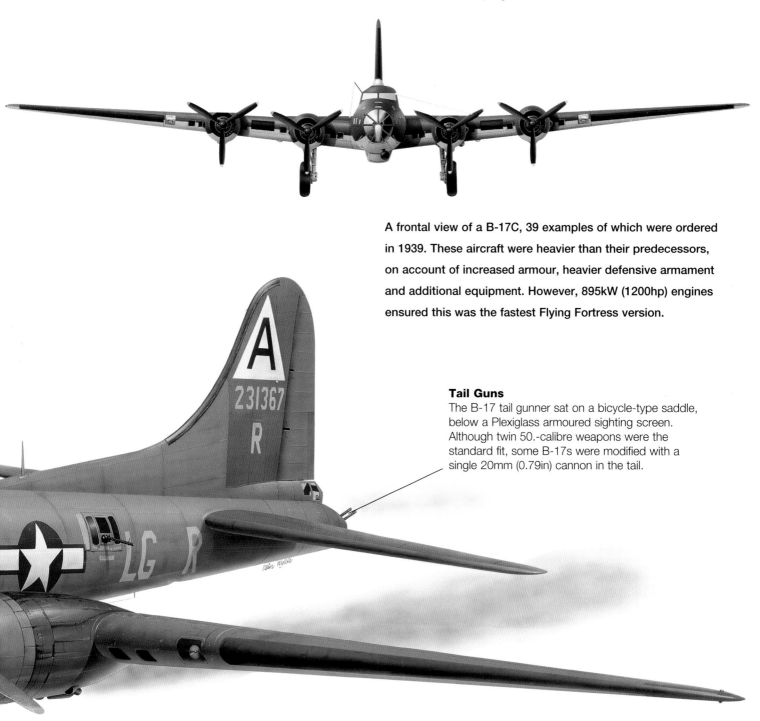

A frontal view of a B-17C, 39 examples of which were ordered in 1939. These aircraft were heavier than their predecessors, on account of increased armour, heavier defensive armament and additional equipment. However, 895kW (1200hp) engines ensured this was the fastest Flying Fortress version.

Tail Guns
The B-17 tail gunner sat on a bicycle-type saddle, below a Plexiglass armoured sighting screen. Although twin 50.-calibre weapons were the standard fit, some B-17s were modified with a single 20mm (0.79in) cannon in the tail.

Assigned to the 322nd Bomb Squadron of the 91st BG, Chowhound was a Boeing-built B-17G that flew its first operational sortie in January 1944. It was destroyed by flak over Caen in August 1944, with the loss of all but one crew member.

Boeing B-17 Flying Fortress

The B-17C introduced a ventral 'bathtub' that was also used on the B-17D, but had flush waist gun positions instead of blisters. The conspicuous markings date from the pre-1941 period.

version were completed. The B-17E featured a revised tail with considerably enlarged control surfaces and a prominent dorsal fin, as well as improved defensive armament in the form of additional machine guns. The B-17E was the first to introduce a tail gun position and also boasted power-operated twin-gun turrets aft of the cockpit and below the centre fuselage. This model was the first USAAF heavy bomber to see combat in Europe with the 8th Air Force, when aircraft from the 97th BG struck railway marshalling yards at Rouen, France.

The B-17F that followed was broadly similar to the B-17E, and 3405 examples were built during 1942–43. Compared to its predecessor, the B-17F was stressed to

carry an increased bomb load and employed an enlarged, frameless Plexiglass nose. In light of combat experience it was also equipped with self-sealing fuel tanks.

The major production version was the definitive B-17G, 8680 of which rolled out of the factories of the Boeing, Douglas and Lockheed-Vega companies. The B-17G was distinguished by its twin-gun chin turret to provide a means of countering head-on fighter attacks. Other armament changes were manifested in a revised tail turret and staggered, enclosed waist gun positions and the aircraft typically packed a total of 13 machine guns. Most B-17Gs also featured improved turbochargers, increasing service ceiling to 10,670m (35,000ft), albeit with a reduction in cruising speed as a result of the weight of all the additional equipment.

Daylight Raids

Typical 8th Air Force tactics over Europe involved enormous 'box' formations of bombers sent day after day into the heart of the Third Reich, using their strength in numbers and formidable defensive armament to provide protection against *Luftwaffe* fighters. In the last deep-penetration raid without 'all the way' fighter escort, 291 B-17s and B-24s were sent against the Schweinfurt ball bearing factory in October 1943. The result was 60 bombers posted missing, 17 crashed or written off on return and 121 that suffered some kind of damage. In the face of such mounting losses, the USAAF introduced escort fighters to protect the bombers all the way to the target and back to their bases in eastern England.

Another defensive measure involved the use of YB-40 escorts, these being even more heavily armed Flying Fortresses, some of which carried as many as

Specification (B-17G)

Type:	Daylight medium/heavy bomber
Dimensions:	Length: 22.78m (74ft 9in); Wingspan: 31.62m (103ft 9in); Height: 5.82m (19ft 1in)
Weight:	32,660kg (72,000lb) maximum take-off
Powerplant:	4 x 895kW (1200hp) Wright Cyclone R-1820-97 radial piston engines
Maximum speed:	462km/h (287mph)
Range:	3220km (2000 miles) with bombload
Service ceiling:	11,280m (37,000ft)
Crew:	10
Armament:	13 x 12.7mm (0.5in) machine guns plus a maximum bombload of 7983kg (17,600lb)

Without camouflage to improve performance, Douglas-built B-17Gs of the 881st BG (352nd and 533rd BS) based at RAF Ridgewell head towards their target in occupied Europe.

'Blitz Week'

In July 1943 the Allies launched their first sustained aerial bombing offensive against key industrial targets deep in the Reich. Beginning with a raid on 24 July, the 'Blitz Week' operations called upon the combined strength of 13 bomb groups of the 8th Air Force under the command of Maj Gen Ira Eaker. The 24 July mission saw a force of B-17s sent to attack targets in Norway, sustaining only one loss in the process. On the following day, 323 B-17s assembled to attack Hamburg and Kiel. Here, they faced much stiffer opposition, losing 15 of their number over Hamburg and four more over Warnemünde. On the 26th, 303 B-17s raided Hamburg and Hannover. The longest raid by VIII Bomber Command thus far took place on 28 July, when 182 B-17s struck Kassel and Oschersleben. The climax of 'Blitz Week' came on 30 July, when 186 B-17s returned to Kassel. Over the course of six days, VIII Bomber Command lost 88 B-17s in 1672 sorties.

30 machine guns. The YB-40 concept was judged ineffective, but by January 1944, B-17s were protected by the superlative P-51 fighter, which could provide escort all the way to Berlin and back.

While the Flying Fortress saw the bulk of its combat service in Europe, smaller numbers served in the Middle East and Far East. In the Pacific theatre, the USAAF B-17 was employed on maritime patrol and reconnaissance duties, in addition to close-support bombing. For long-distance bombing missions in the Pacific, the B-24 was generally preferred on account of its longer range compared to the B-17.

Outside of the USAAF, the B-17s saw wartime service with RAF Bomber and Coastal Commands. In fact, it was an RAF Fortress Mk I (B-17C) that flew the type's first combat mission, during a raid on the port of Wilhelmshaven in July 1941.

By the end of the war, the arrival of the B-29 had rendered the B-17 obsolescent in the bombing role, but in the years that followed, the Flying Fortress continued to play a useful role on second-line and support duties, including air-sea rescue, airborne early warning and drone launch/direction.

Douglas C-47 Skytrain (1935)

The fact that the C-47 remains in front-line military service in the second decade of the twenty-first century goes some way to show the excellence of the basic design, first flown as a commercial airliner in 1935. In World War II, the C-47 played a leading role in decisive air assault operations in Europe and the Pacific.

Evolved from the DC-3, the Douglas C-47 Skytrain military transport is perhaps the best-known transport aircraft in history – and arguably the best known aircraft of all time. The commercial model, first flown in December 1935, introduced new standards of speed and comfort to air travel. In its initial military guise, the DC-3 appeared as the C-41 of late 1939, a one-off command transport with VIP accommodation and

Cockpit
While the C-47 captain occupies the usual left-hand seat, the co-pilot sits on the right, and is also responsible for the radios and throttles.

Cabin
The typical interior layout for trooping operations comprises a row of utility bucket seats fitted along each cabin wall. These can be removed for freighting work.

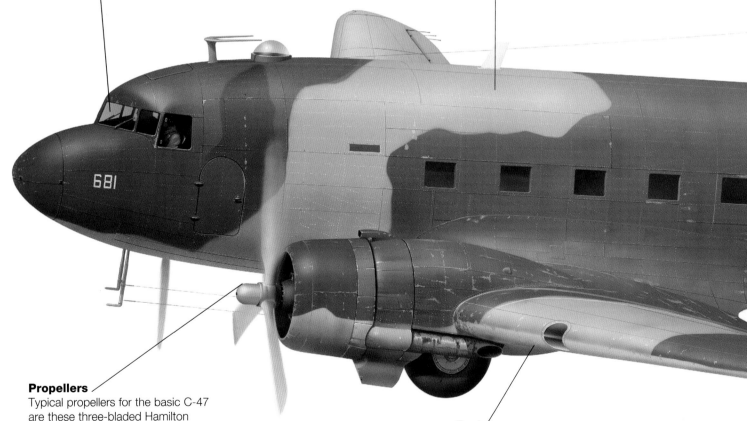

Propellers
Typical propellers for the basic C-47 are these three-bladed Hamilton Standard constant-speed units. The constant-speed unit in the hub controls the pitch of each blade.

Fuel
The main fuel tanks (containing 795 litres/210 U.S. gal) are located in the centre section forward of the wing spar, and are supplemented by two auxiliary tanks (760 litres/201 U.S. gal) aft of the spar.

military communications equipment. In 1940 the aircraft was ordered in quantity by the U.S. Army Air Corps as a troopship, essential changes for its role including the replacement of the airline interior with bucket seats along the cabin sides, and introduction of Pratt & Whitney R-1830 radial engines in place of the previous Wright Cyclones.

The first U.S. Army troopship version, the C-47, was built to a total of 93 aircraft, before production switched to the C-47A with an improved electrical system,

Production of the A-model extended to 4931 aircraft. With the addition of high-altitude superchargers and R-1830-90 engines, the Skytrain became the C-47B, 3241 of which were completed, primarily for use in Southeast Asia. In particular, the C-47B gave valuable service hauling supplies across the Atlantic and over the Himalayan 'hump' into China.

Among the myriad of versions subsequently completed, the 28-seat C-53 Skytrooper was notable as a minimum-change military version of the standard

C-47A serial FAC-681 of the Colombian Air Force is seen as it appeared in the 1980s. A former RAF machine, it was later converted as an AC-47 gunship. In 2014 six AC-47T Fantasma gunships remained in Colombian Air Force service.

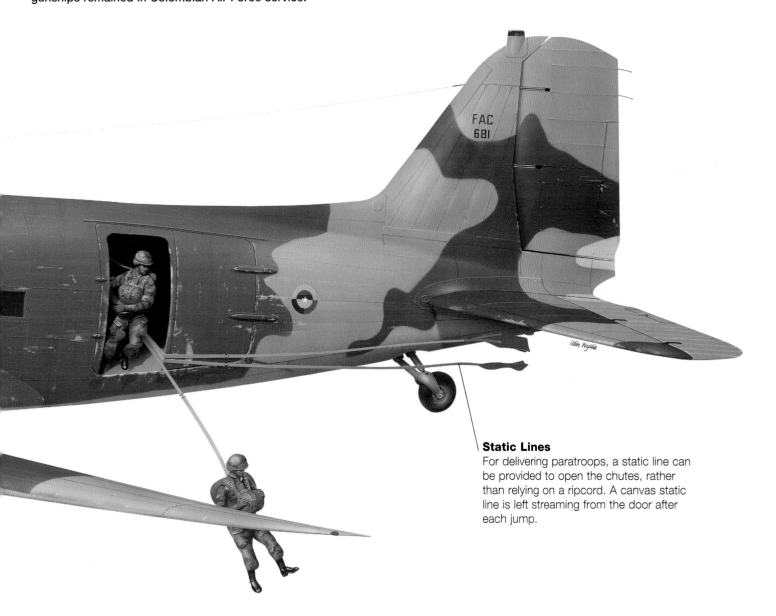

Static Lines
For delivering paratroops, a static line can be provided to open the chutes, rather than relying on a ripcord. A canvas static line is left streaming from the door after each jump.

Douglas C-47 Skytrain

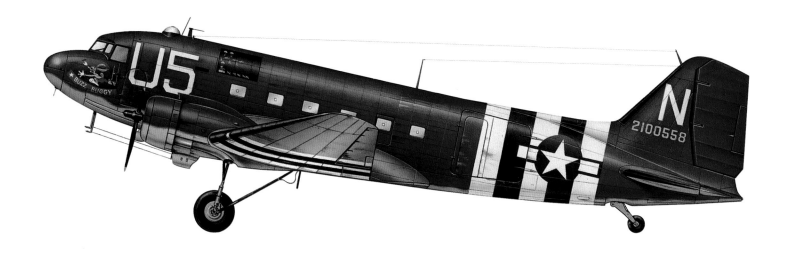

DC-3 airliner. In the course of the war, C-47 production topped 10,000, while close to 5000 more were built under licence in the USSR as the Lisunov Li-2. Licensed foreign production also included the L2D (Navy Type 0 Transport), built by Showa and Nakajima in Japan, and which also saw combat service in World War II.

From 1942, the C-47 served as the USAAF's standard transport and glider tug and as such took part in every U.S. airborne operation during the war. Gen Dwight D. Eisenhower put the C-47 on a pedestal with the bazooka, jeep and atomic bomb as weapons that contributed most to the Allied victory. Among its most incredible wartime exploits were the downing of a

Wearing D-Day recognition stripes, C-47A Buzz Buggy of the 81st Troop Carrier Squadron, 436th Troop Carrier Group was based at Membury, England, from March 1944 to February 1945.

Mitsubishi A6M Zero by a pilot who aimed a Browning Automatic Rifle (BAR) into the slipstream before opening fire; another C-47 in the same China-Burma-India theatre lost a wing, and received a wing from an earlier DC-2 as replacement. Thus modified, the aircraft flew on in service as an asymmetric 'DC-2-and-a-half'. More typical were the stories of everyday bravery in airborne assault missions that took place in Sicily, New Guinea, Normandy, southern France and the bridges at Nijmegen and Arnhem. The type also served as the Dakota with the RAF, in which a total of 1895 examples eventually saw action with no fewer than 25 squadrons. British versions included the Dakota Mk I based on the C-47, Dakota Mk II (C-53), Dakota Mk III (C-47A) and Dakota Mk IV (C-47B).

Post-war Service

The Skytrain remained an important transport for the USAF well into the post-war era, and continued to play an important role with the Military Air Transport Service (MATS) during the Berlin Airlift of 1948–49. Over 1000 examples were still to be found on inventory in 1961. Thereafter, the C-47 continued to excel in a range of specialist and second-line missions, with operators around the globe, including Antarctic exploration, maritime patrol, navigation training, search and rescue (including with a jettisonable lifeboat carried below

Specification (C-47)

Type:	Military transport
Dimensions:	Length: 19.43m (63ft 9in); Wingspan: 29.11m (95ft 6in); Height: 5.18m (17ft 0in)
Weight:	11,793kg (26,000lb) maximum take-off
Powerplant:	4 x 895kW (1200hp) Pratt & Whitney R-1830-92 14-cylinder radial piston engines
Maximum speed:	370km/h (230mph)
Range:	2575km (1600 miles)
Service ceiling:	7315m (24,000ft)
Crew:	3
Armament:	None

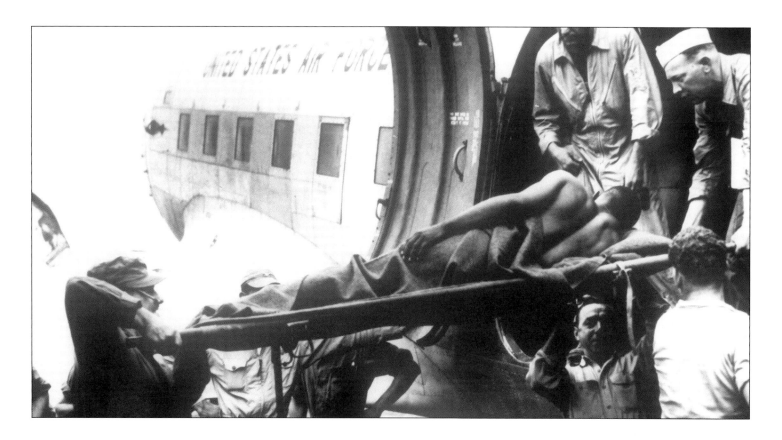

Korean War casualties are loaded on a USAF C-47 at a forward airstrip for evacuation to air bases further south. These patients are being evacuated from the front near Hagaru-ri in late 1950.

Skytrains over Sicily

Codenamed Operation Husky, the invasion of Sicily in July 1943 marked the first major Allied airborne assault. C-47s bore the brunt of the airborne invasion force, and dropped a total of 4381 paratroops. During the night of 9 July, a British force of 137 gliders was towed by aircraft including around 100 C-47s of the U.S. 51st Troop Carrier Wing, but navigational errors meant the paratroops were unable to capture their objective, the Ponte Grande Bridge, and 69 gliders came down in the sea. A similar fate befell the 226 C-47s of the 52nd TCW, which conducted a simultaneous airdrop of paratroops from the 82nd Airborne Division. Navigation errors here meant that many of these paratroops came down far from their objectives. Despite these difficulties, many of the objectives were eventually achieved by the British and American troops. A seaborne assault followed on 10 July, and the taking of Sicily provided a stepping-stone towards Italy itself.

the fuselage), radar countermeasures, staff transport and gunship. The latter role saw the development of the AC-47, which saw service with the USAF in the early years of the Vietnam War. The definitive AC-47D 'Puff the Magic Dragon' gunship was armed with three 7.62mm (0.3in) Miniguns firing through the fuselage door and starboard side windows, provided with 21,000 rounds of ammunition. Other AC-47s have seen action with foreign operators, most notably in Latin America, where Skytrain gunships continue in front-line use.

The naval equivalent to the C-47 was the R4D employed by the U.S. Navy. In later service, the R4D was joined by a military version of the revamped Super DC-3, which appeared in 1949. In U.S. Navy service this was designated as the R4D-8 (later re-designated C-117D). The Super DC-3 featured a reduced-span wing, redesigned tail, refined undercarriage and a strengthened and extended fuselage, with accommodation for 30–38 passengers. While the 'Super' was powered by Wright R-1820-80 Cyclones, subsequent re-engining efforts concentrated on adding turboprops, to create conversions such as the popular Basler BT-67, powered by two Pratt & Whitney Canada PT6A-67R turboprops.

Supermarine Spitfire (1936)

The pre-eminent British fighter of World War II was a thoroughbred with a racing lineage. A masterpiece of design from R.J. Mitchell, the Spitfire is remembered as one of the classic fighters of all time, and saw service in every theatre of combat, from the outbreak of war until the final Allied victory.

The Spitfire owed much of its performance to the successful series of Schneider Trophy seaplanes from the Supermarine stable. The initial production version was the Spitfire Mk I, which took to the air in March 1936, powered by a Merlin II engine and armed with eight machine guns. The Mk I entered RAF service in August 1938 and went on to provide sterling service during the Battle of Britain in summer 1940.

September 1940 saw the arrival of the Spitfire Mk II with Merlin XX engine, and the Mk IIB version that was armed

Propeller
Engine efficiency was improved through the use of a constant-speed propeller, with propeller pitch automatically adjusted based on the flight regime, ensuring optimum engine operating levels.

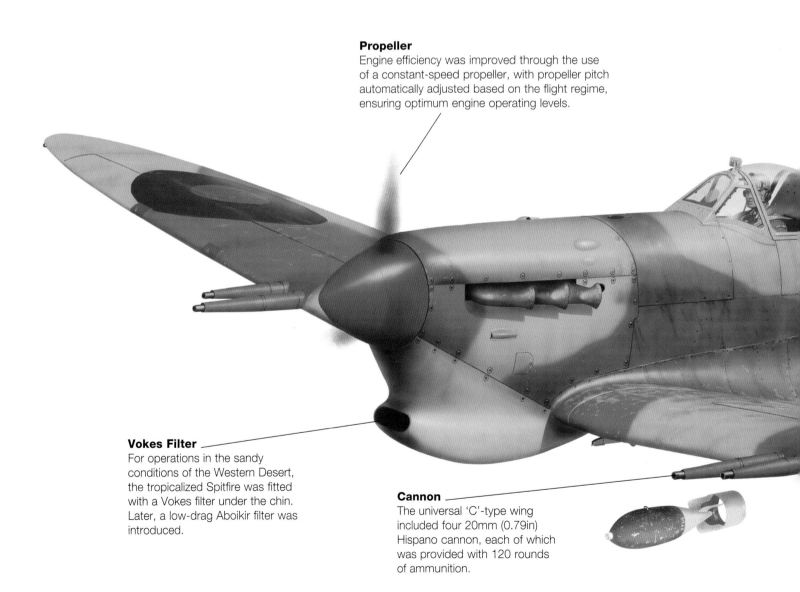

Vokes Filter
For operations in the sandy conditions of the Western Desert, the tropicalized Spitfire was fitted with a Vokes filter under the chin. Later, a low-drag Aboikir filter was introduced.

Cannon
The universal 'C'-type wing included four 20mm (0.79in) Hispano cannon, each of which was provided with 120 rounds of ammunition.

with two 20mm (0.79in) cannon and four machine guns. First of the photo-reconnaissance models, meanwhile, was the Mk IV.

The Mk V, which appeared in March 1941, was the most significant production Spitfire, accounting for 6479 of the total 20,351 aircraft built. As RAF Fighter Command's standard fighter the Mk V introduced the Merlin Mk 45 and was produced in a number of sub-variants including the Mk VB with cannon and machine gun armament, and the Mk VC fighter-bomber with provision for external stores. Most Mk VCs were completed with 'clipped' wings to improve performance at altitudes below 5000ft (1525m). From mid-1941 until mid-1942 the Spitfire Mk VB was the backbone of Fighter Command, until superseded by the Mk IX.

The Spitfire Mk IX was the second most prolific variant, with a production run of 5665. Based on the Mk V, the Mk IX added the Merlin 61 with a two-stage, two-speed supercharger. Developed hastily as a response to the *Luftwaffe's* Fw 190 fighter-bomber, the Mk IX was optimized for performance at medium and high altitudes. However, a clipped-wing version, the Merlin 66-powered LF.Mk IX, was also produced, and served in the UK, Middle East and Far East. The LF.Mk IX could carry two 500lb (227kg) bombs underwing in addition to its fixed gun armament.

Two high-altitude fighter developments of the Mk IX were built in series, comprising the Mks VI and VII, both with extended wingtips. The Mk VIII, meanwhile, was a dual-role fighter and fighter-bomber that saw service

Camouflage and Markings
The RAF Middle East scheme typically comprised Dark Earth/ Middle Stone upper surfaces with Sky or Azure Below below. This aircraft also carries the insignia of No.7 Wing, SAAF, on the tailfin.

This Spitfire Mk V was operated by No.2 Squadron, No.7 Wing, South African Air Force (SAAF), part of the Desert Air Force, in July 1943. The type replaced the Curtiss Kittyhawk with this operator and first saw action flying from bases in Sicily, and later captured airfields on the Italian mainland.

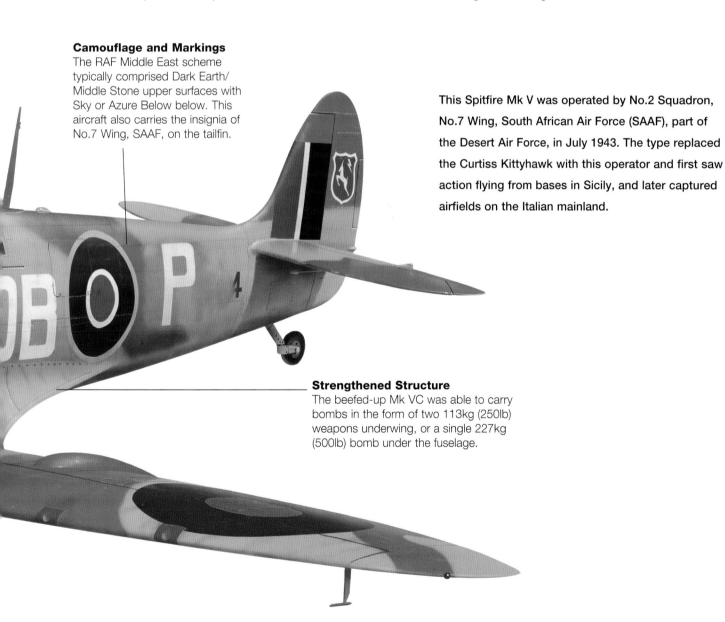

Strengthened Structure
The beefed-up Mk VC was able to carry bombs in the form of two 113kg (250lb) weapons underwing, or a single 227kg (500lb) bomb under the fuselage.

Supermarine Spitfire

An aerial view of this Battle of Britain Spitfire Mk IA reveals the classic tapered wing of the type, as well as the yellow gas detection patch applied on the port wing in summer 1940.

almost exclusively in the Mediterranean and Far East, on account of it receiving tropicalized equipment as standard. In contrast to the hastily developed Mk IX, the Mk VIII was tailored for the Merlin 61/66 engine from the outset and also added a number of other improvements, including a retractable tailwheel. Further PR models followed, in the form of the Mks X and XI, both intended for high-altitude work, and unarmed.

With the introduction of the Mk XVI, the Merlin-engined Spitfire approached its peak performance. Capable of a maximum speed of 652km/h (405mph) on the power of its Packard Merlin 266, the Spitfire Mk XVI was available in fighter and fighter-bomber configurations, being produced in a range of sub-variants analogous to those of the Mk IX. The Mk XVI could also be equipped with rocket projectiles and as such was an important component of the 2nd Tactical Air Force in the final months of the war.

The Merlin was superseded by the Rolls-Royce Griffon, the first production Spitfire with the new powerplant was the Mk XII, with the Griffon IV. Intended to counter the Fw 190 menace once and for all, the

Mk XII was introduced in 1943 and was followed by the Mk XIV fighter/fighter-bomber with the Griffon 65 that entered service in mid-1944 with units based in the UK. A dual-role fighter/reconnaissance model appeared at the end of the war, in the shape of the Mk XVIII with a top speed of 712km/h (442mph). The unarmed Griffon-powered photo-reconnaissance version was the PR.Mk XIX, which flew the final operational RAF Spitfire sortie over Malaya in 1956. Post-war, fighter development continued with the Mk 21 (Griffon 61/64), Mk 22 (Griffon 85) and Mk 24.

In Fleet Air Air Arm service, the Spitfire became the Seafire, a total of 2334 of which were completed. Following trials aboard the carrier HMS *Illustrious* in late 1941, the first production Seafire appeared as the Mk IB, based on the land-based Mk V. In May 1942 it was followed by the Seafire Mk IIC, replacing the 'B'-type wing with the 'C'-type cannon wing. The Seafire L.Mk IIC was intended for low-altitude operations, while the F.Mk III and low-level LF.Mk III introduced a manually folding wing.

In 1945 the Griffon Seafire began to be fielded, the first such model being the F.Mk XV, which was followed

Specification (Spitfire Mk VB)

Type:	Fighter
Dimensions:	Length: 9.11m (29ft 11in); Wingspan: 11.23m (36ft 10in); Height: 3.48m (11ft 5in)
Weight:	3078kg (6785lb) maximum take-off
Powerplant:	1 x 1074kW (1440hp) Rolls-Royce Merlin 45/46/50 V-12 liquid-cooled piston engine
Maximum speed:	602km/h (374mph)
Range:	756km (470 miles)
Service ceiling:	11,280m (37,000ft)
Crew:	1
Armament:	2 x 20mm (0.78in) cannon and 4 x 7.7mm (0.303in) machine guns

by the F.Mk XVII with a clear-view bubble canopy to improve the pilot's vision. The FR.Mk XVII was a fighter-reconnaissance version, while the F.Mk 56 introduced the option of a contra-rotating propeller. Post-war versions were the F.Mk 46 and F.Mk 47, with bubble canopies, provision for reconnaissance equipment and,

This Spitfire Mk IA was flown by South African ace Adolph 'Sailor' Malan in August 1940, when he commanded No.74 Squadron. By year's end, Malan had 18 victories.

ultimately, power-folding wings. The Mk 47 saw combat in the Korean War.

Spitfires in the Med

The Spitfire first saw overseas service in the form of the Mk V. In March 1942, an initial consignment of these fighters was shipped to Malta in order to defend the island fortress against Axis forces. The first aircraft for the Malta operation were flown on to the island from the deck of HMS *Eagle*, and by April Spitfire numbers on the island were in excess of 350, deliveries being aided by Royal Navy and U.S. carriers. In order to extend the Spitfire's range for operations from Malta, Supermarine developed a 90-Imp gal (410-litre) drop tank that could be carried under the fuselage. When the *Luftwaffe* began to deploy the Fw 190 in North Africa in late 1942, the Spitfire Mk IX was called into theatre. The first Mk IXs were active in the Mediterranean in January 1943. Thereafter, they helped to restore Allied air superiority and continued to provide cover for operations aimed at cutting off Axis supply routes in the region. This tropicalized Spitfire Mk VC of No.43 Squadron is seen in Sicily, as the Allied campaign in the Mediterranean turned towards the Italian mainland.

Junkers Ju 88 (1936)

One of the most versatile warplanes to see service in World War II, the Ju 88 excelled in roles as diverse as medium bomber, anti-shipping strike, close support and night-fighter, and was a mainstay of the *Luftwaffe* throughout the conflict.

The Junkers Ju 88 was first conceived as a high-speed medium bomber and in this form the initial Ju 88 V1 prototype was first flown in December 1936. Of all-metal construction, the aircraft was initially powered by a pair of Daimler-Benz DB 600A V-12 engines. After a total of nine prototypes had been completed, in 1939 construction switched to a pre-production batch of 10 Ju 88A-0 aircraft. By now, the basic design had been revised to include a four-man cabin. Since the Ju 88 was also expected to undertake diving attacks, dive brakes were added under the outer wings and the inner wings were strengthened for the carriage of bombs.

By the outbreak of the war, the *Luftwaffe* was receiving series-production Ju 88A-1 bombers, around 60 of which had been completed by the end of 1939. After service with a test unit that summer, the first combat missions were carried out by I./Kampfgeschwader 30 in September that year. A total of seven Gruppen had converted to the Junkers bomber by the time Germany invaded Norway, and production had increased to

Crew
The Ju 88A bomber was usually operated by a crew of four, comprising a pilot, co-pilot/ bomb aimer, radio operator/ventral gunner and a flight engineer/rear gunner.

Defensive Armament
The pilot had acess to a forward-firing MG 15 machine gun that was arranged to fire through the starboard windscreen. One or two similar weapons were usually fitted at the rear of the cockpit.

Bombload
The Ju 88A-5 was capable of carrying 28 50kg (110lb) bombs internally, while additional weapons each of up to 500kg (1102lb) could be carried on four racks under the inner wings.

Ventral Gondola
As well as being armed with a fourth defensive MG 15, this was used by the bomb aimer.

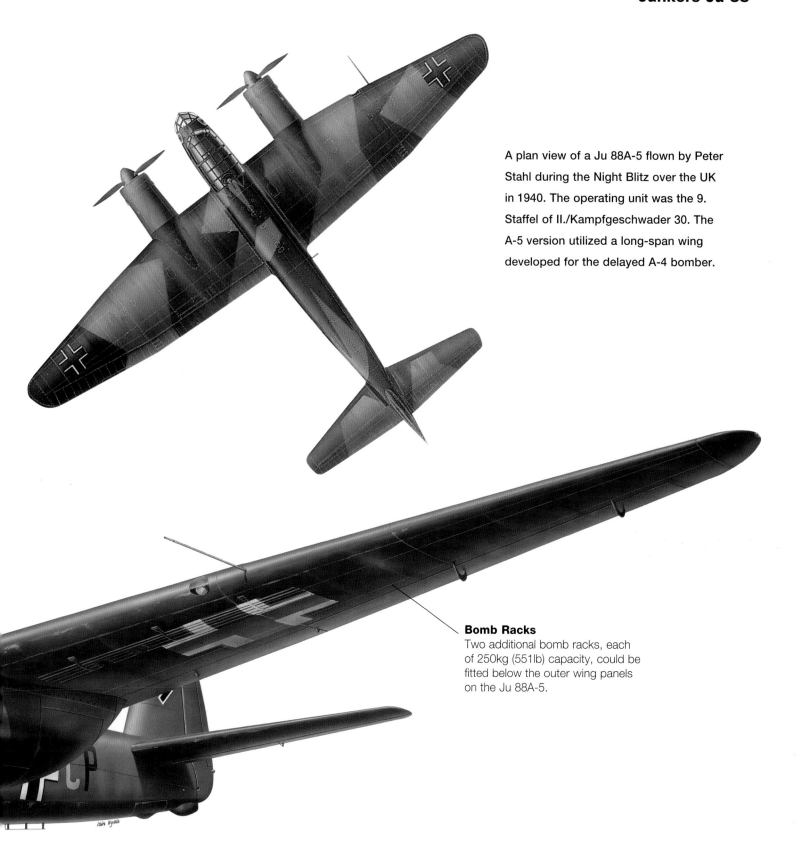

A plan view of a Ju 88A-5 flown by Peter Stahl during the Night Blitz over the UK in 1940. The operating unit was the 9. Staffel of II./Kampfgeschwader 30. The A-5 version utilized a long-span wing developed for the delayed A-4 bomber.

Bomb Racks
Two additional bomb racks, each of 250kg (551lb) capacity, could be fitted below the outer wing panels on the Ju 88A-5.

Another KG 30 Ju 88A-5. Based at Westerland-Sylt, the I. Gruppe of this wing was the first to use the Ju 88 in combat, its initial mission involving an anti-shipping attack on British warships in the Firth of Forth on 26 September 1939.

Junkers Ju 88

300 aircraft a month. 1940 saw the appearance of the Ju 88A-2 version, with provision for rocket-assisted take-off gear, followed by the A-4 and similar A-5, both of which featured Junkers Jumo 211 engines, increased wingspan and strengthened landing gear. The Ju 88A played a significant role in the Battle of Britain and the subsequent Blitz raids later in 1940, the type by now equipping 17 Gruppen.

The Ju 88A remained the principal medium bomber of the *Luftwaffe* until the end of the war, later versions adding such features as a balloon cable fender (Ju 88A-6), maritime search radar (A-6/U), tropicalized equipment (A-9, A-10 and A-11), anti-shipping strike modifications

(A-14), enlarged bomb bay (A-15) and provision for torpedo carriage (A-17). The bombers saw service in the Balkans and Mediterranean, and on the Eastern Front. Perhaps the most successful missions were those flown against the Allied North Cape convoys in 1941–42, when Norway-based Ju 88As from III./KG 26 and KG 30 sunk around 27 merchantmen and seven naval vessels.

Night-fighters

The Ju 88 enjoyed much success as a night-fighter, a role in which it first saw action in summer 1940. The first such aircraft were Ju 88C-2 heavy fighters that were flown as intruders by II./NJG 1, attacking British bomber bases from their base in the Netherlands.

First of the dedicated night-fighters was the Ju 88C-6B equipped with FuG 220 Lichtenstein BC radar. Further improvements were manifest in the Ju 88R series, beginning with the R-1 powered by BMW 801 engines, otherwise similar to the Ju 88C-6, and the Ju 88R-2 with uprated BMW 801D engines and with FuG 217 Neptun tail-warning radar.

While Ju 88C and R night-fighters were built in 1942–43, production capacity was concentrated on the bomber versions, and as a result the Ju 88 night-fighters continued to be outnumbered by adaptations of the Messerschmitt Bf 110. In an effort to counter the British night bombing offensive of 1943, the *Luftwaffe*

Specification (Ju 88G-6c)

Type:	Night-fighter
Dimensions:	Length: 15.58m (51ft 1.5in); Wingspan: 20.00m (65ft 7.5in); Height: 4.85m (15ft 11in)
Weight:	13,100kg (28,880lb) maximum take-off
Powerplant:	2 x 1342kW (1800hp) Junkers Jumo 213E liquid-cooled piston engines
Maximum speed:	625km/h (388mph)
Range:	2250km (1398 miles)
Service ceiling:	10,000m (32,810ft)
Crew:	3
Armament:	4 x 20mm (0.79in) MG 151/20 cannon in nose and 2 x upward-firing 20mm MG 151/20 cannon amidships

introduced new night-fighter, the Ju 88G, which became the most important German night-fighter of the war. The Ju 88G employed an enlarged, square fin, and initial Ju88G-0 pre-production aircraft were powered by BMW 801Ds and equipped with Lichtenstein SN-2 radar and four 20mm (0.79in) cannon. The Ju 88G series was

Mistel

In the final, desperate months of the war, the German war machine called upon ever more unconventional ideas in an effort to turn the tide of the fighting. One such was the use of redundant Ju 88s as unmanned missiles. In the Mistel (Mistletoe) composite aircraft weapon, the Ju 88 provided the explosive-filled lower component, which was guided to the vicinity of the target by a manned fighter mounted above the centre fuselage in a piggyback fashion. Once the bomber had been directed at the target, it was released and the fighter returned to base. The initial Mistel I combining the Ju 88A-4 and a Bf 109F fighter. Among the airframes diverted to the Mistel programme were the small batch of Ju 88G-10 ultra long-range heavy fighters, with lengthened fuselages for additional fuel carriage. The Mistel combinations found some success in the last months of the conflict in Europe.

A Ju 88A-4, this 3./KG 30 machine landed by mistake at RAF Lulsgate Bottom, after a night raid on Birkenhead in July 1941. It was subsequently throroughly tested by the RAF at Farnborough.

built in a variety of sub-variants, including the G-6a and G-6b that were produced in Dessau and powered by BMW 801D radials, and the Bernburg-built G-6c that featured Jumo 213E inline engines. Within these sub-variants there existed a plethora of different equipment and weapons fits, radar including the baseline SN-2 and the later FuG 218 Neptun and FuG 240 Berlin. At the controls of the Ju 88, some of the *Luftwaffe*'s most successful night-fighter aces recorded many of their victories. Helmut Lent, commander of NJG 3, scored 102 night victories, followed by Heinz Rökker of 2./NJG 2 (62 victories) and Paul Zorner of II./NJG 100 (59 victories).

Other roles in which the Ju 88 yielded dedicated versions were heavy fighter and reconnaissance fighter (Ju 88C series, generally with a solid nose containing cannon and machine gun armament), long-range reconnaissance (Ju 88D series) and anti-tank. In the latter role, the Ju 88P-1 was a development of the A-4 with a 75mm (2.95in) Pak 40 cannon and was followed by the P-2 to P-4, with different combinations of heavy anti-tank weapons.

Douglas SBD Dauntless
(1938)

By the end of the war in the Pacific, the venerable Dauntless dive-bomber was showing its age, and yet its contribution to victory in a succession of key naval battles cannot be overstated and its tally of Japanese shipping is unmatched.

Wright Cyclone
The SBD-1 was powered by the R-1820-32 Cyclone that developed 746kW (1000hp) on take-off. An intake atop the engine cowling provided carburettor cooling air.

Bomb Sight
The pilot was provided with a three-power telescopic sight that protruded through the windscreen and could be used for both gun- and bomb-aiming.

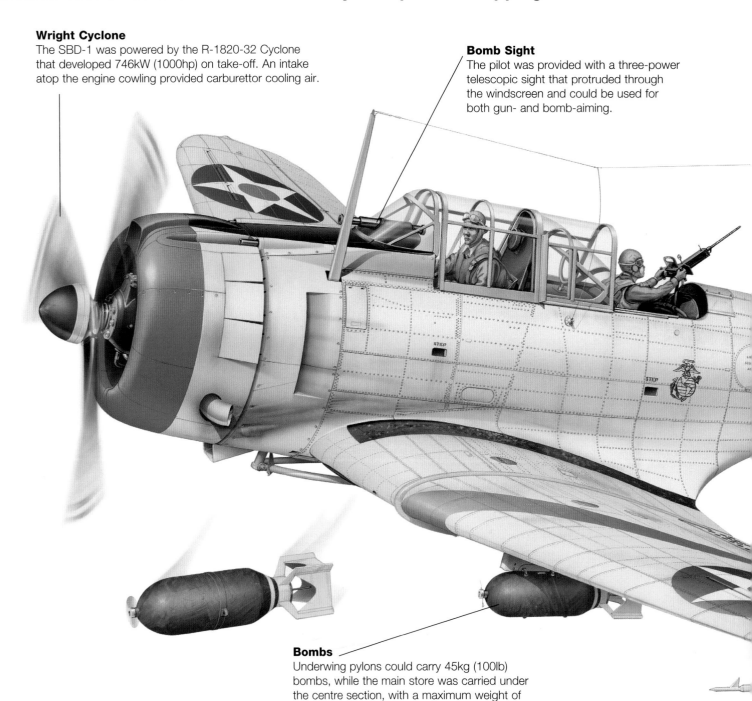

Bombs
Underwing pylons could carry 45kg (100lb) bombs, while the main store was carried under the centre section, with a maximum weight of 725kg (1600lb).

The aircraft that found fame as the Douglas SBD Dauntless began life as a product of the Northrop Corporation, which was responsible for the BT-1 carrier-based dive-bomber of 1938, 54 of which were built to serve on the USS *Yorktown* and *Enterprise*. When Douglas took over Northrop, the BT-1 served as the basis for a reworked prototype XBT-2 of 1938, which was simply a modified development of the Northrop aircraft. In April 1939 the re-designated XSBD-1 won orders from both the U.S. Marine Corps (57 SBD-1 versions) and the U.S. Navy (87 SBD-2s) in order to equip scout and bombing squadrons of the respective service.

Before U.S. forces were thrust into action in the Pacific, Douglas had flown an improved SBD-3, this being outfitted with an additional pair of machine guns in the nose, self-sealing tanks and the Wright R-1820-52 radial engine. The first SBD-3 took to the air in March 1941, and over 500 examples had been delivered by the time Japan attacked Pearl Harbor on 7 December 1941. It fell to an SBD from USS *Enterprise* to sink the first enemy vessel by U.S. air power in World War II: the Japanese submarine *I-70* on December 10.

Similar to the SBD-3, the SBD-4 featured a revised electrical system and was built at the El Segundo,

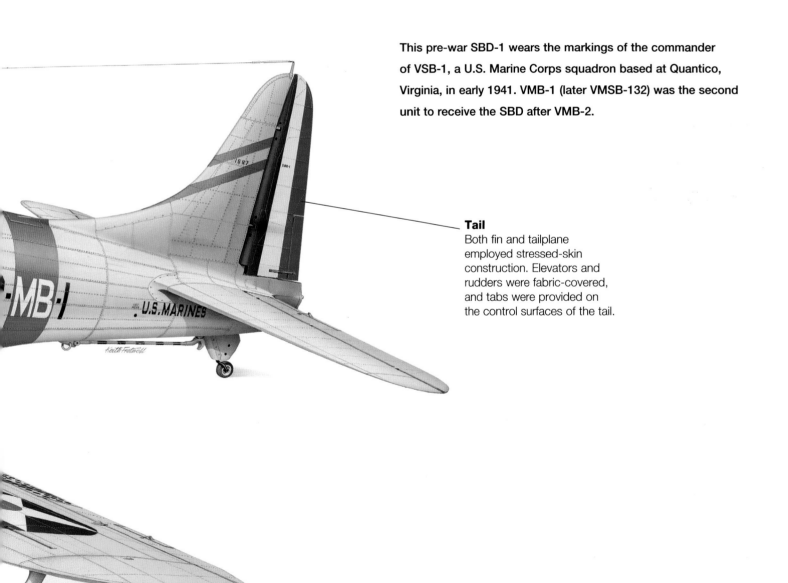

This pre-war SBD-1 wears the markings of the commander of VSB-1, a U.S. Marine Corps squadron based at Quantico, Virginia, in early 1941. VMB-1 (later VMSB-132) was the second unit to receive the SBD after VMB-2.

Tail
Both fin and tailplane employed stressed-skin construction. Elevators and rudders were fabric-covered, and tabs were provided on the control surfaces of the tail.

Douglas SBD-1 Dauntless

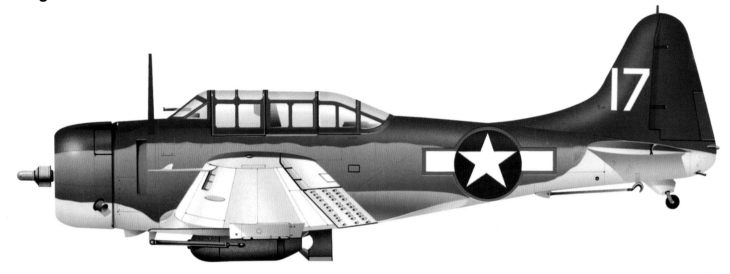

This SBD-4 was operated by VMSB-243, part of the 1st Marine Air Wing, based on Munda on New Georgia, part of the Solomons Islands chain, in August 1943.

California factory, which delivered 780 examples in the course of 1942–43. A number of photo-reconnaissance adaptations of the SBD-1, 2 and 3 were also completed in the period up to 1942. With the establishment of a new Douglas plant at Tulsa, Oklahoma, production here switched to the SBD-5, of which 2409 examples were built. The SBD-5 produced during 1943–44 was powered by an R-1820-60 engine and was followed by

the SBD-6, of which 451 were manufactured with the -66 engine installed. As employed aboard a U.S. Navy carrier, SBDs were generally assigned to one bombing squadron (VB designation) and one scout squadron (VS), part of an overall air wing that also included two squadrons of fighters and one of torpedo-bombers. In practice, both VB and VS units shared similar tasks.

War-winning Dive-bomber

The Dauntless was responsible for sinking a greater tonnage of Japanese shipping than any other aircraft and was central to U.S. naval successes at the Battles of Midway, Coral Sea and the Solomons. This was all the more remarkable considering the fact that the Dauntless was considered obsolescent at the outbreak of the war, and was generally underpowered, vulnerable to enemy fire and limited in terms of endurance. Despite its limited performance, it has been recorded that one Navy SBD crew managed to shoot down seven Japanese A6M Zero fighters in a space of just two days.

In its intended role, the Dauntless made its mark at the Battle of Coral Sea in May 1942. In the course of the battle, SBD-2 and SBD-3 models from USS *Yorktown* combined with Douglas TBD-1 Devastator torpedo-bombers and succeeded in putting the Japanese carrier *Shoho* to the bottom after a 30-minute battle that cost just three U.S. aircraft.

During the Battle of Midway the Dauntless played the pivotal role, when a force of 128 was launched from the decks of Admiral Chester Nimitz's carrier groups to seek out the carriers of Admiral Isoroku Yamamoto in June 1942. The Japanese force was finally discovered

Specification (SBD-5)

Type:	Scout/dive-bomber
Dimensions:	Length: 10.06m (33ft 0in); Wingspan: 12.65m (41ft 6.25in); Height: 3.94m (12ft 11in)
Weight:	4924kg (10,855lb) maximum take-off
Powerplant:	1 x 895kW (1200hp) Wright R-1820-60 radial piston engine
Maximum speed:	394km/h (245mph)
Range:	1770km (1100 miles)
Service ceiling:	7407m (24,300ft)
Crew:	2
Armament:	2 x 12.7mm (0.5in) machine guns, 2 x 7.62mm (0.3in) machine guns plus a bombload of 1 x 726kg (1600lb) bomb under the fuselage and 2 x 147kg (325lb) bombs underwing

with darkness approaching, and the SBDs at the limits of their range and fuel. In the process, 40 of the dive-bombers were lost. The survivors, each armed with a single 1000lb (454kg) armour-piercing bomb, pressed home attacks on the carriers *Kaga*, *Akagi*, *Hiryu* and *Soryu*, sinking all four (three of them set ablaze in the space of just three minutes) and turning the tide of the war in the Pacific.

Subsequent actions in the Pacific saw SBD involved in combat at Rabaul, Guadalcanal and the Solomons, and Truk. By late in the war, the Dauntless had been supplanted by the Curtiss SB2C Helldiver in the dive-bomber role, but this aircraft suffered from a number of shortcomings and was never as successful as the SBD that preceded it. Once the Helldiver was on the scene, however, the earlier aircraft began to be relegated to anti-submarine patrol and close air support duties.

In addition to naval service, the Dauntless was also operated by the U.S. Army Air Forces, which designated the aircraft as the A-24 Banshee. USAAF versions comprised the A-24 (168 SBD-3As), A-24A (170 SBD-4As) and A-24B (615 SBD-5As). By the time production of all versions had come to an end, 5936 SBDs had rolled out of the factories.

Other Operators

U.S. Marine Corps SBDs, carrying centreline and underwing bombs, are seen heading for Japanese targets on Rabaul in 1944. The USMC was the second most prolific Dauntless operator, and certainly the most successful outside the U.S. Navy. In all, 20 Marine squadrons flew the Dauntless. Less auspicious was the service of the A-24, which the USAAF had ordered in January 1941. A-24s saw action in New Guinea and at Makin, but the aircraft proved vulnerable to interception by Japanese fighters. In the face of mounting casualties, the USAAF withdrew the A-24 from the front line. The UK acquired nine Dauntless DB.Mk Is (SBD-5s), but after subjecting the aircraft to test in 1944, rejected it for service. The Royal New Zealand Air Force also took the Dauntless into battle, after receiving SBD-3, SBD-4 and SBD-5 models from Navy and Marine stocks. These saw action at Bougainville. The other combat operator was France, which employed A-24s and SBD-3s at Agadir, Morocco, and in metropolitan France in pursuit of retreating German forces from 1944.

Mitsubishi A6M Zero (1939)

Popularly known as the 'Zero', the Mitsubishi A6M was the world's most capable carrier-based fighter at the time of its appearance, out-performing all land-based contemporaries. Latterly outclassed, it remained in service until the end of the war.

The brainchild of prolific designer Jiro Horikoshi, the Mitsubishi A6M (Allied reporting name 'Zeke') was schemed as a replacement for the same company's A5M carrier fighter. A cantilever low-wing monoplane, the A6M1 prototype completed its maiden flight in April 1939 and in this form was powered by a Mitsubishi Zuisei 13 radial engine. In production form, the A6M2 of early 1940 introduced a new Nakajima Sakae 12 powerplant and was armed with a pair of wing-mounted 20mm (0.79in) cannon, plus two machine guns in the nose. The new engine was a result of early testing, in which the A6M1 had demonstrated excellent performance with the exception of maximum speed, which had failed to meet the original specification.

The official military designation for the new warplane was Navy Type 0 Carrier Fighter and in 1940 initial combat trials were undertaken in China by a pre-production batch. The antiquated Polikarpov fighters flown by the Chinese proved to be no match for the Zero. It was in the course of these operational trials that the Zero recorded its first aerial victory, in September 1940. By the end of that year, the Zero detachment had claimed 59 victories without loss.

Once entering combat in World War II, the highly agile A6M2 proved itself an immediate success, quickly gaining aerial supremacy during the Imperial Japanese Navy's campaigns in the East Indies and Southeast Asia. The A6M2 was the IJN's premier fighter during the raid on Pearl Harbor in December 1941, in which eight Zero fighters were lost from a total of 105 involved in the surprise attack on the U.S. Navy fleet. The A6M remained the service's pre-eminent fighter in theatre as fighting extended to Malaya, the Philippines and Burma. Along the way, it demonstrated its superiority against

Lightweight Construction
In order to achieve the eight-hour endurance specific for operations over the Pacific theatre, the Zero employed a very light construction. The result was an airframe that was vulnerable to hits be even rifle-calibre weapons, and on occasions structural failure could result from a high-speed dive.

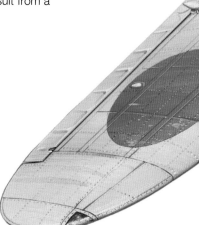

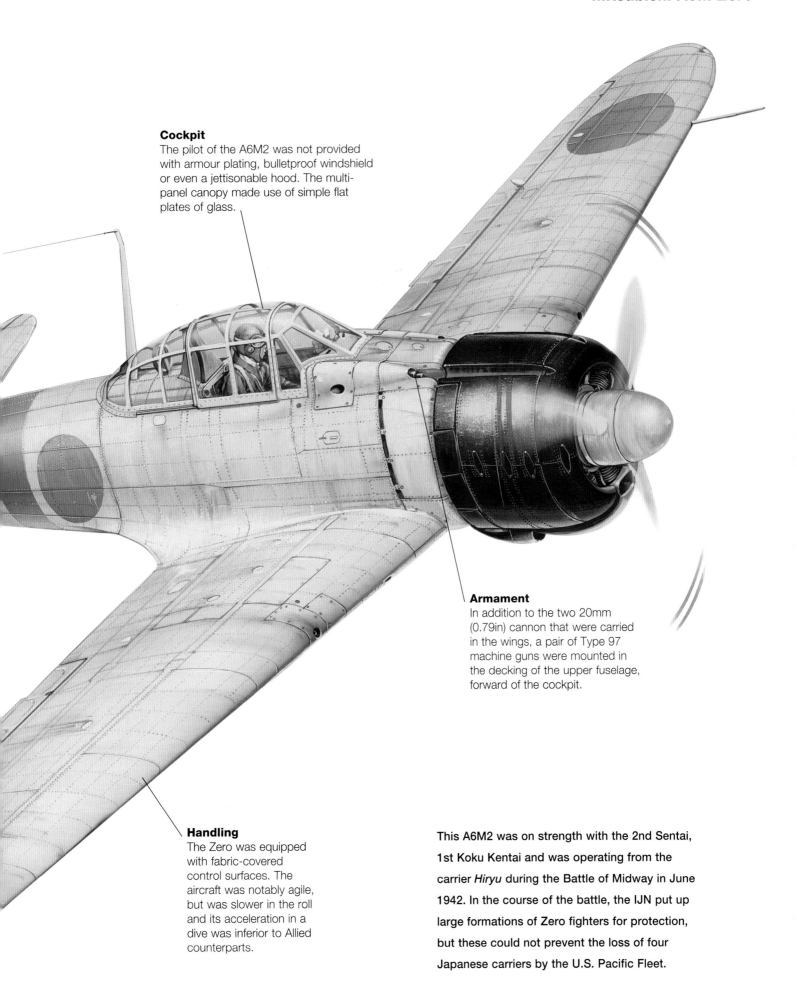

Cockpit
The pilot of the A6M2 was not provided with armour plating, bulletproof windshield or even a jettisonable hood. The multi-panel canopy made use of simple flat plates of glass.

Armament
In addition to the two 20mm (0.79in) cannon that were carried in the wings, a pair of Type 97 machine guns were mounted in the decking of the upper fuselage, forward of the cockpit.

Handling
The Zero was equipped with fabric-covered control surfaces. The aircraft was notably agile, but was slower in the roll and its acceleration in a dive was inferior to Allied counterparts.

This A6M2 was on strength with the 2nd Sentai, 1st Koku Kentai and was operating from the carrier *Hiryu* during the Battle of Midway in June 1942. In the course of the battle, the IJN put up large formations of Zero fighters for protection, but these could not prevent the loss of four Japanese carriers by the U.S. Pacific Fleet.

Mitsubishi A6M Zero

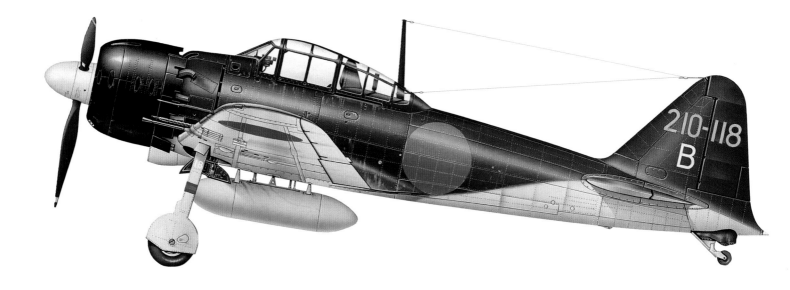

lesser Allied types in theatre, including the Brewster Buffalo, Curtiss P-36 and P-40 and Hawker Hurricane fighters. Japan's leading ace of the Pacific war, Saburo Sakai, flew a Zero, who is believed to have achieved 64 aerial kills.

An improved A6M3 entered service in spring 1942, now powered by a Sakae 21 with two-stage supercharger. Not only supremely manoeuvrable, the Zero was also well equipped for fighting at the extended ranges encountered in the Pacific theatre. The aircraft could carry a fuel tank under the fuselage to increase the endurance of its long-range fighter

Specification (A6M5b)

Type:	Carrier fighter
Dimensions:	Length: 9.12m (29ft 11.1in); Wingspan: 11.00m (36ft 1.1in); Height: 3.51m (11ft 6.2in)
Weight:	2733kg (6025lb) maximum take-off
Powerplant:	1 x 820kW (1100hp) Nakajima NK2F Sakae 21 radial piston engine
Maximum speed:	565km/h (351mph)
Range:	1143km (710 miles)
Service ceiling:	11,740m (38,517ft)
Crew:	1
Armament:	2 x 20mm (0.79in) cannon and 3 x 13.2mm (0.52in) machine guns

The A6M5c sub-variant (93 built) featured improved armament in the form of an additional pair of 13.2mm (0.52in) machine guns fitted outboard of the standard wing cannon.

patrols. Even before the arrival of the powerful Hellcat, however, the A6M had begun to suffer at the hands of the Grumman F4F Wildcat, which, although inferior in terms of performance and agility, was better able to withstand battle damage and possessed heavier-hitting armament, self-sealing tanks and armour protection for the pilot. While the Zero was always fast, it was also underpowered, and as a result the design stressed lightweight construction. This, in turn, led to a fighter that was vulnerable to even machine gun fire, and had little in the way of armour protection.

Changing Fortunes

The Battle of Midway of June 1942 represented a watershed for the Zero, and thereafter the Japanese fighter began to be increasingly outclassed by U.S. opposition, in particular the U.S. Navy's Grumman F6F Hellcat, which proved to be faster than the Zero at all altitudes. While the A6M3 version had helped to offset the appearance of the Wildcat, it could do little in the face of the Hellcat.

In an effort to wring additional performance out of the basic airframe, the IJN introduced the A6M5, with Sakae 21 and an improved exhaust system. This version was actually slower than the A6M2, but enjoyed a superior rate of climb and was faster in the dive. It

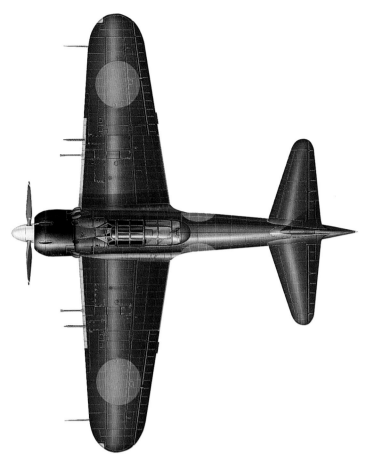

was also built in greater numbers than any of the other Zero models. As the tide of the war turned against the Japanese, the Zero was also used for kamikaze raids, and in one action, five A6M5s sunk the U.S. Navy carrier *St Lo* and damaged three others in October 1944.

Final Models

The last models in the Zero line comprised the A6M6 of late 1944, with a water-methanol boosted Sakae 31, and the A6M7 fighter/dive-bomber of mid-1945 with a rack under the fuselage for the carriage of a single 250kg (551lb) bomb. In total, in excess of 10,000 Zero fighters were completed, including a floatplane version built by Nakajima as the A6M2N (Allied reporting name 'Rufe'). As such, it was the most prolific Japanese fighter of all time.

Although the A6M's vulnerability to the Hellcat in particular was clear by the time of the Battles of the Philippines and Leyte Gulf in 1944, the lack of an adequate replacement meant the Zero was forced to soldier on in IJN service until the bitter end.

Attack on Rabaul

The Japanese attack on Rabaul in January 1942 was typical of the whirlwind successes in which the A6M was pitched in the initial phase of the war in the Pacific. Air power on Rabaul, the key strategic base on the island of New Britain, was provided by Australian Hudson light bombers and Wirraway reconnaissance aircraft, but there was no genuine fighter cover. On 20 January, a force of 120 A6M2s, Aichi D3A1s and Nakajima B5Ns took off from the carriers *Zuikaku*, *Shokaku*, *Kaga* and *Akagi*, attacking installations at Rabaul. Slicing through gallant opposition put up by the Wirraways, the IJN aircraft paved the way for a task force of 5300 men that landed at Simpson Harbour on 23 January, securing the port and the airfield at Kavieng. After capturing Rabaul, Japan established a major base and proceeded to land on mainland New Guinea, advancing towards Port Moresby and Australia.

North American B-25 Mitchell (1939)

The USAAF's definitive light/medium bomber of World War II, the B-25 may have served in more campaigns than any other type in that conflict. The type also gave good service in U.S. Navy and Allied hands, and flew the 'Doolittle raid' on Japan.

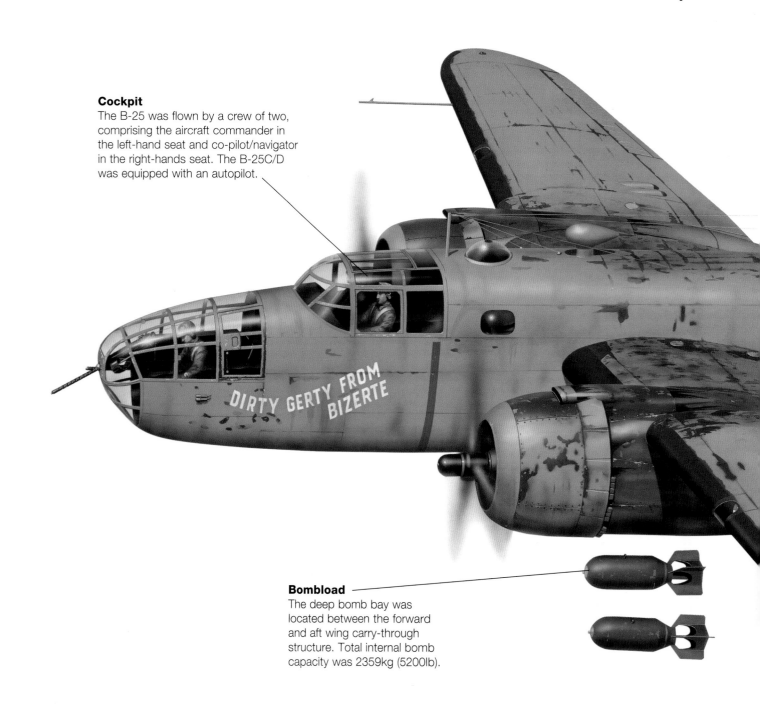

Cockpit
The B-25 was flown by a crew of two, comprising the aircraft commander in the left-hand seat and co-pilot/navigator in the right-hands seat. The B-25C/D was equipped with an autopilot.

Bombload
The deep bomb bay was located between the forward and aft wing carry-through structure. Total internal bomb capacity was 2359kg (5200lb).

The B-25 began as the North American NA-40 that was formulated in response to a U.S. Army Air Corps specification of 1938 calling for an attack bomber. First flown in March 1939, the NA-40 was powered by Pratt & Whitney R-1830 engines and was then adapted as the NA-40B, with Wright R-2600-A71 Cyclones. This led to the NA-26 design that was completed in September 1939. The NA-26 was ordered into production as the B-25, which first flew in August 1940, and which now incorporated various recommendations made by the Army. The result was an aircraft with a good balance of speed, armament and agility; salient features included twin engines on a mid-mounted wing, provision for a cockpit crew of three using side-by-side seating and a retractable

Dorsal Turret
Rear protection was provided by a Bendix dorsal turret, armed with two 0.5in (12.7mm) Browning machine guns.

This B-25D (serial number 41-29896) served in North Africa with the 340th Bombardment Group (Medium) in 1943. The D-model was essentially similar to the B-25C, although the entire production run (2290) was completed by North American at Dallas, Texas, rather than Inglewood, California.

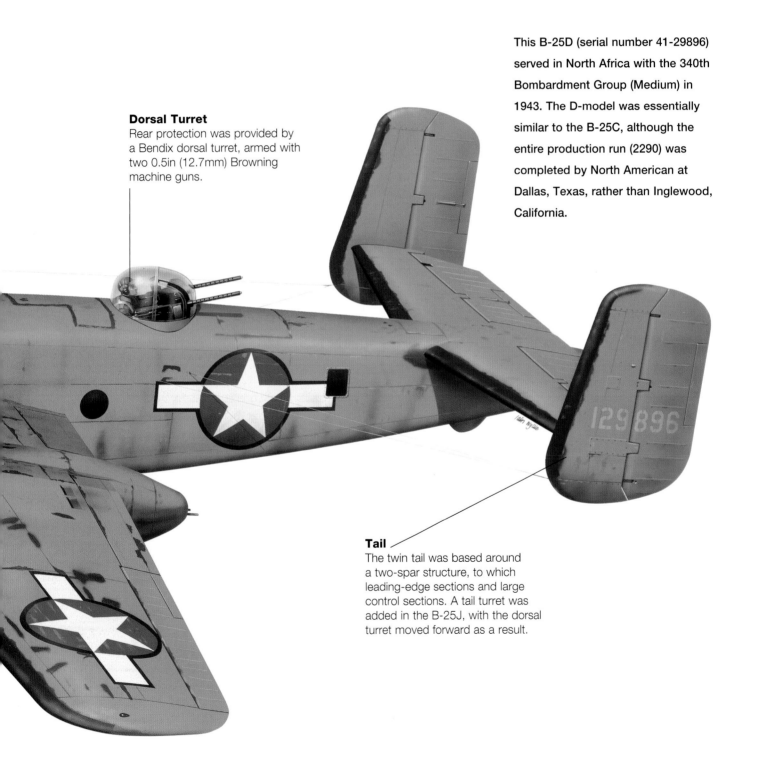

Tail
The twin tail was based around a two-spar structure, to which leading-edge sections and large control sections. A tail turret was added in the B-25J, with the dorsal turret moved forward as a result.

North American B-25 Mitchell

tricycle undercarriage. The Mitchell popular name was applied in honour of William Mitchell, the champion of U.S. air power between the wars.

The 40 B-25As brought further improvements to the basic design, including additional armour and self-sealing tanks. As the initial production variant, the B-25A entered service with the 17th Bombardment Group (Medium) in spring 1941. The unit scored a 'first' when it sunk a Japanese submarine near the mouth of the Columbia River on 24 December 1941. This was the first 'kill' of an enemy submarine in U.S. waters.

Development of the B-25 continued apace, first with the B-25B (120 built) that added power-operated Bendix gun turrets in the dorsal and ventral positions, while the tail guns were deleted. Based on the B-25B, the B-25C

Specification (B-25D)

Type:	Medium bomber
Dimensions:	Length: 16.12m (52ft 11in); Wingspan: 20.60m (67ft 7in); Height: 4.82m (15ft 10in)
Weight:	15,880kg (35,000lb) maximum take-off
Powerplant:	2 x 1268kW (1700hp) Wright R-2600-13 radial piston engines
Maximum speed:	457km/h (284mph)
Range:	2414km (1500 miles)
Service ceiling:	6462m (21,200ft)
Crew:	5
Armament:	6 x 12.7mm (0.5in) machine guns plus a maximum bombload of 1361kg (3000lb)

Wearing the 'Air Apache' badge on the tail, this B-25J was part of the 345th Bombardment Group (Medium), which moved to Leyte in the Philippines in November 1944. The 'bat wings' nose art was associated with the group's 499th Squadron.

differed in its use of Wright R-2600-13 radial engines in place of the earlier R-2600-9s.

The B-25C was the first model to be built in significant numbers, production topping off at 1619, and this variant also added features such as an autopilot and underwing bomb racks. The B-25D, of which 2290 were built, was generally similar to the B-25C, and served as the basis for a reconnaissance version that entered service under the F-10 designation.

B-25 'Gunships'

The B-25 was first taken into battle by the 3rd BG in the Southwest Pacific. The 17th BG, meanwhile, was readied for a daring attack on Tokyo, the famous 'Doolittle raid'. The B-25 also saw action over New Guinea, while in the Mediterranean theatre the 12th Air Force began employing the type in North Africa. B-25s in India came under the command of the 10th Air Force, while the 11th Air Force fought in the Aleutians. In New Guinea, the B-25 excelled as a specialist low-level strike aircraft with the 5th Air Force.

Primary targets included Japanese airfields and shipping, and Maj Paul I. 'Pappy' Gunn supervised the development of dedicated ground-attack versions, armed with up to eight forward-firing Browning machine guns, as well as fragmentation bombs. A dramatic demonstration of the B-25's prowess in the low-level role came during the Battle of the Bismarck Sea in March

A front view of the B-25J from the 499th 'Bats Outa Hell'. The aircraft, which carried the individual name 'Betty's Dream', was fitted with a total of 18 guns, including 12 in the nose.

1943. Combined with Australian Bristol Beaufighters and USAAF B-17s, B-25s and Douglas A-20s of the 3rd and 38th BG hit a Japanese convoy with such force that only four destroyers from a total force of 16 vessels escaped.

B-25s operated by the RAF equipped No.2 (Bomber) Group in Mitchell Mk I and Mk II versions. A total of 850 B-25s were also supplied to the USSR, deliveries of these aircraft beginning in March 1942.

Doolittle's Raid

On 18 April 1942, a force of 16 17th BG B-25Bs led by Lt Col James H. Doolittle took off from the confines of the flight deck of the carrier USS *Hornet*. At the time, the B-25 was the heaviest aircraft to have operated from a carrier. Thus began a flight of 1184km (714 miles) to strike the Japanese capital, together with other targets at Nagoya, Kobe and Yokohama. The B-25Bs were specially prepared for the mission, with increased fuel capacity and with their defensive armament removed.

While the military effects of the raid were limited, the propaganda value was enormous for a U.S. still smarting from the surprise attack on Pearl Harbor. After pressing home their attacks, the surviving B-25s made for China, where most force-landed. In recognition for the raid, Doolittle received the Medal of Honor. Before the end of the year he was a major general, in taken command of the 12th Air Force in North Africa.

Armament experiments saw the creation of the B-25G and B-25H versions in 1943, these carrying different types of 75mm (2.95in) cannon. The first of these gunships, the experimental XB-25G, was tested with a 75mm U.S. Army field gun. In production form, the 405 B-25Gs employed an M4 cannon of the same calibre, complemented by a battery of six machine guns. The B-25H (1000 built) carried even heavier armament in the form of a 75mm cannon and 14 (later increased to 18) machine guns.

The variant to see most widespread use was the B-25J, which was available with either a glazed or solid nose. In RAF hands, the J-model was known as the Mitchell Mk III. The 4390 B-25Js were powered by R-2600-92 engines and armed with 12 machine guns.

The U.S. Navy was another customer for B-25 derivatives under the PBJ-1 designation. In total, the Navy received 706 aircraft, to a similar standard to the B-25J. These were all transferred to the USMC, which operated them as PBJ-1C and PBJ-1D that served in the South Pacific with search radar in the belly and nose, and PBJ-1Js with radar in a starboard wing pod. Nine USMC squadrons saw combat in World War II, with VMB-413 the first into action at Stirling Island in the Solomons in March 1944.

Post-war, the B-25 continued to provide valuable service to a number of foreign air arms, and remained on strength with the U.S. military as a trainer, initially with the AT-25 (advanced trainer) designation, and latterly as the TB-25. In this form, the aircraft remained in U.S. Air Force service well into the 1950s. Indeed, the final U.S. military example, used as a staff transport, was not struck off charge until May 1960.

Focke-Wulf Fw 190 (1939)

At the time of its combat appearance, the Fw 190 was the most capable fighter in service, offering a winning combination of performance and manoeuvrability. Further development ensured it retained its prowess until the end of the war.

Conceived as a replacement for the Bf 109, the Fw 190 entered development in 1937 under the design leadership of Kurt Tank. Powered by an air-cooled BMW radial engine, the cantilever low-wing monoplane fighter first flew in prototype form in June 1939. The second prototype,

V2, featured an armament of two 13mm (0.51in) MG 131 machine guns and two 7.92mm (0.31in) MG 17 machine guns. The pre-production Fw 190A-0 version was powered by a 14-cylinder BMW 801 radial and was built with short- and long-span wings. The long-span model

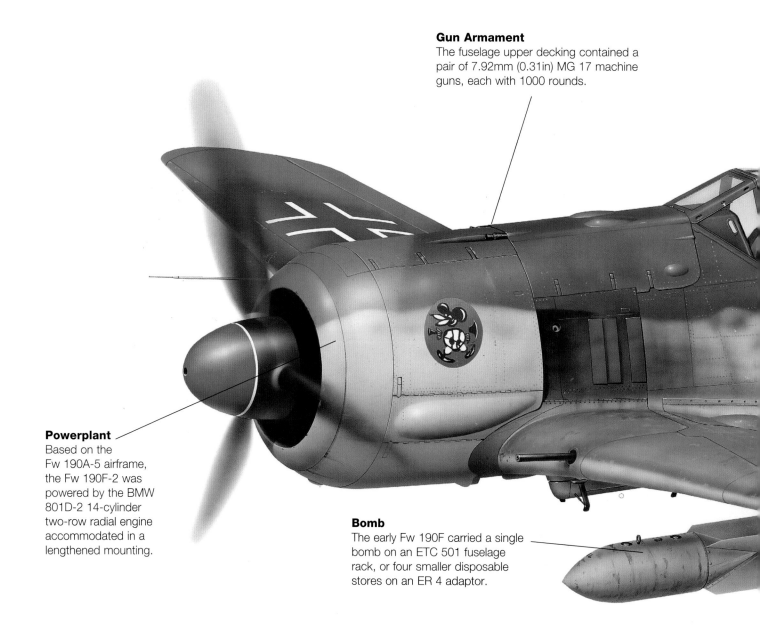

Gun Armament
The fuselage upper decking contained a pair of 7.92mm (0.31in) MG 17 machine guns, each with 1000 rounds.

Powerplant
Based on the Fw 190A-5 airframe, the Fw 190F-2 was powered by the BMW 801D-2 14-cylinder two-row radial engine accommodated in a lengthened mounting.

Bomb
The early Fw 190F carried a single bomb on an ETC 501 fuselage rack, or four smaller disposable stores on an ER 4 adaptor.

proved most promising and was subsequently ordered into production as the Fw 190A-1. Production deliveries commenced in mid-1941, with the first operator being 6./JG 26. Once in combat over Western Europe from September, the fighter quickly proved superior to the RAF's Spitfire Mk V.

The A-series included the Fw 190A-3 with BMW 801D-2 engine and an armament of four 20mm (0.79in) cannon and two machine guns. The A-4 was produced in fighter-bomber, bomber-destroyer and tropicalized sub-variants, all of which featured water-methanol power boosting. In the A-5 the nose was stretched slightly, and this model yielded sub-variants including the A-5/U6 fighter-

bomber, the A-5/U12 with an armament of six 30mm (1.18in) cannon, the long-range A-5/U8 fighter-bomber, the A-5/U11 close-support aircraft with a 30mm MK 103 cannon beneath each wing, and the A-5/U14 and U15 with provision for torpedo carriage. Finally, the A-5/U16 bomber-destroyer added a 30mm MK 108 cannon in the outboard wing position. The A-7 and A-8 were introduced to production in December 1943 and offered increased armament and armour.

Night-fighting was a specialist role for which the Fw 190A-5/U2 was developed. This was used for *Wilde Sau* (wild boar) tactics in which day fighters were eased at night, especially in order to counter the 'Window' jamming

Tailfin
The robust fin was comprised of two spars, one vertical along the rear and one angled along the leading edge. The rudder ran the full length of the fin.

Operating over Kharkov on the Eastern Front in 1943, this Fw 190F-2 was among the dedicated close-support versions that replaced the Ju 87 in this role. This particular aircraft was operated by the 5. Staffel, II. Gruppe of Schlachtgeschwader 1.

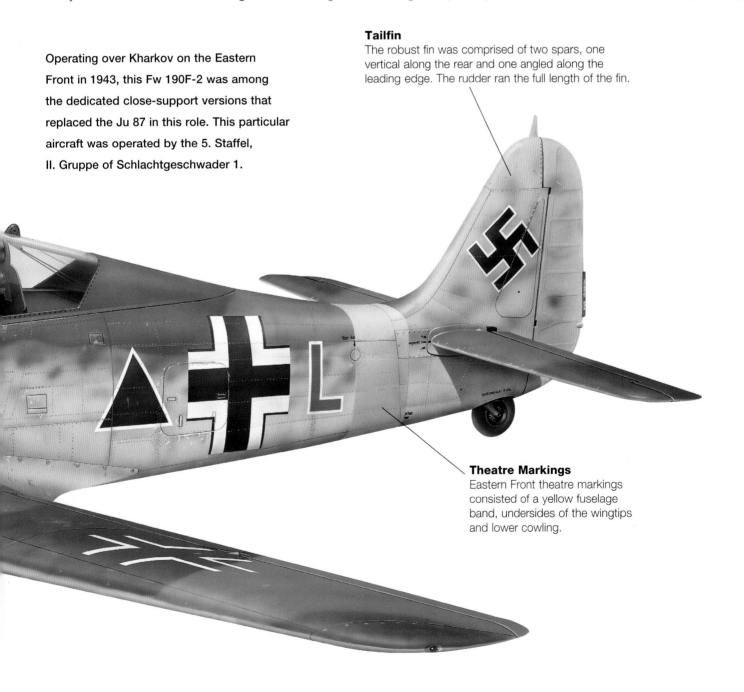

Theatre Markings
Eastern Front theatre markings consisted of a yellow fuselage band, undersides of the wingtips and lower cowling.

Focke-Wulf Fw 190

employed by RAF bombers. The prime exponent of *Wilde Sau* was JG 300, which operated both Fw 190s and Bf 109Gs. The tactics are first employed in August 1943, and eventually proved relatively successful. The Fw 190A-8 became the most numerous wilde Sau fighter.

The 'Dora' series was the next major production version, developed on the basis of a number of Fw 190A-7s that were modified with liquid-cooled Junkers Jumo 213A V-12 engines, and in this form served as prototypes for the Fw 190D-0. The Fw 190D was distinguished by its lengthened nose that mounted the

Specification (Fw 190A-8)

Type:	Fighter
Dimensions:	Length: 8.84m (29ft 0in); Wingspan: 10.50m (34ft 5.4in); Height: 3.96m (13ft 0in)
Weight:	4900kg (10,803lb) maximum take-off
Powerplant:	1 x 1566kW (2100hp) BMW 801D-2 radial piston engine
Maximum speed:	654km/h (405mph)
Range:	805km (500 miles)
Service ceiling:	11,400m (37,402ft)
Crew:	1
Armament:	4 x 20mm (0.79in) cannon and 2 x 7.92mm (0.31in) machine guns

6./JG 26 was based at Coquelles, in the Pas de Calais, in November 1941. As such it received some of the first production Fw 190A-1s. This example was flown by Walter Schneider.

Jumo 213 within an annular cowling. Other changes included provision for a drop tank on each of two underwing racks. The key sub-variant was the Fw 190D-9 that entered *Luftwaffe* service in autumn 1944. Offering a top speed of 685km/h (426mph) it has a strong claim to be the finest piston-engined German fighter of the war. The D-9 was powered by a 1670kW (2240hp) Jumo 213A with water-methanol boosting and was armed with two cannon and two machine guns. The ground-attack-optimized D-12 featured improved armour protection around the engine and was armed with two MG 151/20s plus a single MK 108 cannon firing through the spinner.

The Fw 190F and Fw 190G were developed in order to provide dedicated ground-attack aircraft, with the capability to carry up to 1800kg (3968lb) of disposable stores. The first of the ground-attack models to enter service was the Fw 190G-1. This was based on the Fw 190A-5, but was adapted for the carriage of a 1800kg (3968lb) bomb, which demanded a strengthened undercarriage; wing armament was reduced to a pair of MG 151/20 cannon, while wing racks could accommodate two drop tanks.

The Fw 190F-1 appeared after the first of the G-series, in early 1943. In many respects similar to the Fw 190A-4, the F-1 differed in having additional armour protection for

A plan view of Schneider's Fw 190A-1 demonstrates the excellent view provided by the one-piece, rear-sliding canopy. Powerplant for the A-1 was the 1193kW (1600hp) BMW 801C-1.

the cockpit and powerplant, the outboard 20mm (0.79in) cannon deleted and an ETC 51 bomb rack installed beneath the fuselage. The Fw 190F-2 was distinguished by its bubble canopy, while the F-3 was equipped to carry a 250kg (551lb) bomb beneath the fuselage. Field modifications were supplied in the form of the Fw 190F-3/R1 and F-3/R3, with four ETC 50 underwing bomb racks or two 30mm (1.18in) MK 103 cannon in the same location.

Development of the Fw 190D airframe continued, producing the long-span Focke-Wulf Ta 152 (the designation reflecting the input of chief designer Tank), which offered increased armament and a boosted Jumo 213E/B for a top speed of 760km/h (472mph) at 12,500m (41,010ft).

Fw 190A: First into Combat

Seen here under test in summer 1941 in the form of pre-production Fw 190A-0 series machines (both 'small wing' and the definitive 'large wing' versions), the A-series was the first to enter combat. The operational test unit for the new fighter, dubbed Würger (Shrike), was the II. Gruppe of JG 26, while production aircraft began to roll out of the factory in June 1941. An initial pair of aircraft from the Arado production line were delivered in August, while another two from AGO followed in October. By late September 82 Fw 190A-1s had been accepted. II./JG 26 based at Moorseele, Belgium, and re-equipped fully, and III./JG 26 at Liegescourt in France was in the process of conversion. The Fw 190 demonstrated an immediate performance advantage over the Spitfire Mk V, but the A-1 version suffered from engine overheating, and was replaced in production in autumn 1941 by the A-2, with an improved BMW 801C-2 engine and revised armament, with two 20mm (0.79in) cannon replacing the machine guns formerly carried in the wing roots.

Ilyushin Il-2 *Shturmovik* (1939)

Built in greater numbers than any other military aircraft in history, the Il-2 was a war-winner for the Soviets, with over 36,000 built between 1941 and 1955. The ground-attacker was capable of defeating the best-protected German tanks.

Of robust construction, with generous application of armour, hard-hitting armament and typically operated with heavy fighter protection, the Ilyushin Il-2 *Shturmovik* (attacker) was one of the most effective weapons employed by the Soviet war machine during World War II. The *Shturmovik* concept dated back to the early 1930s, and by 1938 had been refined by Sergey Ilyushin and his team at the Central Design Bureau. The prototype for the Il-2 was

This Il-2M3 was on strength with the 566th Attack Aviation Regiment, 277th Attack Aviation Division, Soviet Frontal Aviation, and served on the Leningrad front in summer 1944. Flown by squadron commander V.I. Mykhlik, the inscriptions on the fuselage read 'For Leningrad' and 'Revenge for Khristenko', a pilot lost in combat in early 1944.

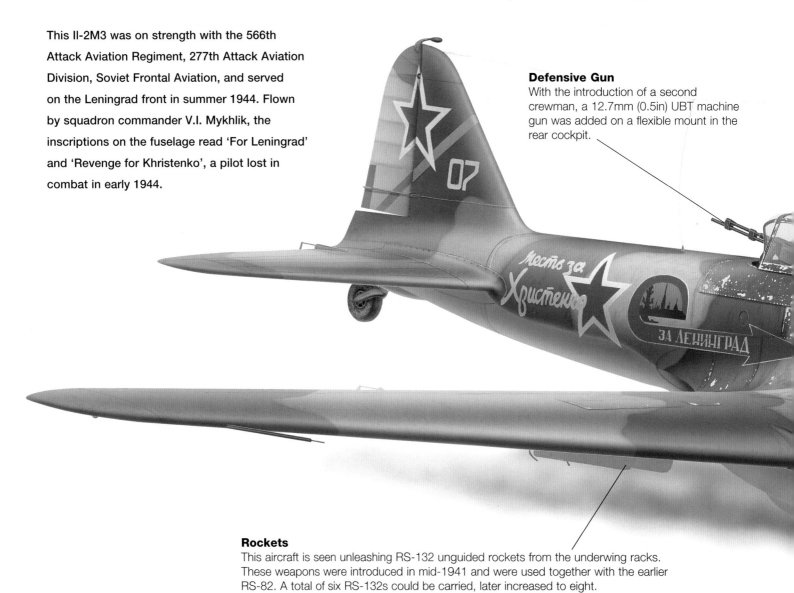

Defensive Gun
With the introduction of a second crewman, a 12.7mm (0.5in) UBT machine gun was added on a flexible mount in the rear cockpit.

Rockets
This aircraft is seen unleashing RS-132 unguided rockets from the underwing racks. These weapons were introduced in mid-1941 and were used together with the earlier RS-82. A total of six RS-132s could be carried, later increased to eight.

a heavily-armoured two-seater with protection for the crew, engine, radiators and fuel tank. The prototype TsKB-55 was first flown in October 1939, before it received the Soviet Air Force designation BSh-2.

Powered by the original Mikulin AM-35 liquid-cooled engine, the BSh-2 was found to be overweight and underpowered. The Ilyushin *Shturmovik* was thus redesigned as the single-seat TsKB-57, with the more powerful Mikulin AM-38 engine, optimized for low level operation. First flown on October 1940, the TsKB-57 passed state acceptance trials in March 1941, and was re-designated as the Il-2 in April. Deliveries to operational units commenced in May 1941.

Although only around 250 examples had been completed by the time Nazi Germany invaded the Soviet Union in June

1941, production ramped up once the aircraft factories in western Russia were moved east of the Ural Mountains. Stalin himself announced that the Red Army needed the Il-2 'like air, like bread', further accelerating the production tempo.

The Il-2 first saw combat with the 4th Attack Aviation Regiment (4th ShAP) over the Berezina River in the days after the German invasion began. Since pilots and ground crew alike had received little formal training on the new type, losses were initially high. Before long, however, tactics were refined, and the Il-2 was typically flown in an echeloned assault by four to 12 aircraft, which simultaneously attacked their target in a shallow, turning dive. Meanwhile, rocket projectiles were found to be capable of taking out most armour with a single hit, but

Cockpit Armour
The pilot was seated in an armoured tub, with a thickness of 5–12mm (0.2–0.5in) and which also extended to protect the engine, and was capable of defeating all small arms fire.

Engine
The Il-2M3 was powered by a Mikulin AM-38F liquid-cooled V-12, developing 1285kW (1720hp). Introduced in July 1942, it was capable of running on motor fuel.

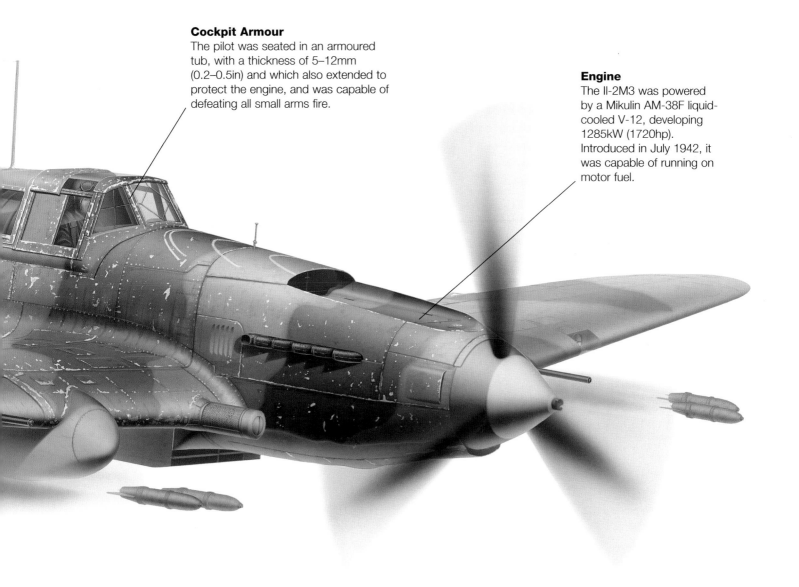

required considerable skill to aim. As a result, many pilots favoured the fixed armament of two forward-firing 20mm (0.79in) cannon and two machine guns, or otherwise PTAB shaped-charge bomblets, the latter first being employed on a large scale during the Battle of Kursk in July 1943.

Continued losses to enemy fighters forced the reintroduction of a rear gunner. As a stopgap measure, Il-2s were modified in the field, with an aperture cut in the fuselage behind the cockpit for a gunner armed with a 12.7mm (0.5in) UBT machine gun in an improvised

A frontal view of the Il-10. Powered by a Mikulin AM-42 driving a three-bladed propeller, the Il-10 demonstrated greatly enhanced perforrnance compared to the Il-2.

mounting. A more definitive response to the Il-2's vulnerability to enemy fighters appeared in February 1942 in the form of the two-seat Il-2M. In this version the rear gunner was seated under an elongated canopy. The Il-2M entered service in September 1942 and surviving single-seaters were modified to a similar standard.

Other improvements introduced during the course of the war included the replacement of the original 20mm (0.9in) cannon with weapons of 23mm (0.9in) (in early 1942) or 37mm (1.45in) calibre, aerodynamic improvements, wooden as opposed to wooden outer wing panels and increased fuel capacity.

The Il-2M3 of 1943 incorporated redesigned wings with 15 degrees of sweepback on the outer panels of the wing leading edge, and nearly straight trailing edges. The 'arrow wing' *Shturmovik* offered much improved performance and handling and the Il-2M3 became the most numerous model. The Il-2M3 was available for service in January 1943 in time to take part in the closing stages of the Battle of Stalingrad. In one celebrated incident in July 1943, Il-2M3s reportedly destroyed 70 of the German 9th Panzer Division's tanks in a period of just 20 minutes. Two hours of constant attacks then succeeded in destroying 270 tanks of the 3rd Panzer Division.

Outside of the Soviet Air Force, wartime Il-2s served with Polish, Czech, Yugoslav and Bulgarian units. As

Specification (Il-2M3)

Type:	Ground-attack aircraft
Dimensions:	Length: 11.60m (38ft 1in); Wingspan: 14.60m (47ft 11in); Height: 4.20m (13ft 9in)
Weight:	6380kg (14,065lb) maximum take-off
Powerplant:	1 x 1285kW (1285hp) Mikulin AM-38F V-12 liquid-cooled piston engine
Maximum speed:	414km/h (257mph)
Range:	720km (450 miles)
Service ceiling:	5500m (18,045ft)
Crew:	2
Armament:	2 x 23mm (0.9in) forward-firing cannon, 2 x 7.62mm (0.3in) forward-firing machine guns, 1 x 7.62mm machine gun in rear cockpit, plus up to 600kg (1320lb) of disposable stores underwing

This Il-10 was operated by a Soviet Air Force unit based in Poland in 1945. Three regiments took Il-10s into battle before the end of the war in the west, with another active in the Far East.

a follow-on *Shturmovik*, Ilyushin produced the Il-10, with a new AM-42 powerplant, and this aircraft entered front-line service in October 1944. Since the Soviets now enjoyed air superiority over the *Luftwaffe*, the Il-10 was able to do away with a certain amount of armour,

although it retained the rear gunner. Structure of the aircraft was now all-metal and the basic armament of two 23mm (0.9in) cannon and two machine guns in the wing was retained. A new 20mm (0.79in) weapon was available as an alternative to the previous defensive machine gun. The Il-10 was also license-built in Czechoslovakia and was exported in considerable numbers to China and North Korea after World War II, and saw action in the Korean War.

The Battle of Kursk

During the Battle of Kursk in the summer of 1943, Vasily Ryazanov, commander of the 1st Attack Aviation Corps, made notably effective use of the Il-2 as part of a combined-arms force that used the *Shturmoviks* alongside infantry, armour and artillery. Prior to the battle, the Soviets assembled 35 per cent of their entire combat aircraft strength at Kursk, and these enjoyed superior maintenance and larger forward fuel reserves than their *Luftwaffe* counterparts. The Il-2s operated over Kursk in large numbers,

harassing German armour and racking up huge victory claims, although their own losses were significant. Ryazanov twice received the Gold Star of Hero of the Soviet Union, and his 1st Attack Aviation Corps became the first unit to be awarded the honorific title of Guards. The victory at Kursk stands as a turning point in the war, after which the Red Army held the strategic initiative until the end of the war.

De Havilland Mosquito (1940)

Immortalized as the 'Wooden Wonder' on account of its construction, the Mosquito was the RAF's most flexible warplane of World War II, excelling as a high-speed reconnaissance aircraft, light bomber, night-fighter, fighter-bomber and anti-shipping aircraft. Its service career lasted well into the 1950s.

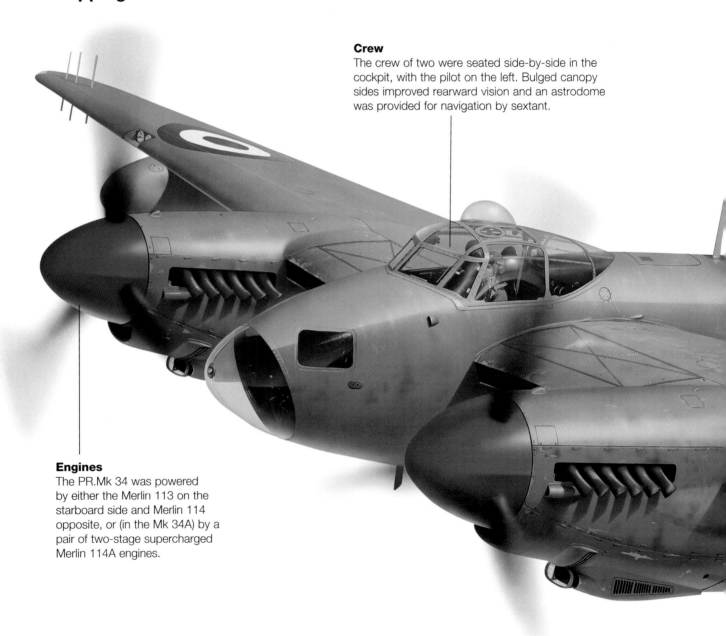

Crew
The crew of two were seated side-by-side in the cockpit, with the pilot on the left. Bulged canopy sides improved rearward vision and an astrodome was provided for navigation by sextant.

Engines
The PR.Mk 34 was powered by either the Merlin 113 on the starboard side and Merlin 114 opposite, or (in the Mk 34A) by a pair of two-stage supercharged Merlin 114A engines.

Under a design team led by Geoffrey de Havilland, work on the D.H.98 Mosquito began as a private venture in October 1938, the original proposal scheming a light bomber that would make use of primarily wooden construction in order to avoid the constraints of wartime reliance on strategically vital materials. In total 50 of the aircraft were ordered in 1940 under Specification B.1/40, and a first prototype Mosquito made its maiden flight in November 1940, powered by a pair of 1089kW (1460hp) Rolls-Royce Merlin 21s. The aircraft immediately displayed impeccable performance, including a top speed in excess of any of the RAF's then front-line fighters.

This Mosquito PR.Mk 34 was flown by No.81 Squadron, based at RAF Tengah, Singapore, in 1955 as part of the Far East Air Force. A total of 50 of this ultimate mark of photo-reconnaissance Mosquito were completed by Percival.

Wooden Construction
The fuselage employed an oval tapering cross-section constructed of balsa, sandwiched between plywood sheets.

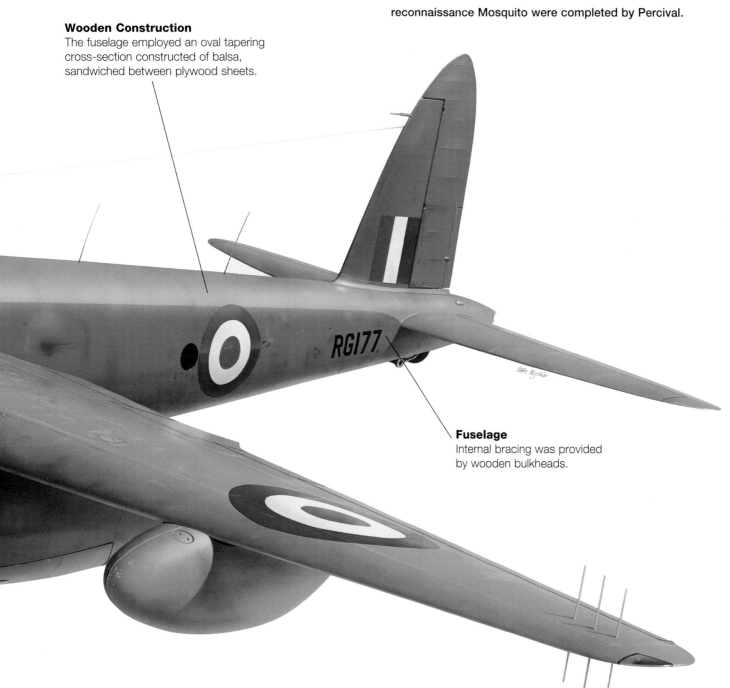

Fuselage
Internal bracing was provided by wooden bulkheads.

De Havilland Mosquito

An initial production batch involved 10 aircraft that were completed as Mosquito B.Mk IV Series I light bombers with glazed nose and an internal bomb bay, the first example of which flew in September 1941. It paved the way for the definitive B.Mk IV Series II, with Merlin 21, 23 or 25 engines in lengthened nacelles. The Series II entered service with No.105 Squadron and completed its first combat mission in May 1942, during a raid on Cologne. Such was its speed that the Mosquito light bomber was fielded unarmed, and employed its performance to escape the attentions of enemy fighters.

Later in the war the light bomber Mosquito range was expanded to include aircraft with bulged bomb bays for the carriage of 4000lb (1814kg) 'Cookie' bombs, while the Mosquito B.Mk VII was Canadian-built, with

Frontal view of a Mosquito B.Mk IV Series II light bomber, which introduced various refinements including extended nacelles, enlarged tailplane and flame dampeners on the exhausts.

Packard Merlin Mk 31s. The B.Mk IX featured increased bombload and Merlin 72 engines. The B.Mk XVI added a pressurized cabin, improved navigation equipment and bulged bomb bay. The final wartime bombers were the B.Mk XX and B.Mk 25, both built in Canada.

Photo Reconnaissance

Photo reconnaissance was always a primary role of the Mosquito, and of the three prototypes, the last to fly, in June 1941, was equipped for this role. The PR version, was, however, the first to see service, completing a daylight reconnaissance sortie over occupied France in September of the same year. The sole Mosquito PR.Mk I was followed by a number of conversions of the B.Mk IV, creating the PR.Mk IV with provision for up to four cabinets. The similar PR.Mk VIII introduced Merlin 61 engines with two-stage superchargers.

Built in more significant numbers was the PR.Mk IX that was based on the B.Mk IX, with Merlin 72 engines and increased fuel capacity. The first pressurized PR version was the Mosquito PR.Mk XVI, a variant of the B.Mk XVI that also added an astrodome. The PR.Mk 32, meanwhile, was a high-altitude model, similar to the Mosquito NF.Mk XV night-fighter, with a lightened airframe and Merlin 113s. The ultimate reconnaissance version was the PR.Mk 34, which saw active post-war service, and was equipped for very long-range missions with additional fuel in a bulged bomb bay.

Specification (Mosquito NF.Mk 30)

Type:	Night-fighter
Dimensions:	Length: 12.73m (41ft 9in); Wingspan: 16.51m (54ft 2in); Height: 4.65m (15ft 3in)
Weight:	9798kg (21,600lb) maximum take-off
Powerplant:	2 x 1275kW (1700hp) Rolls-Royce Merlin 76 V-12 liquid-cooled piston engines
Maximum speed:	655km/h (407mph)
Range:	1143km (710 miles)
Service ceiling:	11,885m (39,000ft)
Crew:	2
Armament:	4 x 20mm (0.79in) cannon

The Mosquito B.Mk IV Series II of No.105 Squadron, RAF Bomber Command, based at Marham in 1943. The first of these aircraft had been delivered to the unit in late 1942.

The second prototype Mosquito was completed as a night-fighter, and first flown in May 1941. Compared to the bomber, this had a strengthened wing, flat windscreen, AI Mk IV radar and an armament of four 20mm (0.79in) cannon and four machine guns in the nose. The original production model was the Mosquito NF.Mk II that entered service in May 1942, with a top speed of 595km/h (370mph).

Operation Jericho

One of the most extraordinary episodes of the type's wartime career took place on the morning of 18 February 1944, when a squadron of RAF Mosquito bombers, flying as low as 15m (50ft) over occupied France, demolished the walls of the civil prison at Amiens in Operation Jericho. The aircraft involved were Mosquito FB.Mk VIs from Nos.21, 487 and 464 Squadrons, No.2 Group. The Mosquitoes were covered by Hawker Typhoon fighters which in the process tangled with Fw 190s near Amiens. Despite poor visibility, the attack succeeded in breaching the prison walls using delayed-fuse 250lb (113kg) bombs, and as such freed a 258 prisoners, including a number from the French Resistance. Two Mosquitoes were lost in the course of the raid. However, the precise reasons behind the raid remain a mystery to this day, and a considerable number of those prisoners released were later recaptured.

Next in line was the NF.Mk XII of December 1942, which had cannon-only armament and AI Mk VIII radar. While the Mk XII was produced by conversion, the similar NF.Mk XIII was newly built. Of these latter, a number were converted with U.S.-made AI Mk X radar in an enlarged nose radome, becoming NF.Mk XVII aircraft.

Another new-built variant was the NF.Mk XIX, with increased weight and Merlin 25s. For high-altitude operations, the RAF fielded the Mosquito NF.Mk XV. This had armament reduced to four machine guns, increased wingspan and Merlin 76/77s.

Arriving in service from July 1944 was the last of the wartime night-fighter models, the NF.Mk 30, with Merlin 72/73, 76/77 or 113/114 engines and a top speed of 655km/h (407mph).

As a fighter-bomber, the Mosquito initially made its mark in the form of the FB.Mk VI, which effectively combined the gun armament of the night-fighter with the internal bombload of the light bomber. The FB.Mk VI was adopted by Coastal Command, with which it pioneered the use of rocket projectiles as an anti-shipping weapon. The FB.Mk VI entered service in November 1943 and was later joined by small numbers of the FB.Mk XVIII armed a single 57mm (2.24in) Molins gun in the nose.

Post-war, the Mosquito saw service with a number of foreign operators, the eventual production run totalling 7785 aircraft from factories in the UK, Canada and Australia. In RAF service, PR Mosquitoes remained in front-line use in the Far East until 1955, and in second-line service Mosquitoes were on RAF strength as late as 1961.

North American P-51 Mustang (1940)

With a strong claim to be the finest piston-engined fighter of World War II, the superlative P-51 emerged from potential obscurity when re-engined with the British-designed Merlin powerplant. It became a war-winning long-range escort after its service entry in late 1943, and later saw combat action in the Korean War.

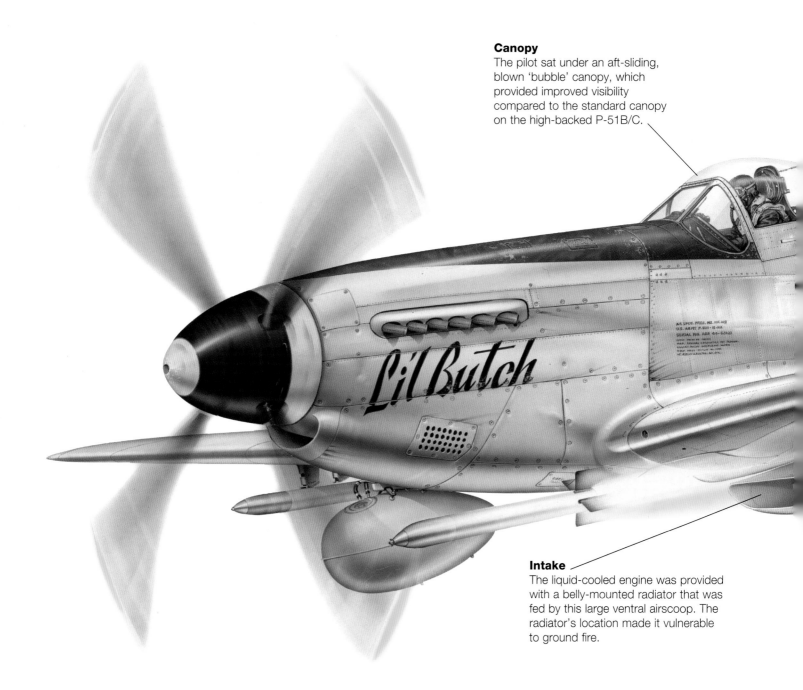

Canopy
The pilot sat under an aft-sliding, blown 'bubble' canopy, which provided improved visibility compared to the standard canopy on the high-backed P-51B/C.

Intake
The liquid-cooled engine was provided with a belly-mounted radiator that was fed by this large ventral airscoop. The radiator's location made it vulnerable to ground fire.

The P-51 emerged from an urgent British wartime requirement received by North American in April 1940. After its completion in a period of just 120 days, the NA-73 prototype was flown with an Allison V-1710-F3R engine in October 1940. A first production machine took to the air in May 1941 and in November that year a first example arrived in the UK for evaluation by the RAF. Two early examples also underwent evaluation with the USAAC, under the destination XP-51, but initially at least, no U.S. orders were forthcoming. As a result, it was left to the RAF to become the major early operator, taking 320 Mustang Mk I models. These initial Mustangs excelled at low level and possessed good range, and were therefore adopted for the army cooperation role, making use of the relatively heavy armament of four 12.7mm (0.5in) and four 7.62mm (0.3in) machine guns.

It had also been observed that the Allison engine struggled badly at altitudes over 3660m (12,000ft). Camera-equipped Mustang Mk Is first entered service with the RAF in April 1942 and eventually served with 23 squadrons within Fighter Command; a follow-on British order added another 300 Mustang Mk Is.

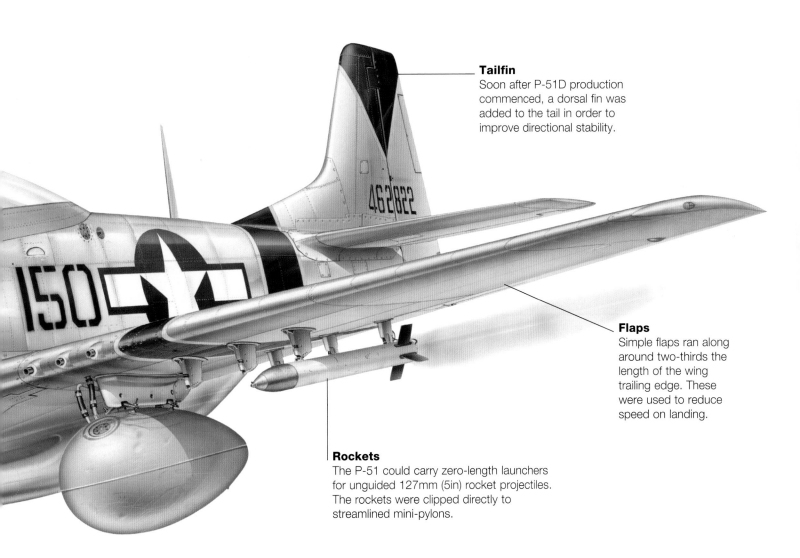

Tailfin
Soon after P-51D production commenced, a dorsal fin was added to the tail in order to improve directional stability.

Flaps
Simple flaps ran along around two-thirds the length of the wing trailing edge. These were used to reduce speed on landing.

Rockets
The P-51 could carry zero-length launchers for unguided 127mm (5in) rocket projectiles. The rockets were clipped directly to streamlined mini-pylons.

Li'l Butch was a P-51D of the 47th Fighter Squadron, 15th Fighter Group, U.S. 7th Air Force, based at Iwo Jima in the Pacific in 1945. Prominent wing and fuselage bands, spinner and fin triangle were added to prevent confusion with Japanese aircraft.

North American P-51 Mustang

The USAAC ordered 150 P-51s for supply to the UK under the Lend-Lease programme. These aircraft differed in their use of self-sealing fuel tanks and armament of four 20mm (0.79in) cannon and served with the RAF as the Mustang Mk IA, of which 93 were delivered. A derivative was the camera-equipped F-6A that was used for tactical reconnaissance by the USAAF.

Once the U.S. entered the war, official attitudes changed and an order was placed for the NA-73, initially in the form of the A-36A intended for ground support and first flown in September 1942. The USAAF's Apaches, 500 of which were eventually completed, were

Specification (P-51D)

Type:	Long-range fighter
Dimensions:	Length: 9.85m (32ft 3.75in); Wingspan: 11.28m (37ft 0.25in); Height: 3.71m (12ft 2in)
Weight:	5262kg (11,600lb) maximum take-off
Powerplant:	1 x 1112kW (1490hp) Packard Rolls-Royce Merlin V-1650-7 V-12 liquid-cooled piston engine
Maximum speed:	704km/h (437mph)
Range:	3347km (2080 miles)
Service ceiling:	12,770m (41,900ft)
Crew:	1
Armament:	6 x 12.7mm (0.5in) machine guns plus provision for up to 2 x 454kg (1000lb) bombs or 6 x 127mm (5in) rockets

Nooky Booky IV was a P-51K flown by Leonard Carson of the 362nd Fighter Squadron at Leiston, Suffolk, in 1945. Carson was leading ace of the 357th Fighter Group, with 18.5 victories.

armed with six machine guns in the wing and upper fuselage and fitted with bomb shackles under the wing. Dive brakes were installed on the upper and lower surfaces of the wing. The Apache saw combat in North Africa and Southeast Asia from mid-1943.

A first USAAF fighter version appeared in the form of the P-51A, with four machine guns in the wing and an Allison V-1710-81. A total of 310 of this model were ordered in 1942 and the version was contemporaneous with the Apache. Some 50 P-1As were diverted to the RAF, as Mustang Mk IIs, while others were equipped for reconnaissance as the USAAF's F-6C.

Meanwhile, the turning point for the Mustang was the British decision to re-engine the aircraft with the Merlin, an initial batch of four aircraft being converted to Rolls-Royce power on an experimental basis. The new engine transformed the performance of the fighter and led to the appearance of the P-51B in 1943, which employed a Packard-built V-1650-3 Merlin. The new engine was complemented by a strengthened fuselage, redesigned ailerons and an armament of four 12.7mm (0.5in) machine guns. Boasting a top speed of 710km/h (441mph) at 9085m (29,800ft), the P-51B was soon ordered in significant quantities. A total of 1988 P-51Bs was completed at Inglewood, California, while the similar P-51C (1750 built) was manufactured at Dallas, Texas. As production of these versions continued, an effort was

Although capable of a high rate of fire, with six 12.7mm Browning machine guns in the wing the P-51K was less heavily armed that the P-47, or the various cannon-armed fighters of the RAF.

RAF, as the Mustang Mk III, and in a reconnaissance capacity by the USAAF as the F-6C.

The definitive P-51D (RAF Mustang Mk IV; reconnaissance F-6D) added a cut-down rear fuselage and a 'teardrop' canopy for much improved pilot visibility. A six-gun wing was fitted from the outset. The 'D' was the most numerous version, with 7956 examples completed. With the addition of an Aeroproducts propeller, the P-51D became the P-51K, of which 1500 were completed, including F-6K reconnaissance machines and Mustang Mk IVs for the RAF (this earlier designation being retained).

Fastest of the wartime Mustangs was the P-51H, which could attain 784km/h (487mph). A total of 555 were built before the conflict ended and further contracts were cancelled. In total, 15,586 P-51s of all versions were built, including Mustangs for the Royal Australian Air Force that were built locally by the Commonwealth Aircraft Corporation.

made to increase the P-51's lethality, increasing the fixed armament to six wing machine guns. As the USAAF embarked on its day bomber offensive, so the P-51 was upgraded with increased fuel capacity, enabling the fighter to cover a distance of 3347km (2080 miles) – as far as Berlin. The P-51B/C was also operated by the

'Little Friends'

Carrying a long-range drop tank, this P-51D served with the 8th Air Force's 357th Fighter Squadron, 361st Fighter Group, and was typical of the escort fighters that protected the USAAF 'heavies' on their daylight bombing raids over occupied Europe. The first P-51Bs arrived in England in November 1943 and instantly proved superior in terms of range and high-altitude performance than the P-47 hitherto used as a bomber escort. Furthermore, they were more reliable than the P-38 Lightning. Availability of the Mustang allowed USAAF bombers to receive protection during raids on targets deep inside Germany, and thereby, in concert with

RAF Bomber Command, keep up the pressure on the Reich around the clock. Such was the success of the P-51 that it was planned to re-equip all fighter groups of the 8th Air Force with the fighter, and although this was not realized, by the end of 1944, P-51s equipped no fewer than 15 fighter groups of the 'Mighty Eighth'.

Yakovlev Yak-1/3/7/9 (1940)

The most important Soviet fighter line of World War II, the Yakovlev series of single-seaters were built in greater numbers than their contemporaries, and scored more victories than all other Soviet fighter types combined.

The first of the Yakovlev single-seat fighter dynasty was the Yak-1, product of a design competition launched in early 1939. From the start, the plan was to devise a fighter built around the Klimov M-105P inline engine with an integral cannon. The Soviet authorities also stipulated the use of wooden or composite materials. The resulting

I-26 prototype took to the air in January 1940, a low-wing monoplane of welded steel tube and wooden construction. While the wing and tail unit had fabric covering, the forward fuselage had metal covering.

In May 1940 the I-26 was authorized for production, with the armament of a 20mm (0.79in) cannon firing

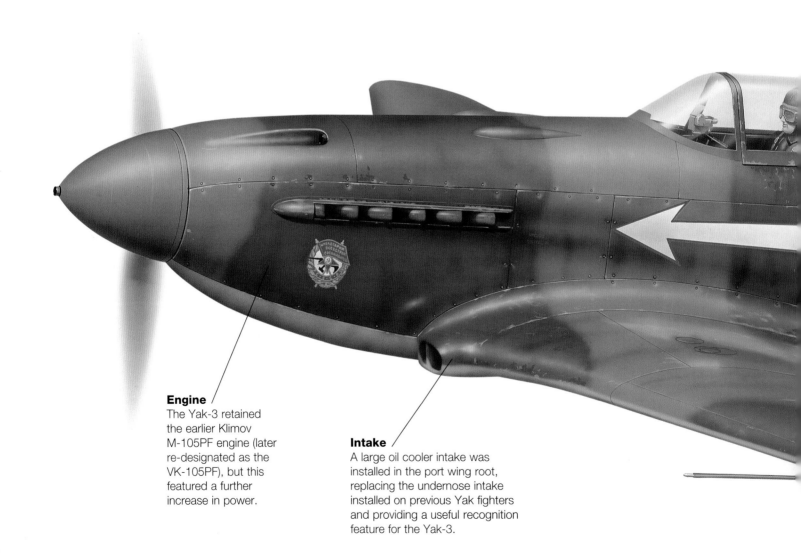

Engine
The Yak-3 retained the earlier Klimov M-105PF engine (later re-designated as the VK-105PF), but this featured a further increase in power.

Intake
A large oil cooler intake was installed in the port wing root, replacing the undernose intake installed on previous Yak fighters and providing a useful recognition feature for the Yak-3.

through the propeller hub, and two machine guns mounted in the decking above the engine. While 18 pre-production Yak-1s were built in summer 1940, only 64 aircraft were completed in 1940; a second unit did not receive its aircraft until April 1941. Only one regiment in the west had re-equipped with the Yak-1 by the time of the German invasion in June 1941. As the Red Army was pushed back, Yak-1 production was moved to factories in Siberia and elsewhere.

While the pace of Yak-1 production increased, Yakovlev set about creating a stopgap solution to provide additional fighters for the Soviet Air Force. For this, the company took the Yak-7UTI, a two-seat trainer based on the Yak-1. In August 1941 the trainer model was reconverted to become a fighter – the Yak-7. This retained the rear cockpit canopy but demonstrated performance similar to the Yak-1, as well as additional fuel capacity. In September 1941, production of the Yak-7UTI trainer switched over to the Yak-7 fighter. In early 1942 the design was refined as the Yak-7A, with a re-modelled cockpit, while the Yak-7B of mid-1942 replaced the original 7.62mm (0.3in) machine guns with 12.7mm (0.5in) weapons.

A Yak-3 of the 303rd Fighter Aviation Division, First Soviet Air Army, on the 3rd Ukrainian Front, in 1944. Pilot of this aircraft was 303rd commander Georgii Nefedovich, who eventually accumulated 23 kills.

Canopy
Combined with the lowered rear fuselage deck, the canopy provided excellent all-round vision, and the windscreen on the Yak-3 was a one-piece, low-drag model.

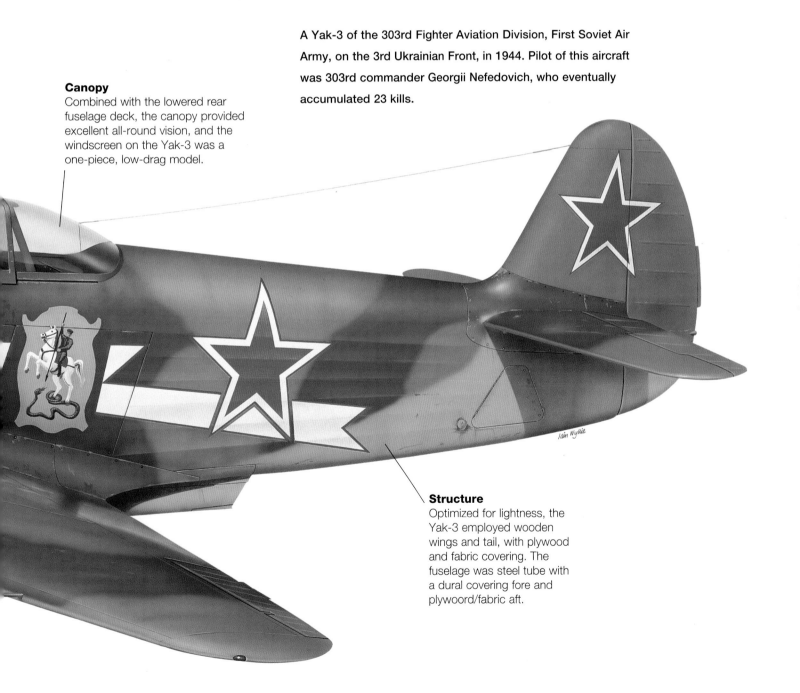

Structure
Optimized for lightness, the Yak-3 employed wooden wings and tail, with plywood and fabric covering. The fuselage was steel tube with a dural covering fore and plywoord/fabric aft.

Yakovlev Yak-1/3/7/9

In March 1942 a small batch of lightened Yak-1s was completed, featuring boosted M-105PF engines but with the machine guns deleted. June 1942 saw another addition to the line, the Yak-1b featuring a reduced-depth rear fuselage, and a new cockpit canopy improving all-round vision. This feature was adopted on subsequent Yak fighters. Armament comprised a 20mm (0.79in) cannon and one 12.7mm (0.5in) gun.

In a bid to counter the Bf 109F/G, both the Yak-1 and Yak-7B were re-engined with the M-105PF engine from August 1942, in time to see action over Stalingrad. Some Yak-7Bs were also completed with the M-105PA

This Yak-9D was flown by the famous 'Normandie-Niemen' Regiment in 1944. This French-manned unit was established in 1943 and fought with distinction over Byelorussia and Lithuania.

engine that incorporated a new 37mm (1.45in) cannon. After 8734 Yak-1s, production switched to the Yak-3 in July 1944.

In summer 1942, the availability of new alloys permitted new weight-saving features to be incorporated in the Yak-7, in turn allowing additional fuel capacity, and producing the long-range Yak-7D. In total, 6399 Yak-7s of all models were completed by the time production ended in July 1944. In June 1942 a Yak-7B fuselage and M-105PF engine had been combined with the wings of the Yak-7D, and a cut-down rear fuselage and canopy similar to the Yak-1B. The vacant rear cockpit area could be used to house additional fuel, small bombs or cameras. The resulting aircraft was ultimately designated Yak-9, and became the standard 'heavy' version in the Yak fighter line.

Numerically, the Yak-9 became the most important Soviet fighter of the war, and first saw significant action at Stalingrad. The new fighter replaced most of the earlier wooden components and featured an armament of one 20mm (0.79in) cannon and one 12.7mm (0.5in) machine gun. Production facilities gradually switched over from the Yak-7 to the Yak-9 and in the meantime some features of the former were included in production Yak-7Bs.

Specification (Yak-9D)

Type:	Long-range fighter
Dimensions:	Length: 8.55m (28ft 0in); Wingspan: 9.74m (31ft 11in); Height: 3.00m (9ft 10in)
Weight:	3117kg (6858lb) loaded
Powerplant:	1 x 880kW (1180hp) Klimov M-105PF V-12 liquid-cooled piston engine
Maximum speed:	591km/h (367mph)
Range:	1360km (845 miles)
Service ceiling:	9100m (30,000ft)
Crew:	1
Armament:	1 x 20mm (0.78in) cannon and 1 x 12.7mm (0.5in) machine gun

A frontal view of the Yak-9D. The fighter utilized a lightweight armament comprising a single 20mm (0.79in) ShVAk firing through the spinner and one 12.7mm (0.5in) UBS machine gun.

The Yak-3 was developed from the lightened Yak-1 of March 1942. Superbly agile, the Yak-3 served as the 'light' complement to the Yak-9, and was powered by a further boosted M-105PF. Other changes included the lowered rear deck and rear-view canopy, and a new wing of reduced span. The Yak-3 entered front-line service in spring 1944 and a total of 4848 Yak-3s of all sub-variants were produced by mid-1946, when production ended. The Yak-9 remained in production until late 1948, by which time 16,769 of these aircraft had been completed in a range of sub-variants. The key post-war versions of the Yak-3 and Yak-9 included the Yak-9P, which introduced all-metal construction and saw combat in the Korean War, and the Yak-3P, the latter featuring three-cannon armament and VK-105PF engine.

Wartime Yak-9 Variants

Yak-9Bs of the 130th Fighter Aviation Division wear the inscription 'Little Theatre: Front' (i.e., donated by Moscow's Little Theatre to the Front). The Yak-7B was a fighter-bomber version, but was produced in only limited numbers. More successful was the Yak-9D long-range version with a range of 1360km (845 miles) thanks to additional fuel capacity in the former rear cockpit. The improved Yak-9DD increased range to 2285km (1420 miles) thanks to additional wing fuel tanks. The Yak-9T and Yak-9K were respectively armed with 37mm (1.45in) and 45mm (1.78in) cannon for anti-tank missions. Last of the wartime line were the strengthened Yak-9M and the Yak-9U with more powerful VK-107A engine.

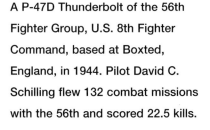

Republic P-47 Thunderbolt (1941)

The pugnacious P-47 was one of the stand-out Allied fighters of World War II, equally adept as a long-range bomber escort over occupied Europe or as a potent ground-attack aircraft in theatres that ranged from Burma to the Mediterranean.

The P-47 was an evolution of the Seversky P-43, designed by a team led by the innovative Alexander Kartveli. Both fighters were radial-engined, and the P-47 was first flown in prototype form as the XP-47B in May 1941. The big fighter was designed around the Pratt & Whitney R-2800 Double Wasp with an exhaust-driven turbocharger in the rear fuselage. Armament comprised eight machine guns in the wings. Otherwise, the P-47 featured a cantilever low wing, conventional all-metal construction with the exception of fabric-covered control surfaces, a retractable

tailwheel and accommodation for the pilot under an upward-hinged canopy. After minor refinements, the P-47B entered production and arrived with units stationed

A P-47D Thunderbolt of the 56th Fighter Group, U.S. 8th Fighter Command, based at Boxted, England, in 1944. Pilot David C. Schilling flew 132 combat missions with the 56th and scored 22.5 kills.

Rockets
127mm (5in) M8 unguided rockets were launched from triple-round tube launchers underwing and were capable of knocking out heavily armoured German Tiger and Panther tanks.

Engine
The P-47 was powered by the reliable Pratt & Whitney R-2800 series Double Wasp. This was an 18-cylinder radial air-cooled unit. In the P-47D-25 as illustrated this was an R-2800-21 or -59 with a new water-injection system and an improved turbo-supercharger.

in the UK in January 1943. Here, the initial operators were the 56th and 78th Fighter Groups, and the Thunderbolt first saw combat in April of the same year, as an escort fighter for the B-17 day bombers.

Early combat usage revealed that the Thunderbolt was limited in terms of rate of climb and agility, but that it was able to absorb considerable battle damage. With a lengthened fuselage and provision for a drop tank under the fuselage, the next production model was the P-47C. The major production version, however, was the P-47D. A total of over 12,000 D-models was produced, this featuring a cut-down rear fuselage with a 'bubble' hood on later variants, as well as water-injection power boost.

The P-47D saw widespread service, fighting over northern Europe, in the Mediterranean and Far East.

As the P-51D assumed the mantle of long-range escort, the P-47 found itself increasingly used in the ground-attack role, and proved a formidable asset to the Allies after their invasion of Normandy. In the meantime, a number of aces scored heavily on the Thunderbolt, the most prominent among them being Francis S. Gabreski, who scored 31 victories, including three ground kills, flying the P-47D. By the time the war came to an end, the P-47 had been credited with 4.6 enemy aircraft destroyed for each of one of its own number, in the course of over half a million combat sorties. The loss rate of the type was an

Bubble Canopy
The Block 25 P-47D introduced a bubble cockpit canopy as standard. As a result, the pilot's all-round vision was much improved compared to that found on the earlier 'razorback' models.

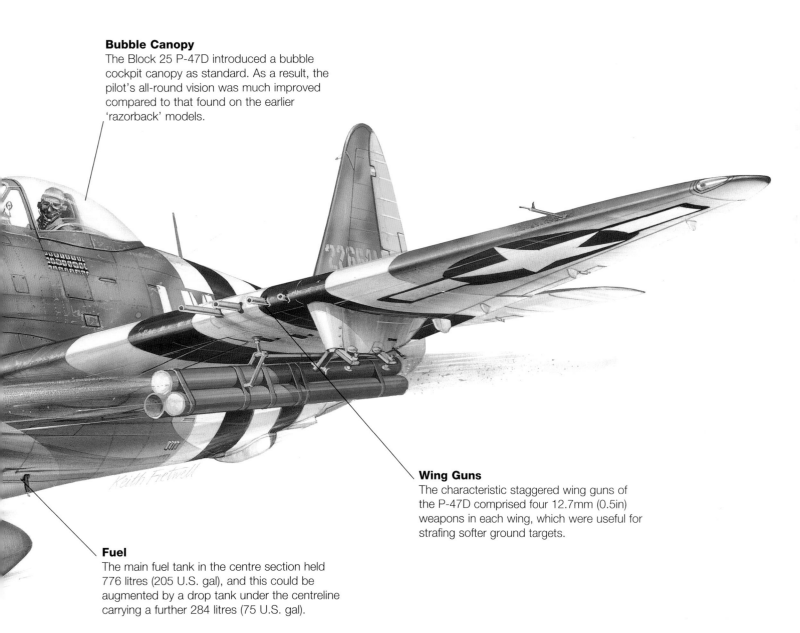

Wing Guns
The characteristic staggered wing guns of the P-47D comprised four 12.7mm (0.5in) weapons in each wing, which were useful for strafing softer ground targets.

Fuel
The main fuel tank in the centre section held 776 litres (205 U.S. gal), and this could be augmented by a drop tank under the centreline carrying a further 284 litres (75 U.S. gal).

Republic P-47 Thunderbolt

exceptionally low 0.7 per cent per mission. In one single remarkable day in April 1945, P-47s of the 78th FG posted claims for 135 German aircraft – all destroyed on the ground by strafing.

In an effort to boost the straight-line performance of the Thunderbolt, Republic developed the P-47M with an improved supercharger and a top speed of 763km/h (473mph) at 9755m (32,000ft). The P-47M began to be issued to units in Europe at the end of 1944. In the Pacific, meanwhile, the ultimate wartime model was the P-47N that was fitted with an enlarged wing with blunt tips and increased fuel capacity. This was the fastest

A P-47D of the 527th Fighter Squadron, 86th Fighter Group, based in Italy in 1944. As well as pursuing retreating German forces in Italy, the unit flew escort missions for bombers.

and heaviest production version, and a total of over 1800 P-47Ns was completed. During the war these served primarily as escorts for B-29 bombers during raids over Japan in 1945.

Ground-attack Specialist

In all, P-47 production amounted to 15,675 aircraft, making it the most numerous American-made fighter in history. Of this total, a significant number were adapted for ground-attack duties, the P-47D featuring provision for underwing racks that could carry a pair of 454kg (1000lb) bombs, in addition to the 568-litre (125-U.S. gal) drop tank under the fuselage. P-47Ds from later production batches had increased external storers capacity, including up to 10 127mm (5in) rockets.

In the fighter-bomber role, the P-47D entered service with the 384th FG in Australia, from where they struck Japanese targets in New Guinea. Thereafter, P-47D fighter-bombers served with the U.S. 9th and 15th Air Forces in the UK and Mediterranean respectively. The RAF flew the P-47 in Burma, a total of 16 squadrons receiving no fewer than 826 Thunderbolt Mk I (P-47B) and Thunderbolt Mk II (P-47D) aircraft. British Thunderbolts served primarily in the fighter-bomber role, and in Burma they proved successful in mounting 'cab rank' patrols over the jungle, attacking Japanese

Specification (P-47D)

Type:	Long-range fighter
Dimensions:	Length: 11.01m (36ft 1.75in); Wingspan: 12.43m (40ft 9.5in); Height: 4.32m (14ft 2in)
Weight:	8800kg (19,400lb) maximum take-off
Powerplant:	1 x 1716kW (2300hp) Pratt & Whitney R-2800-59 radial piston engine
Maximum speed:	689km/h (428mph)
Range:	2028km (1260 miles)
Service ceiling:	12,800m (42,000ft)
Crew:	1
Armament:	8 x 12.7mm (0.5in) machine guns; 2 x 454kg (1000lb) bombs underwing; up to 10 127mm (5in) unguided rockets

A frontal view of the 527th FS P-47D reveals the external stores, comprising 1000lb (454kg) bombs underwing and one of the nine different types of drop tank, carried on the centreline.

targets earmarked by mobile control officers on the ground. Other wartime operators of the P-47 included Brazil, France, Mexico and the USSR. As the last of the Thunderbolts, the P-47N version remained in U.S. service long after the war, examples passing to the Air National Guard before being phased out in 1955, by which time they had been given the new designation of F-47N. Foreign operators continued to fly the Thunderbolt for some years longer, notably in Latin America and with the Republic of China.

56th Fighter Group

This formation of 'razorback' P-47Bs was put up by the 56th Fighter Group in October 1942. The aircraft nearest the camera was flown by one of the leading Thunderbolt aces, Hubert Zemke. The 56th was the leading exponent of the P-47, credited with the destruction of 665.5 aircraft in air-to-air combat, giving it more air-to-air kills than any other fighter group in the Eighth Air Force, and making it the top-scoring P-47 group during World War II. The kill tally also puts it second in terms of top-scoring USAAF fighter groups. In addition to its aerial victories, the 56th also claimed 311 fighters destroyed on the ground. Leading pilots of the 56th included Zemke, Bud Mahurin, Robert Johnson, Jerry Johnson and Gabby Gabreski. Of these, Johnson became the first to break Eddie Rickenbacker's then record of 26 victories. This milestone occurred on 8 May 1944. All Johnson's kills came at the controls of P-47s.

Avro Lancaster (1941)

The most celebrated British heavy bomber of World War II, the Lancaster found fame for daring missions such as the 'Dambusters raid' and the attack on the *Tirpitz*, although its origins in the Avro Manchester were far less auspicious.

The prototype Lancaster was based on a converted Avro Manchester airframe, according to a design by Avro's chief designer, Roy Chadwick. The Manchester was a twin-engined heavy bomber but suffered as a result of its Rolls-Royce Vulture engines, which were underdeveloped, underpowered and unreliable. In September 1941 Avro received a contract for two new prototype aircraft, the first of which was to fly within four months. The first of the revised bombers retained the Manchester's triple tail configuration, but added enlarged outer wing panels

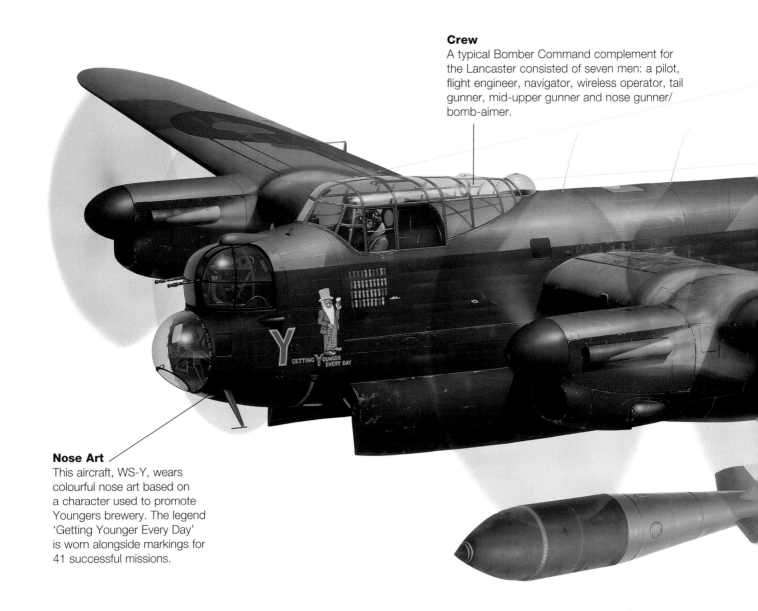

Crew
A typical Bomber Command complement for the Lancaster consisted of seven men: a pilot, flight engineer, navigator, wireless operator, tail gunner, mid-upper gunner and nose gunner/ bomb-aimer.

Nose Art
This aircraft, WS-Y, wears colourful nose art based on a character used to promote Youngers brewery. The legend 'Getting Younger Every Day' is worn alongside markings for 41 successful missions.

and four of the proven 854kW (1145hp) Rolls-Royce Merlin X engines. Subsequently it received a new twin fin and rudder assembly that would become standard on production Lancasters. The prototype first flew in January 1941 before commencing intensive flying trials.

The Ministry of Aircraft Production had given consideration to closing down the Manchester production line entirely after completing its contract for 200 Manchesters. Happily for Bomber Command, the plan was vetoed and Avro continued development work on the Manchester Mk III (which would later be named the Lancaster). A first series-built machine was flying by October 1941.

The Manchester was replaced in service by the Lancaster, but the production numbers were so prodigious

that it was putting a strain on the supply of engines. One expedient was to procure licence-built Packard Merlins from the U.S. Another measure saw the Lancaster re-engined with Bristol Hercules VI or XVI radial engines. The Hercules developed 1294kW (1735hp) compared to the 954kW (1280hp) of the Merlin XX and 22 or 1208kW (1620hp) of the Merlin 24 used in the other production aircraft.

Defensive armament for the bomber was to include a ventral turret, but this was abandoned, leaving the B.Mk I protected by three Frazer-Nash turrets. Each of these hydraulically operated turrets was armed with 7.7mm (0.303in) machine guns, comprising two each in the nose and mid-upper dorsal positions and four in the tail turret. In terms of offensive weapons, these were carried in a capacious bomb bay that was originally intended to

Twin Fins
Compared to the Manchester with its triple fins, the production Lancaster employed a twin-fin tail unit, with tailfins of considerably increased height.

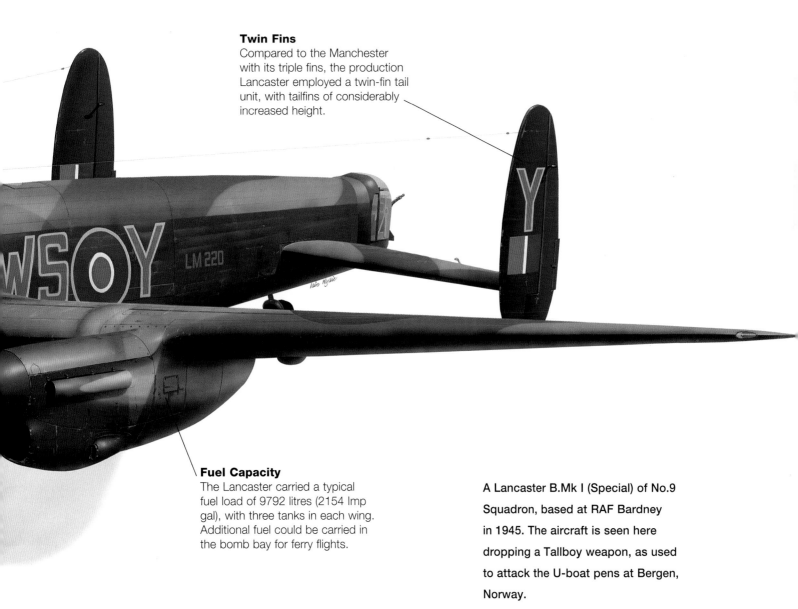

Fuel Capacity
The Lancaster carried a typical fuel load of 9792 litres (2154 Imp gal), with three tanks in each wing. Additional fuel could be carried in the bomb bay for ferry flights.

A Lancaster B.Mk I (Special) of No.9 Squadron, based at RAF Bardney in 1945. The aircraft is seen here dropping a Tallboy weapon, as used to attack the U-boat pens at Bergen, Norway.

Avro Lancaster

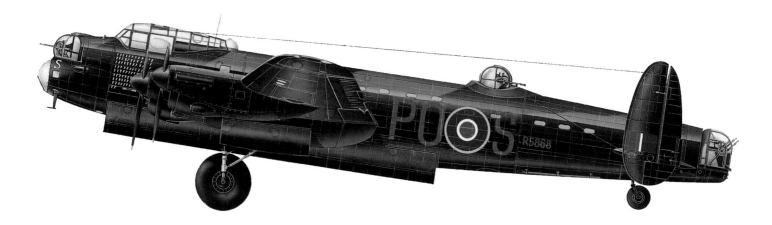

accommodate 1814kg (4000lb) of weapons. Throughout the Lancaster's career, the bomb bay was enlarged to carry larger bombs. These began with 3629kg and 5443kg (8000lb and 12,000lb) weapons and eventually included the Barnes Wallis-designed Grand Slam bomb, weighing a colossal 9979kg (22,000lb).

Lancaster in Service

First of the Lancaster squadrons was No.44 (Rhodesia) Squadron, based at Waddington, which received its initial aircraft in December 1941. The unit flew its first mission with the new bomber during the night of 10–11 March 1942 as part of a raid on Essen. In April 1942,

Specification (Lancaster B.Mk I)

Type:	Heavy bomber
Dimensions:	Length: 21.18m (69ft 6in); Wingspan: 31.09m (102ft 0in); Height: 6.10m (20ft 0in)
Weight:	31,751kg (70,000lb) maximum take-off
Powerplant:	4 x 1223kW (1640hp) Rolly-Royce Merlin XXIV V-12 piston engines
Maximum speed:	462km/h (287mph)
Range:	4070km (2530 miles) with bombload
Service ceiling:	7470m (24,500ft)
Crew:	7
Armament:	8 x 7.7mm (0.303in) machine guns, plus bombload comprising one bomb of up to 9979kg (22,000lb) or smaller bombs up to a total weight of 6350kg (14,000lb)

Now preserved at the RAF Museum, Lancaster B.Mk I R5868 was built by Metropolitan-Vickers, as part of a batch ordered as Manchesters, but was completed as a Lancaster.

Lancasters from Nos.44 and 97 Squadrons took part in a daring, low-level daylight attack on the MAN diesel engine factory at Augsburg.

In early 1943, Guy Gibson was selected to recruit the best Bomber Command pilots to form a new, elite squadron for a special mission. The result was No.617 Squadron, which was tasked with perfecting low-altitude flying before being assigned the target of three dams in the heart of Germany's industrial Ruhr region. The dams raid of May 1943 was a propaganda success, and one of the most daring bombing missions in history, but its strategic effect was limited.

After its raid on the dams, No.617 Squadron employed 12,000lb Tallboy and 22,000lb Grand Slam attacks on the battleship *Tirpitz*, which was finally sunk in late 1944. Other missions for the Lancaster included the Battles of Hamburg, the Ruhr and Berlin in 1943 and early 1944, and the attack on Peenemünde in August 1943. In all, Lancasters served with at least 59 Bomber Command squadrons during the conflict. Between them, these flew over 156,000 sorties in the course of which they dropped over 600,000 tons of high-explosive bombs, as well as over 50 million incendiaries. Almost half of all Lancasters delivered during the war (3345 out of 7373) were lost on operations with the loss of over 21,000 crew members.

The basic Lancaster B.Mk I and Hercules-powered B.Mk II were followed by the B.Mk III with improved Merlins. The last of the line to be built in significant

numbers was the Canadian-made B.Mk X. The B.Mk I remained in production throughout the war, demonstrating the excellence of the basic design, and the final example was delivered in February 1946.

A head-on view of the Lancaster B.Mk I. Lancaster production was undertaken by Avro, Armstrong Whitworth, Austin Motors, Metropolitan Vickers, Vickers-Armstrong and Victory Aircraft.

Battle of Britain Memorial Flight

Lancaster PA474 is part of the RAF's Battle of Britain's Memorial Flight and one of only two airworthy survivors of the type. PA474 was completed at Broughton in May 1945, just missing the war in Europe, and was later used for photo-reconnaissance work in Africa during 1948–52. After a period with Flight Refuelling Ltd, PA474 went to the Royal College of Aeronautics at Cranfield as a trials platform. In 1964 the bomber was adopted by the Air Historical Branch and took part in two films, before being prepared for display at the RAF Museum. After restoration, PA474 received permission to fly again in 1967. PA474 joined the Battle of Britain Memorial Flight in 1973 and since then has served as living memorial to the men of Bomber Command, performing at air displays and events.

Grumman F6F Hellcat (1942)

The best carrier fighter of World War II, the Hellcat built on the earlier success of Grumman's F4F Wildcat and was responsible for destroying 5156 enemy aircraft in aerial combat – 75 per cent of all U.S. Navy aerial victories in the conflict.

The F6F Hellcat continued the development path established by the earlier Wildcat, 7885 of which played a significant part in wresting air superiority from the Japanese in the early months of the war in the Pacific. The aircraft incorporated all lessons from combat experience gained by U.S. Navy Wildcat pilots as well as making use of other Allied combat reports. In contrast to the F4F, the new design shifted the position of the wing from mid-set to low-set, but otherwise retained a

basic commonality of appearance. The relocated wing allowed the main landing gear to retract neatly into the centre section of the wing, rather than into the fuselage as was the case in the Wildcat. Other features were an all-metal construction with flush-rifted skinning and folding outer wing panels for carrier stowage. Basic armament

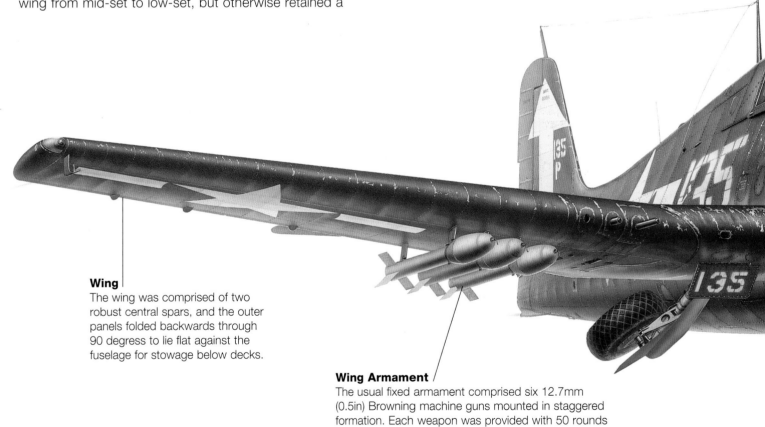

Wing
The wing was comprised of two robust central spars, and the outer panels folded backwards through 90 degress to lie flat against the fuselage for stowage below decks.

Wing Armament
The usual fixed armament comprised six 12.7mm (0.5in) Browning machine guns mounted in staggered formation. Each weapon was provided with 50 rounds of ammunition. This aircraft also carries six 127mm (5in) rocket projectiles to attack ground targets.

comprised six 12.7mm (0.5in) machine guns mounted in the leading edges of the wings.

The new fighter was first flown under the power of a Wright R-2600-10 Cyclone two-stage turbocharged radial, as the XF6F-1 in June 1942, but was soon re-flown with a series of more powerful engines. This resulted in the XF6F-2 with the turbocharged R-2600-16, the XF6F-3 with the R-2800-10 Double Wasp with two-stage turbocharger and the XF6F-4 with the R-2800-27.

Before the re-engining process had been completed, however, the Hellcat was ordered into production in the form of the F6F-3. The first F6F-3 Hellcats were delivered to front-line units in January 1943, the first examples serving with VF-9 on board the USS *Essex*. The first unit to take the fighter into combat against the Japanese was VF-5, aboard the USS *Yorktown* in August 1943. In October that year, Robert W. Duncan became the first Hellcat pilot to down two A6M Zero fighters in a single engagement. Still more impressive was the action near Kwajalein in December, when a force of 91 Hellcats entered battle with 50 Zeros and downed 28, with the loss of just two of their own. In two days of fighting in February 1944, during the course of carrier strikes near Truk, Hellcats from 10 squadrons were responsible for downing

Nose Band
The yellow nose band was applied on the cowling during a series of raids on Tokyo. This marking was worn for a period of only two weeks before the cowling reverted to blue.

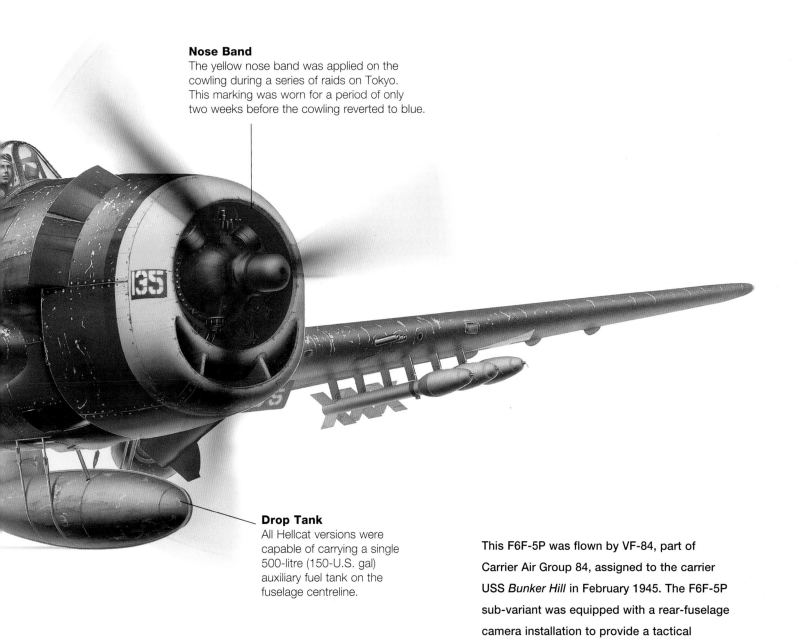

Drop Tank
All Hellcat versions were capable of carrying a single 500-litre (150-U.S. gal) auxiliary fuel tank on the fuselage centreline.

This F6F-5P was flown by VF-84, part of Carrier Air Group 84, assigned to the carrier USS *Bunker Hill* in February 1945. The F6F-5P sub-variant was equipped with a rear-fuselage camera installation to provide a tactical reconnaissance capability.

Grumman F6F Hellcat

127 Japanese aircraft in the air, as well as destroying 86 on the ground. Such success was repeated over a two-day period that March, when 150 Japanese aircraft fell to the guns of F6Fs launched from 11 aircraft carriers around Palau. The basic airframe soon demonstrated its potential to assume other roles, and produced the F6F-3E and F6F-3N night-fighters that were equipped with radar in a wing-mounted pod. Typically, a total of four Hellcat night-fighters operated within each fighter squadron aboard a carrier.

A new version with enhanced capabilities as a fighter-bomber was the F6F-5 of April 1944, which added

Specification (F6F-5)

Type:	Carrier fighter/fighter-bomber
Dimensions:	Length: 10.24m (33ft 7in); Wingspan: 13.05m (42ft 10in); Height: 3.99m (13ft 1in)
Weight:	6991kg (15,413lb) loaded
Powerplant:	1 x 1491kW (2000hp) Pratt & Whitney R-2800-10W radial piston engine
Maximum speed:	612km/h (380mph)
Range:	1521km (945 miles)
Service ceiling:	11,369m (37,300ft)
Crew:	1
Armament:	6 x 12.7mm (0.5in) machine guns, or 2 x 20mm (0.79in) cannon and 4 x 12.7mm machine guns, plus provision for 2 x 454kg (1000lb) bombs

An F6F-5 of VF-27, serving aboard USS *Princeton*, during the Battle of Leyte Gulf, October 1944. VF-27 produced 10 aces, among which the top-scorer was Carl A. Brown, Jr (10.5 kills).

provision to carry up to 907kg (2000lb) of bombs or other ordnance. In some F6F-5s, the inner wing machine guns were replaced by harder-hitting 20mm (0.79in) cannon. Other changes manifest in the F6F-5 were a redesigned engine cowling, new ailerons, strengthened tail surfaces and the installation of a water-injection system to boost the power of the R-2800-10 engine. When equipped for night-fighting, the F6F-5 became the F6F-5N, with a radome mounted on the starboard wing. The 'Dash 5' replaced the F6F-3 in production in mid-1944 after a total of 4402 of the earlier version had been completed. Ultimately, production of the F6F-5N series extended to 7868 aircraft.

Battle of the Philippine Sea

Perhaps the most dramatic demonstration of the Hellcat's prowess came during the Battle of the Philippine Sea in June 1944, a huge operation involving 15 U.S. Navy carriers that between them embarked 480 F6Fs, in addition to 222 dive-bombers and 199 torpedo-bombers. In a week-long campaign, the U.S. Task Force 58 destroyed over 400 Japanese aircraft and sank three carriers.

Pilots associated with the Hellcat include the U.S. Navy's 'ace of aces', 34-kill David McCampbell, who shot down nine aircraft in a single engagement in October 1944.

A frontal view of the fully armed VF-27 F6F-5 reveals details
of its weaponry, including machine guns in the wing, bombs
on the inner underwing stations and rocket projectiles outboard.

The British Fleet Air Arm was the other wartime
operator of the Hellcat, taking 252 F6F-3s as Gannet
(later Hellcat) Mk Is, and 930 F6F-5s as Hellcat
Mk IIs. In the UK the initial operator was 800 Naval Air

Squadron of the Fleet Air Arm. In all, 12,275 Hellcats of
all versions had been completed by the time production
came to an end in November 1945, including over
2500 in 1943 alone. The type remained in U.S. service
for several years after the war, and subsequently with
a small number of export operators, including France,
which took the Hellcat into battle once again
in Indochina.

Post-war Hellcats

A radar-equipped F6F-5N night-fighter and three
F6F-5s are seen in post-war U.S. Navy service.
These brightly marked aircraft were typical of
Hellcats that served with 13 reserve units around
the U.S. after VJ-Day. Aboard carriers, the last
U.S. Navy Hellcats bowed out in 1948, although
the type made a brief return to sea in 1953, when
problems delayed the jet-powered Grumman
F9F Panther. The last of the night-fighting
F6F-5Ns were not disposed of by the front line
until 1954. In Latin America, the Hellcat flew with
the naval air arms of Argentina, Paraguay and
Uruguay, the last of these keeping the type in
service until 1961. France's air force and navy
took delivery of 179 F6F-5s and -5Ns and these
served in Indochina between 1950 and 1952 in a
ground-attack role. As well as being land-based,
the French Hellcats flew combat missions from
the carrier *Arromanches* in 1953 and 1954.

Messerschmitt Me 262 (1942)

Assured its place in history as the first jet fighter to enter service, the *Luftwaffe*'s Me 262 was the most advanced fighter to reach operational status during World War II, and ushered military aviation into the jet age.

Exploiting German research into gas turbines that had begun prior to the outbreak of the war, the Me 262 was the first turbojet-aircraft to achieve operational status. Its design origins date back to late 1938 and, after Messerschmitt had been requested to produce specifications for the new aircraft in January 1939, the first prototype airframes were available in 1941. It was always planned that the new fighter would be powered by two examples of a new gas turbine engine then under development with BMW (a single-engine design had been drafted, but the early turbojets were considered to offer insufficient power).

Me 262A-1a 'Yellow 7' was on strength with the 11. Staffel of Jagdgeschwader 7, based at Prague in April 1945. The aircraft was eventually captured by the Allies at Lechfeld and is now preserved in the National Air and Space Museum in Washington.

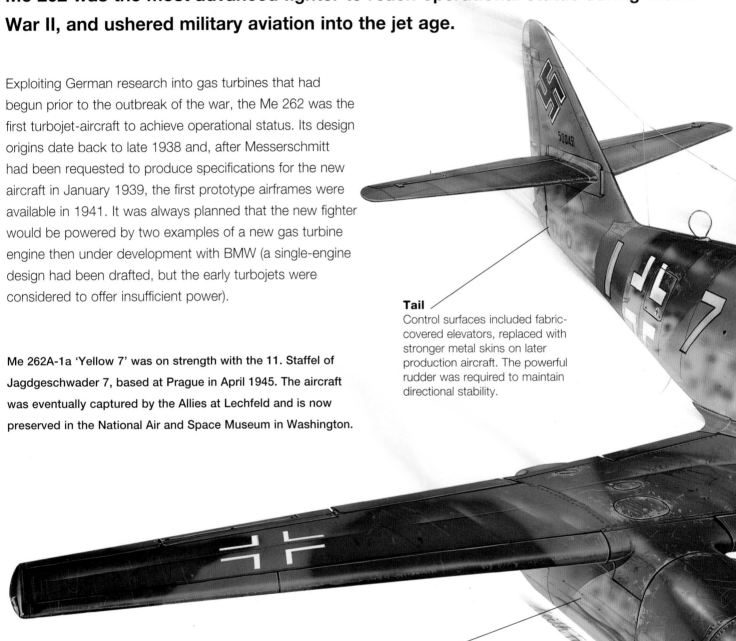

Tail
Control surfaces included fabric-covered elevators, replaced with stronger metal skins on later production aircraft. The powerful rudder was required to maintain directional stability.

Engines
Power was provided by a pair of Junkers Jumo 004B-1 axial-flow turbojets, which suffered from poor reliability and limited service life, primarily due to the effect of Allied bombing on production facilities, and the lack of certain materials required for the turbine blades.

The planned BMW P.3302 jet engines took longer to refine, and it was not until April 1942 that the aircraft made its maiden flight, the initial prototype V1 being powered by a single Jumo 210G piston engine mounted in the nose. A first flight under turbine power followed in March, the powerplant being the intended pair of BMW 003 turbojets, in addition to the Jumo 210 should it be required in an emergency. During the maiden flight with jet power, both turbojets failed soon after take-off, and the prototype was forced to land on piston power alone.

While the first prototypes were equipped with tailwheel undercarriage, the aircraft was equipped with a tricycle landing gear arrangement when production of the new fighter began in 1944. Meanwhile, the failure of the BMW 003 turbojets in the prototype had been attributed to the compressor blades, and work was underway to redesign the engine.

Despite this setback, testing continued under the power of Junkers Jumo turbojets, which were larger and heavier than the BMW units. With the prototype

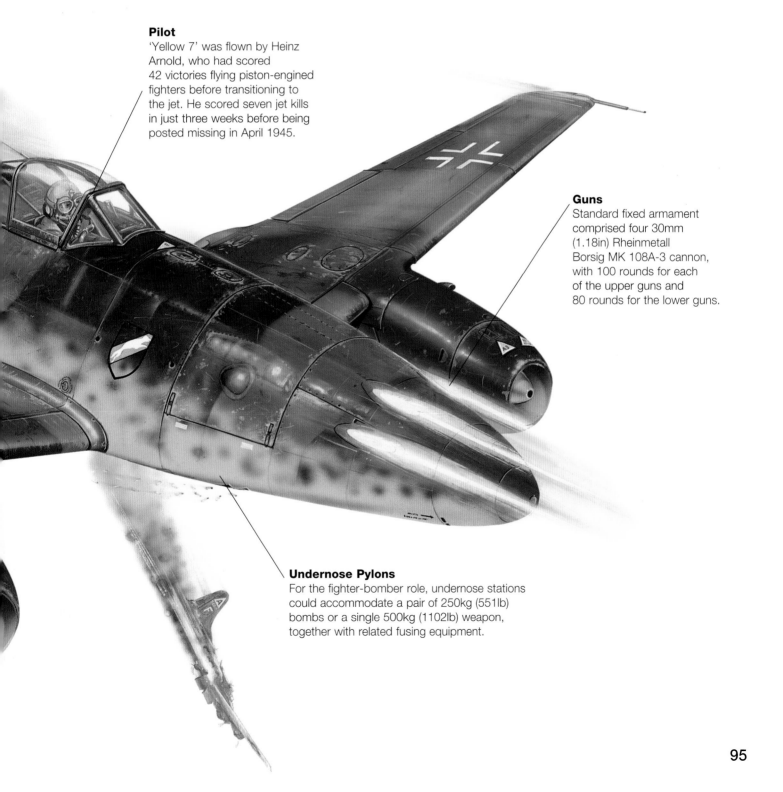

Pilot
'Yellow 7' was flown by Heinz Arnold, who had scored 42 victories flying piston-engined fighters before transitioning to the jet. He scored seven jet kills in just three weeks before being posted missing in April 1945.

Guns
Standard fixed armament comprised four 30mm (1.18in) Rheinmetall Borsig MK 108A-3 cannon, with 100 rounds for each of the upper guns and 80 rounds for the lower guns.

Undernose Pylons
For the fighter-bomber role, undernose stations could accommodate a pair of 250kg (551lb) bombs or a single 500kg (1102lb) weapon, together with related fusing equipment.

Messerschmitt Me 262

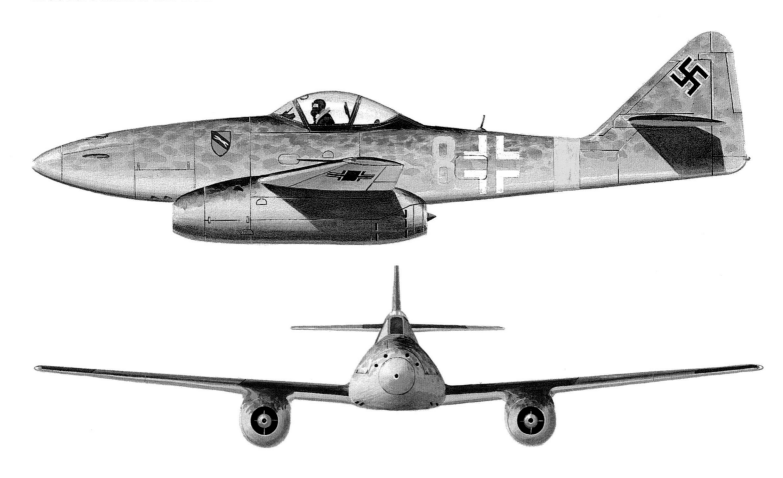

appropriately redesigned, the Me 262 returned to the air on July 1942, now powered by two examples of the Jumo 004A. The improved Jumo 004B-1 turbojet came on line in November 1943, when it was flown in prototype V6. These units were lighter than the interim Jumo 004As and became the standard for the production

A three-view of 'Yellow 8', a Me 262A-1a of 3./JG 7 that was discovered by advancing Allied forces at Stendal in April 1945. The unit emblem of JG 7 was a leaping greyhound.

aircraft. After the completion of 10 prototypes, efforts switched to 20 pre-production machines.

Specification (Me 262A-1a)

Type:	Interceptor fighter
Dimensions:	Length: 10.61m (34ft 9.5in); Wingspan: 12.50m (41ft 0.125in); Height: 3.83m (12ft 6.75in)
Weight:	6775kg (14,936lb) maximum take-off
Powerplant:	2 x 8.8kN (1890lb) Junkers Jumo 004B-1 turbojets
Maximum speed:	870km/h (541mph)
Range:	845km (525 miles)
Service ceiling:	11,000m (36,090ft)
Crew:	1
Armament:	4 x 30mm (1.18in) cannon

Into Service

Thanks to the engine tribulations, development of the jet fighter was not unsurprisingly slow, and it was July 1944 before the Me 262 entered Luftwaffe service. The first to achieve operational status was the Me 262A-1a armed with four 30mm (1.18in) cannon that joined a trials Kommando at Lechfeld. In July 1944, Alfred Schreiber was flying a Me 262A-1a when he engaged an RAF Mosquito reconnaissance aircraft that was reportedly lost when it subsequently landed.

In the same month, the unit was re-designated Kommando Nowotny, and the trials unit began operational missions against the Allies in August. In addition to the baseline Me 262A-1a, the Me 262A-1a/U1 added another pair of cannon, while the Me 262A-1a/U2 was equipped for poor-weather operations and the

the Führer did favour development of this version, the Me 262A-2a, the degree to which this hindered the type's overall progress and pace of deliveries is debatable. As well as the engine problems, Allied raids on the Me 262 production centre forced the evacuation of the manufacturing effort from Regensburg to Oberammergau, where problems were exacerbated by the lack of a suitable workforce.

The Me 262A-2a was equipped to carry up to 500kg (1102lb) of bombs in addition to the basic four-cannon armament and was also developed as a two-seater, the Me 262A-2a/U, with a bomb-aimer in a glazed nose.

Night-fighter Role

The Me 262 also saw some limited success in the night-fighter role. A dedicated night-fighter model appeared before the end of the war, in the form of the radar-equipped Me 262B-1a/U1. As a daytime bomber-destroyer, the Me 262 could also be armed with 24 underwing R4M unguided rockets. Ultimately, however, the Me 262 was a case of 'too little, too late' (a total of around 1430 were completed) and despite its undoubted performance advantage was unable to do anything to alter the course of the war.

Me 262A-1a/U3 was a reconnaissance version with the armament deleted.

The Me 262's delay into service has often been described as a result of Hitler's insistence that the Me 262 take on an offensive bomber role. Although

Me 262B-1a/U1 Night-fighter

The Me 262B-1a/U1 night-fighter was created on the basis of the Me 262B-1a dual-control trainer, which differed from the basic fighter in having a second seat in the aft section of an elongated cockpit. Since this resulted in a reduction in internal fuel capacity, auxiliary fuel tanks were added below the forward fuselage. The first trials of the night-fighter were undertaken at Rechlin in October 1944, using Lichtenstein SN-2 radar. The production version featured a radar operator in the rear seat and FuG 218 Neptun V radar that featured a nose-mounted antenna array. At the end of the war, work was underway on an improved night-fighter, the Me 262B-2a, with an extended fuselage, increased range and upwards-firing cannon.

Northrop P-61 Black Widow (1942)

Without doubt one of the finest night-fighters of the war, the powerful P-61 was one of the few Allied aircraft that was specifically designed for the task. The Black Widow served with particular distinction in the Pacific, often as a night intruder on offensive missions against land and sea targets.

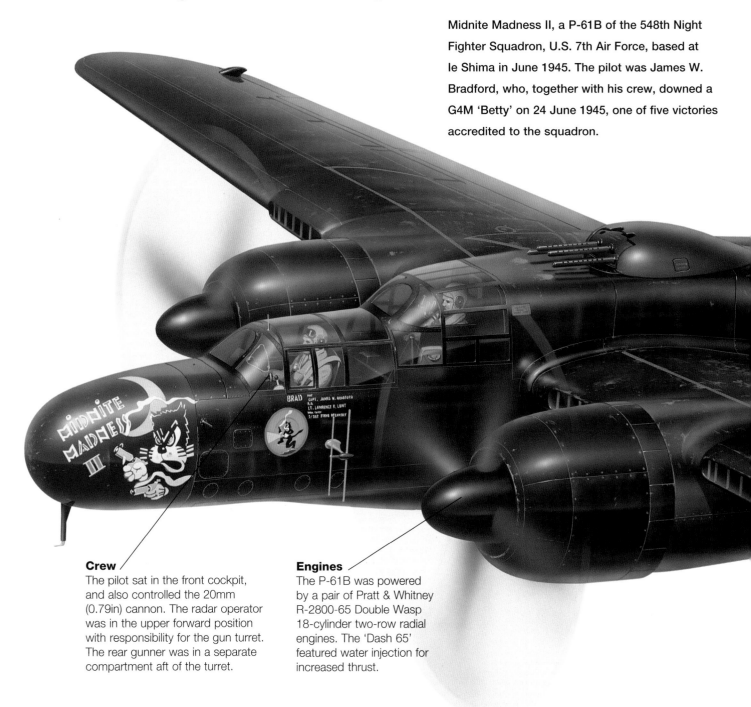

Midnite Madness II, a P-61B of the 548th Night Fighter Squadron, U.S. 7th Air Force, based at Ie Shima in June 1945. The pilot was James W. Bradford, who, together with his crew, downed a G4M 'Betty' on 24 June 1945, one of five victories accredited to the squadron.

Crew
The pilot sat in the front cockpit, and also controlled the 20mm (0.79in) cannon. The radar operator was in the upper forward position with responsibility for the gun turret. The rear gunner was in a separate compartment aft of the turret.

Engines
The P-61B was powered by a pair of Pratt & Whitney R-2800-65 Double Wasp 18-cylinder two-row radial engines. The 'Dash 65' featured water injection for increased thrust.

With the beginning of the night bombing offensive in Europe in 1940, U.S. interest in the field of specialist night-fighters was increased. The U.S. Army Air Corps issued a general requirement for a new night-fighter. The Northrop response involved a large, twin-engine aircraft with a twin-boom tail and accommodation for three crew as well as an airborne interception (AI) radar of a type then still under development. A heavy cannon armament was also provided.

Further impetus for the programme was derived from British work on the cavity magnetron, of which the U.S. had been informed via the Tizard mission, which provided details of Britain's advanced-technology military projects. Use of the cavity magnetron allowed radars to operate in the more effective centimetric wavelength. After Anglo-American work on the radar, this finally emerged as the SCR-70 AI radar for installation in the night-fighter.

In January 1941 two XP-61 prototypes were ordered and within the next 13 months contracts were awarded for a total of 573 aircraft. A first flight by a prototype was completed in May 1942 but it was another year and a half before production P-61As became available. In the meantime, development testing continued using a total of 13 YP-61 service test aircraft.

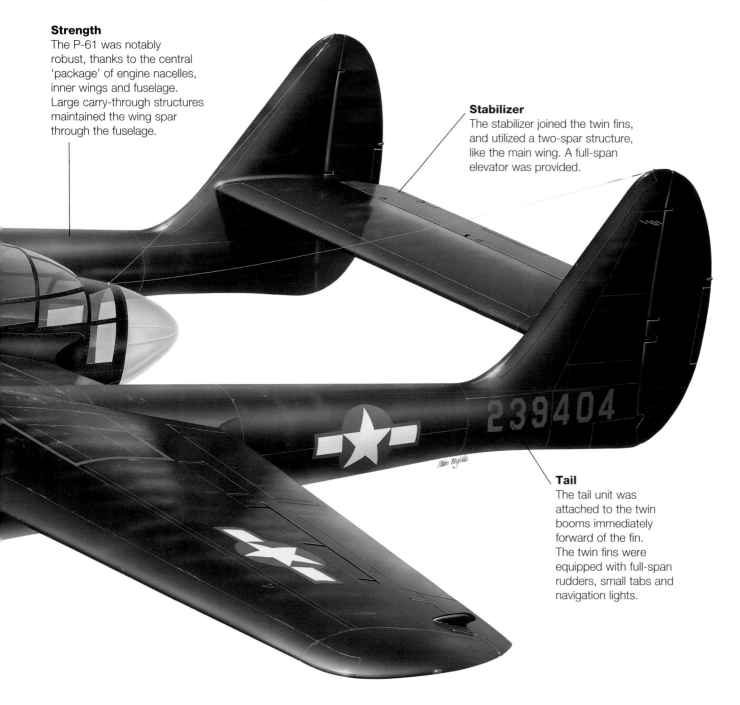

Strength
The P-61 was notably robust, thanks to the central 'package' of engine nacelles, inner wings and fuselage. Large carry-through structures maintained the wing spar through the fuselage.

Stabilizer
The stabilizer joined the twin fins, and utilized a two-spar structure, like the main wing. A full-span elevator was provided.

Tail
The tail unit was attached to the twin booms immediately forward of the fin. The twin fins were equipped with full-span rudders, small tabs and navigation lights.

Northrop P-61 Black Widow

In the first batch of 37 production aircraft, the P-61A was armed with a remotely controlled dorsal turret that mounted four 12.7mm (0.5in) machine guns. This was complemented by four fixed 20mm (0.79in) cannon carried in the belly. The dorsal turret, however, was found to create aerodynamic problems when slewed to the beam position, and was removed from the 38th aircraft onwards. Initial deliveries were made to the 18th Fighter Group stationed at Guadalcanal. The unit achieved a first Black Widow victory in July 1944, with the downing of a Japanese Mitsubishi G4M bomber, and the aircraft went on to replace the Douglas P-70 that had been issued previously as a stopgap night-fighter.

Specification (P-61B)

Type:	Night-fighter
Dimensions:	Length: 15.11m (49ft 7in); Wingspan: 20.12m (66ft 0in); Height: 4.46m (14ft 8in)
Weight:	13,472kg (29,700lb) maximum take-off
Powerplant:	2 x 1491kW (2000hp) Pratt & Whitney R-2800-65 radial piston engines
Maximum speed:	589km/h (366mph)
Range:	4506km (2800 miles)
Service ceiling:	10,090m (33,100ft)
Crew:	3
Armament:	4 x 20mm (0.79in) cannon, plus 4 x 12.7mm (0.5in) machine guns in later aircraft, and provision to carry up to 4 x 726kg (1600lb) bombs

Two views of P-61B serial 42-39403 was fitted with the dorsal gun barbette. Other features of the B-model included a longer nose, Curtiss Electric propellers and four external pylons.

The initial production P-61A exhibited certain shortcomings, in particular in regard to the Pratt & Whitney .R-2800-65 engines, which suffered from reliability problems. In all, 200 P-61As were completed before production switched to the improved P-61B, deliveries of which began in July 1944.

'Widow' Intruders

Although always classed as a night-fighter, the P-61B version saw increasing use as a night intruder, and was capable of carrying weapons loads including four 726kg (1600lb) bombs, or four 1136-litre (300-U.S. gal) drop tanks under the wings. Serving in the Far East, some aircraft were further adapted in field in order to carry 127mm (0.5in) rocket projectiles that were employed against Japanese shipping. In the last 250 P-61Bs, the dorsal turret was reinstated.

The final production version was the P-61C that was powered by the 2088kW (2800hp) R-2800-73 engines, and which had a maximum speed of almost 644km/h (400mph). Only 41 P-61Cs were completed before the war's end, at which point contracts for a further 476 such aircraft were cancelled.

Although best associated with the war in the Pacific, Black Widows also saw combat with the USAAF in Europe. Here, the initial operator was the 422nd Night Fighter Squadron at Scorton, England, which received P-61As in May 1944. During their very first combat

mission in theatre, P-61s based in England succeeded in downing four German bombers. The Black Widows of the 422nd Night Fighter Squadron were later joined in England by those of the 425th NFS, and between them these units were intended to provide night protection of U.S. bases in the run-up to D-Day.

Another European mission involved interception of V-1 flying bombs, with limited success, before the Normandy invasion saw the European Black Widows move to bases on the Continent, from where they harassed the remnants of the *Luftwaffe* in the final months before VE-Day.

The F-15A Reporter was a two-seat reconnaissance version of the P-61E, the latter which had been planned as a long-range escort fighter to accompany the B-29 over Japan, but which won no orders. A total of 36 production F-15As were produced for post-war service, using part-completed P-61C airframes. Compared to the Black Widow, the Reporter featured slimmer engine nacelles and a 'teardrop' cockpit canopy.

P-61 Armament

This early P-61A reveals the original General Electric dorsal turret that was subsequently removed after it was found to be prone to buffeting. This was the same turret as used in the B-29, and was armed with four 12.7mm (0.5in) machine guns, each of which was provided with 800 rounds of ammunition. In service, however, and in order to both increase firepower and make use of the assigned three-man crew, some units in the Pacific flew aircraft with the dorsal turret still mounted, but in a fixed, forward-firing position. The dorsal turret (if fitted) was complemented by four 20mm (0.79in) Hispano cannon that were mounted in the belly, below the fuselage, in a staggered installation. Containers were provided fore and aft for a total of 200 rounds per gun.

Boeing B-29 Superfortress
(1944)

Even without the atomic missions that the type flew against Japan in August 1945, the B-29 – the most advanced heavy bomber of the war – can be considered a war-winner on account of the devastating raids it conducted against the Japanese mainland in the preceding months.

Following the outbreak of war in Europe, in 1939 the U.S. Army Air Corps issued a requirement for a Very Heavy Bomber, a strategic bomber capable of carrying 9072kg (20,000lb) of weapons over a distance of 8582km (5333 miles) at a speed of 644km/h (400mph). When the Japanese attacked Pearl Harbor, the project assumed priority status. By now, the Very Heavy Bomber had been renamed as the Very Long Range project, with a view to deployment over the vast distances of the Pacific theatre.

After receiving the go-ahead from USAAC chief Henry H. 'Hap' Arnold, the project got underway in early 1940. Requests for proposals were issued to five manufacturers in January of that year, with contracts awarded to Boeing

Guns
The pressurized fuselage demanded the use of remote-controlled gun barbettes, provided in the form of four twin-gun turrets located above and below the fuselage, and one in the tail.

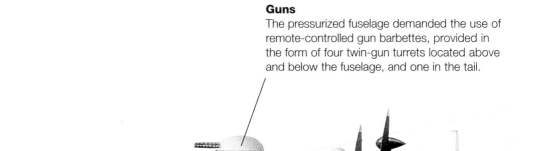

Crew
The Washington was flown by a usual crew of nine, comprising a captain/1st pilot, 2nd pilot, flight engineer, navigator/bombardier, radar navigator, signaller, central fire controller and two gunners. The rear turret was usually unmanned.

Radar
The AN/APQ-13 bombing radar was located between the twin bomb bays. The radome housed a 0.76m (30in) rotating dish antenna.

and Consolidated for the construction of two (later three) prototypes. The first of these to fly was the Consolidated XB-32, but it suffered development delays that led to a protracted service entry.

As of 1940, Boeing's design had advanced much further than that of rival Consolidated, and the manufacturer convinced the USAAC that the finished aircraft would be available within two or three years. The big new four-engined bomber was soon ordered in significant numbers, with a request for 1500 examples received even before the first flight of a prototype XB-29, which occurred in September 1942. Among the futuristic features of the B-29 were its electrically-retractable tricycle undercarriage, pressurized accommodation for the crew and defensive gun turrets that were sighted from adjacent blister windows. The powerplant consisted of four Wright R-3350 Cyclone twin-row radial piston engines, each unit being provided with two superchargers.

In May 1943 plans were drawn up to employ the Superfortress exclusively in combat against Japan. As a result, production B-29 bombers were to be assigned to the 20th Air Force at bases in China and India. The initial aircraft delivered to service units were taken from the batch of 14 YB-29 test aircraft, the first of which flew in June 1943, and which were accepted by the 58th Very Heavy Bombardment Wing in July 1943.

Pending the arrival of significant numbers of Avro Lincolns, 88 ex-USAF B-29s were loaned to the RAF between 1950 and 1955 under the name Washington B.Mk 1. This aircraft was assigned to No.90 Squadron at RAF Marham, one of eight squadrons equipped with Washingtons.

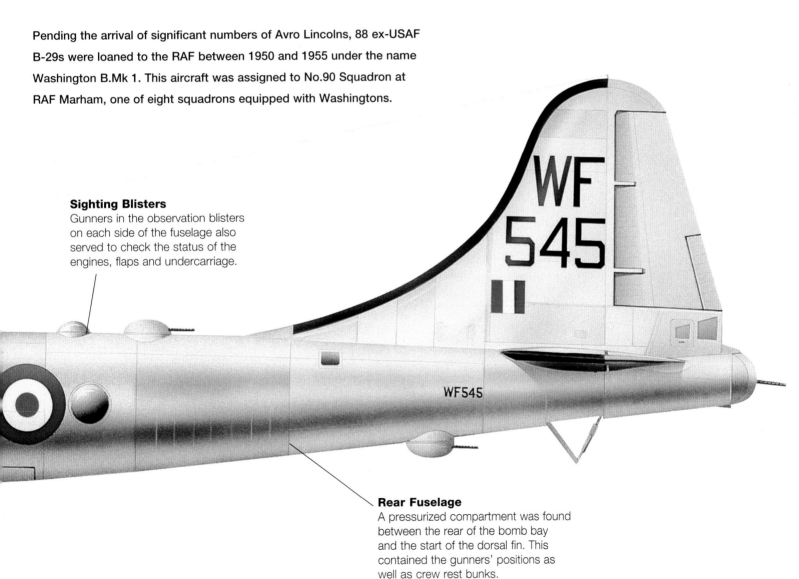

Sighting Blisters
Gunners in the observation blisters on each side of the fuselage also served to check the status of the engines, flaps and undercarriage.

Rear Fuselage
A pressurized compartment was found between the rear of the bomb bay and the start of the dorsal fin. This contained the gunners' positions as well as crew rest bunks.

Boeing B-29 Superfortress

The first true production bombers were the B-29-BW aircraft that were manufactured by Boeing at Wichita and at a new plant in Renton, as well as by Bell in Marietta and Martin in Omaha. In addition to these final-assembly plants, the Superfortress production effort made use of over 60 new factories, all of which provided major components as part of a complex supply chain.

Specification

Type:	Heavy strategic bomber
Dimensions:	Length: 30.18m (99ft 0in); Wingspan: 43.36m (142ft 3in); Height: 9.01m (29ft 7in)
Weight:	64,003kg (141,100lb) maximum take-off
Powerplant:	4 x 1641kW (2200hp) Wright R-3350-57 radial piston engines
Maximum speed:	576km/h (358mph)
Range:	6598km (4100 miles)
Service ceiling:	9695m (31,800ft)
Crew:	10–11
Armament:	12 x 12.7mm (0.5in) machine guns in remote-controlled turrets, 1 x 20mm (0.79in) cannon and 2 x 12.7mm (0.5in) machine guns in tail, plus bombload of up to 9072kg (20,000lb)

Renton-built B-29A-5-BN serial 42-93869 seen soon after leaving the production line. The huge Wright Duplex Cyclone engines drove 5.05m (16ft 7in) diameter four-bladed propellers.

The first B-29s were deployed in theatre in early 1944, initially in India. From here, the Superfortress made a first raid in June 1944 against Bangkok. A first raid on the Japanese mainland was undertaken later in the same month, flying from a hastily prepared base in Chengdu, China. In October 1944 the B-29s began flying missions against Japan from bases on Tinian, Saipan and Guam – newly captured islands in the Marianas chain.

Devastating Raids

During their initial nine months of service, the B-29s were employed mainly for high-level daylight raids, but tactics switched in March 1945, when they began low-level night attacks from the Marianas islands. These were the most destructive raids of the war in terms of casualties, with the first night-time incendiary raid on Tokyo killing around 80,000 people.

Total B-29 production amounted to 3970 aircraft. Two main sub-variants appeared during the war, the Renton-built B-29A-BN with a four-gun forward upper turret, changes to the fuel system and increased wingspan, and the Marietta-built B-29-BA with an increased bombload but a reduced gun armament to bring down its weight.

A top view of the Washington B.Mk 1 reveals the slender wing, designed to withstand massive loading and maximise cruise performance. Fowler flaps generated extra lift at low speed.

It was two Omaha-built B-29-45-MOs, named Enola Gay and Bock's Car, of the 393rd Bombardment Squadron, that were responsible for dropping the atomic bombs Little Boy and Fat Man on the cities of Hiroshima and Nagasaki on 6 and 9 August 1945, respectively.

A total of 118 B-29s were converted for reconnaissance duties, being equipped with cameras and serving as F-13 and F-13A aircraft. These were used to provide reconnaissance for raids on Japan from December 1944.

B-29s remained in use after the war, converted for several other duties including in-flight refuelling, weather reconnaissance and rescue. The B-29 saw military service again in Korea between 1950 and 1953. The final example was retired from service in September 1960.

After the War

War-surplus B-29s stand at Kingman Army Air Field, Arizona, after VJ-Day. While many of the B-29s completed before the end of the war met this fate, some of them being disposed of direct from the production line, the Superfortress continued to provide useful service to the post-war Air Force. Five B-29 bombardment groups took part in the Korea War, where the type flew its first combat missions against North Korean forces in June 1950. A total of 16 B-29s were lost to enemy action during Korea operations, while B-29 gunners shot down 33 enemy fighters. In addition to their primary strategic bombing role, a total of 92 aircraft were converted to KB-29M tanker configuration, with a hose and reel in the aft fuselage. This was followed by the KB-29P (116 conversions), a tanker that made use of the 'flying boom' method, involving an operator that 'flew' the boom nozzle into a receptacle on the receiving aircraft.

Lockheed F-80 Shooting Star (1944)

The P-80 (later F-80) holds the distinction of being the first USAF jet aircraft to enter combat, and although it was subsequently outclassed by swept-wing fighters, it provided good service, especially in the fighter-bomber role in the Korean War and served as the basis for the successful T-33 trainer.

The Shooting Star was not the first U.S. jet to enter service, that honour falling to the Bell P-59 Airacomet, but it was the first to be used operationally and the first to be built in significant quantities. The Shooting Star's origins

lie in a General Operational Requirement issued in mid-June 1943. Thereafter, the design and manufacture of a prototype proceeded at a rapid pace, such that the XP-80 was able to make a maiden flight in January 1944. The

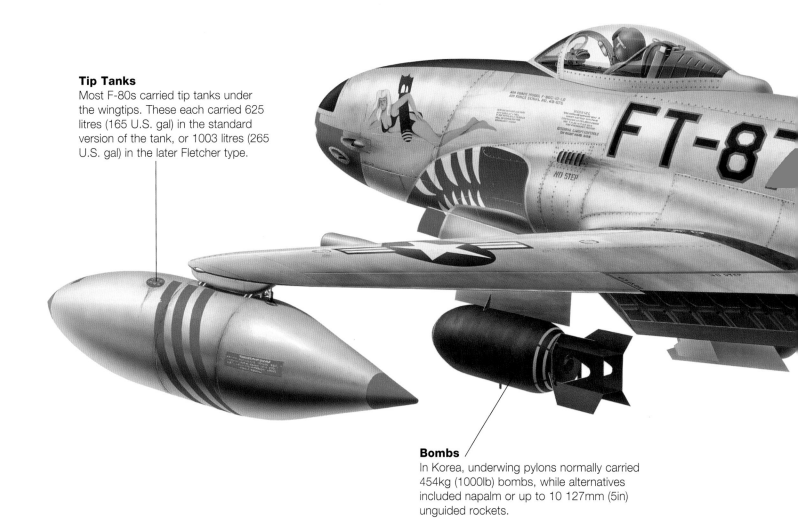

Tip Tanks
Most F-80s carried tip tanks under the wingtips. These each carried 625 litres (165 U.S. gal) in the standard version of the tank, or 1003 litres (265 U.S. gal) in the later Fletcher type.

Bombs
In Korea, underwing pylons normally carried 454kg (1000lb) bombs, while alternatives included napalm or up to 10 127mm (5in) unguided rockets.

original XP-80 with a British-made Halford H-1B engine developing 13.34kN (3000lb) gave way to the improved XP-80A, comprising two prototypes, each of which was fitted with a more powerful General Electric I-40 engine of 29.25kN (4000lb) thrust.

The General Electric powerplant was retained for the pre-production YP-80A aircraft. In April 1944 the Lockheed fighter was ordered into production, and although cancellations affected the programme after VJ-Day, deliveries of the P-80A had already begun before the war came to an end. This initial production model was powered by a 17.12kN (3850lb) General Electric J33-GE-11 engine and had an armament of six 12.7mm (0.5in) machine guns in the nose.

A total of 16 Shooting Stars was flying before the final Allied victory, and these were to be found both in the U.S. and in Europe, the latter deployment intended for operational evaluation. Although plans to build as many as 5000 Shooting Stars were ditched, the fighter was nonetheless selected to form the front-line equipment

A late-production F-80C of the 36th Fighter-Bomber Squadron, 8th Fighter-Bomber Wing, based at Itazuke, Japan, in June 1950. The 36th FBS later converted back to the piston-engined F-51 Mustang, considered more suitable for operations in Korea. It ended the war equipped with F-86 Sabres.

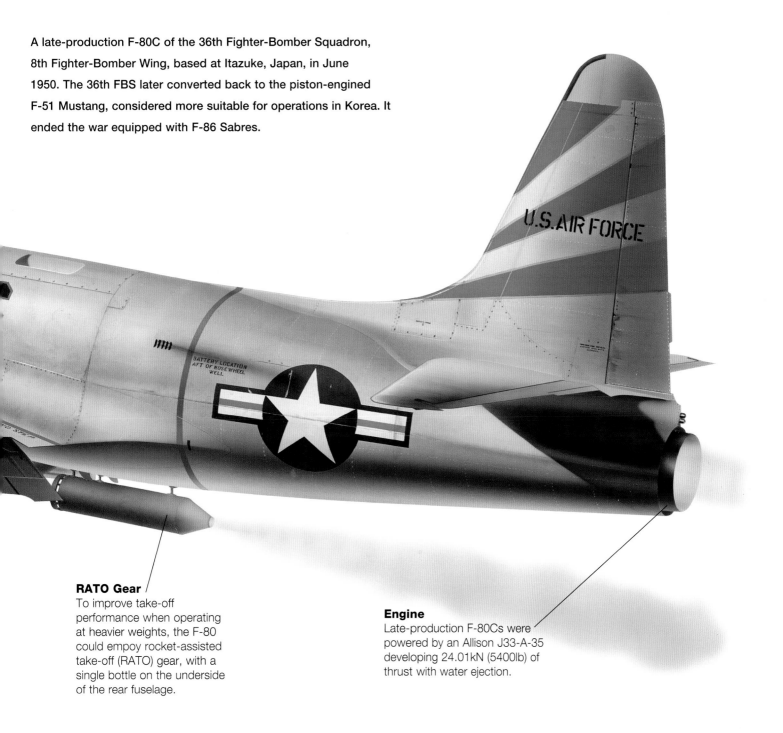

RATO Gear
To improve take-off performance when operating at heavier weights, the F-80 could empoy rocket-assisted take-off (RATO) gear, with a single bottle on the underside of the rear fuselage.

Engine
Late-production F-80Cs were powered by an Allison J33-A-35 developing 24.01kN (5400lb) of thrust with water ejection.

Lockheed F-80 Shooting Star

of USAAF (later USAF) fighter groups, including those in service with the Far East Air Force in Southeast Asia. In June 1947 a specially modified XP-80R became the fastest aircraft in the world, establishing a new speed record of 991.0km/h (615.8mph) in the hands of Albert Boyd. The Allison-powered record-breaker featured a number of modifications, including flush air intakes and a low-profile canopy. Among other early achievements of the type was the first west-to-east transatlantic crossing by jet, accomplished in July 1948 by 16 F-80s of the 56th Fighter Group. (The revised F-80 designation had replaced P-80 in 1947.) The Shooting Star also provided the equipment for the USAF's first jet display team, the Acrojets, established in 1948.

In July 1950, Francis B. Clark of the 35th Fighter-Bomber Squadron destroyed a North Korean Yak-9 and damaged another in Salty Dog, the F-80C illustrated on these pages.

The next version to enter large-scale service was the F-80B, incorporating numerous improvements including thinner wings with thicker skin, increased power, an ejector seat for the pilot and provision for the carriage of rocket-assisted take-off (RATO) equipment.

After 240 F-80Bs had been completed, production switched to the F-80C that was the definitive Shooting Star model. The F-80C had a further increase in power, and improved armament, and a total of 670 were completed by the end of 1950. The initial powerplant for

Specification (F-80C)

Type:	Fighter-bomber
Dimensions:	Length: 10.52m (34ft 6in); Wingspan: 12.15m (39ft 10.5in); Height: 3.45m (11ft 4in)
Weight:	7646kg (16,856lb) maximum take-off
Powerplant:	1 x 24.01kN (5400lb) Allison J33-A-35 turbojet
Maximum speed:	956km/h (594mph)
Range:	1706km (1060 miles)
Service ceiling:	13,030m (42,750ft)
Crew:	1
Armament:	6 x 12.7mm (0.5in) machine guns and up to 907kg (200lb) of external ordnance or 10 127mm (5in) rockets

The forward fuselage of the F-80C contained a concentrated battery of six Colt-Browning M2/M3 12.7mm (0.5in) machine guns, supplied with 300 rounds of ammunition per weapon.

the C-model was an Allison J33-A-23 rated at 20.46kN (4600lb) thrust, but this gave way in later production machines to a J33-A-35 developing 24.01kN (5400lb) of thrust. Provision was also added for underwing rockets.

Korean War Service

It was the F-80C that saw service in the Korean War, this being the most modern fighter type available to

Shooting Star Drones

Work to create an unmanned version of the P-80 began as early as 1945. In 1946 Bell was responsible for modifying two P-80As to pilotless configuration, and the resulting aircraft were used in experiments in which they were operated under radio control from a 'mother ship'. Under Project Bad Boy, a further eight F-80s were converted by Sperry in 1951, becoming QF-80 drones for primary use as airborne targets. A second batch of Sperry-modified aircraft were completed as QF-80 gunnery targets and were equipped with enlarged wingtip tanks that contained cameras to record gunnery patterns. Finally, another contract of 1954 called for Sperry to modify another 55 aircraft as QF-80s, together with 10 DT-33 drone controllers. Among the tasks of the QF-80s was the atmospheric sampling of radioactive particles in the wake of nuclear tests.

the Far East Air Force when the conflict broke out. In November 1950 an F-80C flown by Russell J. Brown of the 51st Fighter Interceptor Wing reportedly downed a MiG-15 in what the U.S. claimed was the first conclusive aerial jet combat between two jet fighters. Soviet records indicate that the MiG survived the encounter with Brown's aircraft. Against swept-wing opposition like the MiG-15, however, the Shooting Star was obsolescent and was demoted to the fighter-bomber role.

The eventual production total for the F-80 amounted to 1732 aircraft. This included 38 airframes that started out on the production line as P-80As before being converted to become RF-80A reconnaissance jets, and a further 114 new-build RF-80As. Another 70-odd aircraft were modified to RF-80C standard, with a fighter-style nose.

With up to three cameras in the nose, these aircraft provided useful service in Korea, where they flew the first photo-reconnaissance sortie of the war in June 1950, and later undertook the first ever combat mission involving aerial refuelling, with support from a KB-29M tanker, in July 1951.

Further Developments

The F-80 served as the basis for two further successful developments, the F-94 Starfire all-weather interceptor, and the T-33, at one time the most widespread two-seat jet trainer in the world. In fact, the T-33 'T-bird' provided the airframe for the subsequent F-94, to which was added a radar in the nose and unguided rocket armament. In this form, Air Defense Command's F-94 became the first gunless rocket-armed interceptor to enter service anywhere in the world.

Cold War and Modern Era

In World War II, military aeroplanes had introduced the turbine engine and the atomic bomb to the world, and combat aircraft would continue to lead the way in technological developments in the years after 1945. The superpower rivalry of the Cold War saw the limits of science pushed yet further, as aircraft designers battled to provide the ultimate combination of performance, agility, weapons and sensors. As the Cold War came to an end, stealth added another possible requirement to the designer's remit, while in the twenty-first century network-centric warfare and precision-guided munitions are the order of the day.

Opposite: A U.S. Air Force B-52H Stratofortress from the 5th Bomb Wing at Minot AFB, North Dakota, prepares to refuel from a tanker over the western United States in 2002. This venerable Cold War warrior entered service in 1955 and remains a potent weapon in the second decade of the twenty-first century.

North American F-86 Sabre (1949)

Perhaps the finest jet fighter of its generation, the F-86 won its spurs over Korea and went on to enjoy unprecedented success in a variety of combat roles and with dozens of different air arms around the world, serving for close to 50 years. With nearly 10,000 built, it is the most prolific Western jet fighter of all time.

Best known for its MiG-killing exploits over Korea, the F-86 was first flown in prototype form in 1947, and remained in front-line service in Bolivia as late as 1994. Originally developed to meet a USAAF specification, the design was intended to be a day fighter, albeit one that would also be capable of operating as an escort fighter or dive-bomber. The result was the North American NA-140 design.

Cockpit
The pilot sat below an aft-sliding canopy on a North American ejector seat, in a pressurized cockpit with air conditioning. The display was dominated by a screen for the fire-control system.

Intake
Adding radar in the D-model demanded a redesign of the entire nose, which now incorporated an engine intake in the chin position, with air being ducted below the cockpit.

Rockets
The 24 Mighty Mouse rockets were the sole armament of the F-86D. These folding-fin weapons were intended to attack bomber formations, each rocket carrying a 3.4kg (7.5lb) warhead.

The USAF's Sabre was evolved from an earlier, straight-wing North American jet fighter, the FJ-1 Fury that was built for the U.S. Navy. The addition of a swept wing on the F-86 ensured that it would be one of the finest dogfighters of its era, with performance that far exceeded the previous generation of jet fighters. In late 1944 North American received a contract for two XP-86 prototypes, but these were originally to be straight-winged. The acquisition of technical data from Nazi Germany after the war forced a major rethink, and the XP-86 was redrafted with swept wing and tail surfaces. The result was a year's delay to the programme, pushing back the maiden flight to October 1947. The XP-86 as initially flown was powered by a General Electric TG-180 turbojet developing 16.68kN (3750lb) of thrust. It was re-engined in April 1948 with a General Electric J47, becoming the YP-86A, capable of exceeding Mach 1 in a shallow dive.

The initial-production P-86A version was powered by a 21.57kN (4850lb) J47-GE-1 and first took to the air in May 1948. The first recipient of the F-86A (as it had been renamed in June 1948) was the 94th Fighter Squadron of the USAF's 1st Fighter Group at March Field, California, in February 1949. It was swiftly followed

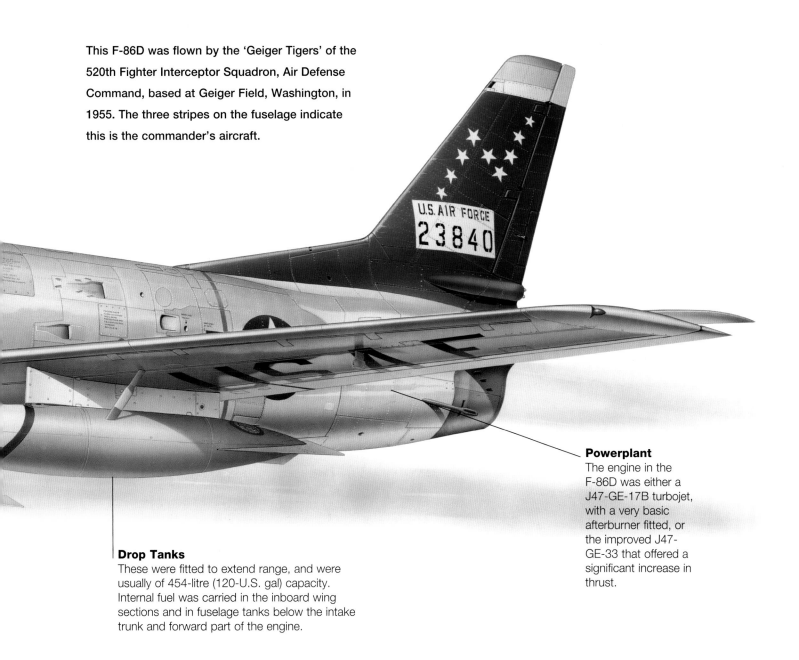

This F-86D was flown by the 'Geiger Tigers' of the 520th Fighter Interceptor Squadron, Air Defense Command, based at Geiger Field, Washington, in 1955. The three stripes on the fuselage indicate this is the commander's aircraft.

Powerplant
The engine in the F-86D was either a J47-GE-17B turbojet, with a very basic afterburner fitted, or the improved J47-GE-33 that offered a significant increase in thrust.

Drop Tanks
These were fitted to extend range, and were usually of 454-litre (120-U.S. gal) capacity. Internal fuel was carried in the inboard wing sections and in fuselage tanks below the intake trunk and forward part of the engine.

North American F-86 Sabre

by the 4th and 81st FGs. The A-model was also the first to see combat, when the 4th FG was despatched to Japan in late 1950 for service in the Korean War. A total of 554 F-86As were completed, most being powered by the 23.13kN (5200lb) J47-GE-3, -7, -9 or -13 turbojets.

The improved F-86E, and the definitive F-86F day-fighter model also saw action in Korea, and between them Sabres were initially credited with almost 800 MiG-15s destroyed, for the loss of only around 80 of their own, to give a victory ratio of 10:1. More recent research suggests that the actual ratio was closer

A Korean War F-86E of the 25th Fighter Interceptor Squadron, 51st Fighter Interceptor Wing. The pilot of this aircraft, named Elenore 'E', was William Whisner, an ace with 5.5 MiG kills.

to 2:1. Meanwhile, of the 41 American pilots who achieved ace status during the Korean War, all but one flew the F-86. The F-86E added an all-moving tailplane, while handling was further improved in the F-86F (of which 1539 were built), which featured an extensively modified wing.

Last of the fighter line from North American production was a dedicated fighter-bomber, the F-86H, with a more

Specification (F-86H)

Type:	Fighter-bomber
Dimensions:	Length: 11.84m (38ft 10in); Wingspan: 11.93m (39ft 1.5in); Height: 4.57m (15ft 0in)
Weight:	9912kg (21,852lb) maximum take-off
Powerplant:	1 x 39.7kN (8920lb) General Electric J33-GE-3D turbojet
Maximum speed:	1114km/h (692mph)
Range:	835km (519 miles)
Service ceiling:	15,485m (50,800ft)
Crew:	1
Armament:	4 x 20mm (0.79in) cannon and 2 x 227kg (500lb), 340kg (750lb) or 454kg (1000lb) bombs, or 16 127mm (5in) rockets

In the neat undercarriage of the Sabre, the nosewheel unit retracted backwards to lie in the forward fuselage, while the mainwheels retracted inwards to lie in the fuselage.

powerful J73 engine contained within a much-redesigned fuselage, additional fuel capacity and nuclear-weapons capability. A total of 477 were built.

While the day fighters are the best known Sabre variants today, the most numerous member of the family was the F-86D all-weather fighter that was intended for

Fury: Sabres at Sea

A first-generation naval jet fighter, the North American FJ-1 Fury had provided the initial basis for the design of the land-based Sabre. Successive marks of F-86 then contributed to the further development of swept-wing FJ Fury derivatives for use by the U.S. Navy and Marine Corps. The experimental XFJ-2 was essentially a naval version of the F-86E, equipped with arrester hook, extending nose gear and catapult hitches. A total of 200 FJ-2 production models followed, these being equipped with folding wings. The next development was the FJ-3 (538 built) that featured a deeper fuselage containing a more powerful Wright J65-W-2 or J65-W-4 turbojet, developing 35.76kN (7800lb) or 34.02kN (7650lb) of thrust respectively. The 152 FJ-4s were dedicated attack variants with 34.25kN (7700lb) Wright J65s, followed by 222 FJ-4B improved attack aircraft with an entirely new airframe.

service with Air Defense Command. Originally designated the F-96 on account of its considerable changes, the F-86D incorporated an interception radar and fire-control system and carried an armament of 27 70mm (2.75in) Mighty Mouse rockets in a retractable ventral tray. The other new-build model was the F-86K (120 built), essentially a D-model adapted for service with NATO allies, and with gun armament. 'Sabre Dogs' accounted for 2504 of the total production run of 9860 North American F-86s. A total of 827 'Sabre Dogs' were subsequently rebuilt as F-86Ls, featuring an increased-span wing and updated avionics.

This total was added to by licensed production in Australia by the Commonwealth Aircraft Corporation (112 aircraft) and in Canada by Canadair (1815). The CAC Sabre differed in its use of the 33.35kN (7500lb) thrust Rolls-Royce Avon 26 engine and armament of two 30mm (1.1in) cannon. A total of 100 were built. Canadair produced F-86Es for the USAF, as well as the similar Sabre Mk 2 (290 aircraft) for Canada and NATO allies. The 438 Sabre Mk 4s built by Canadair were supplied to the UK, with General Electric engines, while the 370 Sabre Mk 5s had 28.26kN (6355lb) Orenda 10 turbojets.

Last of the Canadian production models was the Sabre Mk 6, 655 of which were completed with the 32.35kN (7275lb) Orenda 14. Finally, Fiat in Italy was responsible for assembly of 221 F-86Ks that were provided in kit form by North American Aviation, and Mitsubishi of Japan assembled a further 300 Sabres.

Mikoyan-Gurevich MiG-17 (1950)

Scourge of the U.S. air arms operating over Vietnam, the MiG-17 was a refinement of the Korean War-era MiG-15, rectifying the earlier fighter's shortcomings. The result was an agile fighter and fighter-bomber that also gave good service in successive battles fought by Arab air forces against Israel into the 1970s.

Out-performed and with only very basic weapons and avionics, the MiG-17 should have been no match for the sophisticated American warplanes, led by the superb F-4 Phantom II that it encountered in the skies over Vietnam. However, in the hands of the North Vietnamese People's Air Force, the MiG-17 (which received the Western codename 'Fresco') made full use of its excellent agility, diminutive size and hard-hitting cannon. Three North Vietnamese pilots attained ace status flying the MiG-17, led by Nguyen Van Bay with seven victories.

Engine Intake
The prominent intake divided the incoming airflow as it entered before it was ducted below the cockpit to feed the engine, roughly in line with the wing trailing edge.

Nosewheel
The single nosewheel retracted forward for stowage. The simple undercarriage was designed to enable operations from semi-prepared airfields and rough strips.

Underwing Tanks
Endurance was extended through the use of 400-litre (880-gal) drop tanks that could be carried underwing. In definitive form, four pylons were provided underwing, although drop tanks could only be carried inboard.

Mikoyan-Gurevich began work on the MiG-17 just as the MiG-15 was entering quantity production. The latter type would prove itself in the Korean War, but it suffered from some instability in the high-speed regime. The new fighter would be similar in appearance, but would importantly add aerodynamic refinements, primarily in the form of a wing of increased sweepback and reduced thickness: chord ratio. Indeed, in the early stages, the new aircraft was known by the designation MiG-15bis-45, on account of the 45 degrees of wing sweep. The result was a fighter with improved transonic performance. Armament remained unchanged from that of the MiG-15: one 37mm (1.45in)

and two 23mm (0.9in) cannon in the nose, and initially at least, the Klimov VK-1 engine was retained as well. Design work was completed in spring 1949 and resulted in the prototype SI-2 that was first flown in January 1950. It soon displayed impressive performance, including a maximum speed of 1114km/h (692mph) in level flight.

The loss of the first flying prototype during a test flight delayed the programme by a year, but after completion of the state test flight programme using two new prototypes in June 1951, the new fighter was ordered into series production as the MiG-17 in September of the same year. However, with the MiG-15 already being built in

This non-afterburning MiG-17 was flown by Lt Bomba of the Mozambique Air Force when he defected to South Africa in 1980, where the fighter was tested before being returned to Mozambique.

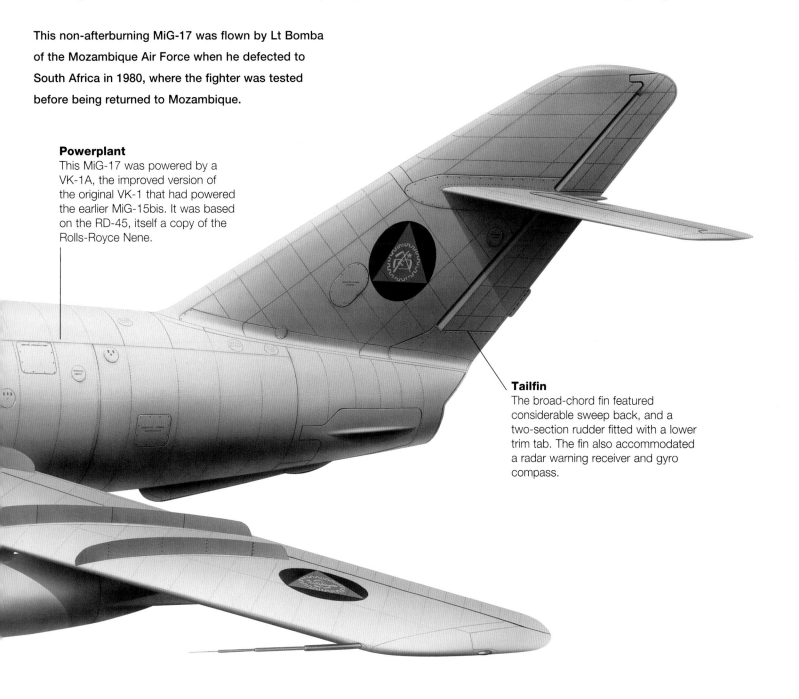

Powerplant
This MiG-17 was powered by a VK-1A, the improved version of the original VK-1 that had powered the earlier MiG-15bis. It was based on the RD-45, itself a copy of the Rolls-Royce Nene.

Tailfin
The broad-chord fin featured considerable sweep back, and a two-section rudder fitted with a lower trim tab. The fin also accommodated a radar warning receiver and gyro compass.

Mikoyan-Gurevich MiG-17

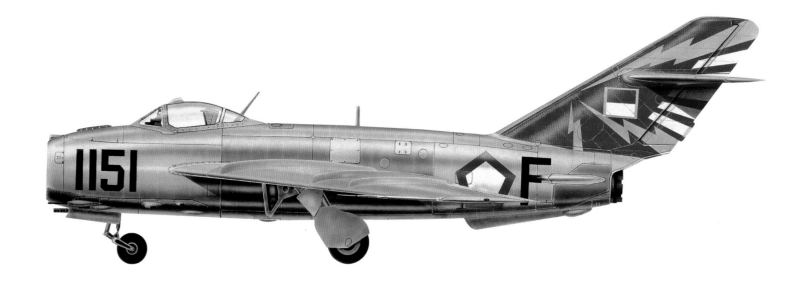

large numbers, it was not until late 1953 that the type was adopted by the Soviet Air Force. Compared to the MiG-15, the new aircraft brought improvements in rate of climb, top speed and agility. When the U.S. Air Force encountered the MiG-17 over Vietnam, beginning in 1965, Robin Olds, commander of the 8th Tactical Fighter Wing, described the Soviet-designed fighter as 'a very dangerous little animal. Its manoeuvrability is phenomenal!'

As production of the MiG-17 ramped up, the original VK-1 was replaced by the improved VK-1A that offered increased durability for the same thrust rating, and additional pylons (for a total of four) were added

This MiG-17F wears the colourful markings of an aerobatic team provided by No.11 Squadron, Indonesian Air Force, that operated the type in the early 1960s.

underwing to carry air-to-ground ordnance and drop tanks. MiG-17s eventually equipped over 40 air forces around the world, and production was also undertaken in Czechoslovakia, Poland and in China, where a range of variants were produced as the Shenyang J-5 series. In total, just short of 8000 MiG-17s were produced at five different factories in the USSR, and when foreign production is added to this number, the grand total exceeded 10,000.

Successive Improvements

The first major improvement to the MiG-17 line was manifest in the MiG-17F that added an afterburning engine, the VK-1F. First flown in September 1951, the MiG-17F began to replace the basic version in production in November 1952 and became the most important production version. The addition of an afterburner unit demanded some changes to the aircraft, which included a cut-back rear fuselage, a ventral strake below the rear fuselage and redesigned airbrakes.

A first radar-equipped interceptor version, the MiG-17P began testing in summer 1951 and became the radar fighter to serve with the Soviet Union, serving in small numbers from winter 1953–54. While the scanning radar was mounted in a radome above the intake lip, the tracking radar was contained in a fairing within

Specification (MiG-17F)

Type:	Fighter-bomber
Dimensions:	Length: 11.26m (36ft 11.5in); Wingspan: 9.63m (31ft 7in); Height: 3.80m (12ft 5.5in)
Weight:	5350kg (11,770lb) maximum take-off
Powerplant:	1 x 22.5kN (5046lb) Klimov VK-1F afterburning turbojet
Maximum speed:	1145km/h (711mph)
Range:	2060km (1280 miles) with drop tanks
Service ceiling:	16,600m (54,450ft)
Crew:	1
Armament:	1 x 37mm (1.45in) cannon and 2 x 23mm (0.9in) cannon, plus up to 500kg (1102lb) of external stores on underwing pylons

In its day-fighter versions, the MiG-17 packed a punch with a nose armament of one 37mm (1.45in) N-37D cannon to starboard, and single 23mm (0.9in) NS-23 cannon on the port side.

the centre of the intake. The definitive radar-equipped model was the MiG-17PF, which combined the radar nose with the afterburning VK-1F. Indeed, the addition of an afterburning engine had originally been planned as a means of improving the otherwise diminished performance of the radar-equipped version of the fighter.

The MiG-17PF succeeded the MiG-17P in production in late 1953, and was ultimately equipped with the RP-5 Izumrud radar with a range of 12km (7.5 miles) against a bomber-size target. With the addition of missile armament matched to RP-1U radar, the interceptor became the MiG-17PFU, built in small numbers in 1955. As such, the MiG-17PFU, with its armament of four RS-2US (AA-1 'Alkali') beam-riding air-to-air missiles was the first missile-armed interceptor to enter production in Europe.

MiG-17 Warbirds

The MiG-17's high-subsonic performance, robust construction and the relative availability of both complete aircraft and spare parts have made it a popular performer on the warbird scene. In the U.S. alone there are around 27 privately owned MiG-17s, many of these originating from Polish production, where locally built variants of the 'Fresco' remained in service until the early 1990s. This particular ex-Polish Air Force example, fitted with underwing smoke generators for airshow performances, was flown by the late Bill Reesman, a former U.S. Air Force and Air Guard pilot who flew 320 combat missions over Vietnam in the F-100 Super Sabre. The jet is now operated by Red Bull.

Boeing B-52 Stratofortress (1952)

Still in front-line service after 60 years, the mighty B-52 remains a powerful symbol of American military power, and has served as both a nuclear deterrent and as a front-line type in conflicts extending from Vietnam to the Global War on Terror. As a rolling upgrade programme continues, B-52s are set to serve at least until 2040.

The B-52 is the longest-serving bomber in U.S. military history. First drafted as a turboprop-powered replacement for the same company's B-50 in 1948, the planned bomber took a change in direction when the 33.36kN (7500lb) thrust Pratt & Whitney J57 turbojet engine became available. As a consequence

of the appearance of this powerplant, then superior to anything else on offer, Boeing and the USAF decided to develop a jet-powered strategic bomber. The Boeing design faced competition from the Convair YB-60, a cheaper jet-powered alternative that was based on the existing piston-engined B-36 Peacemaker. In the event,

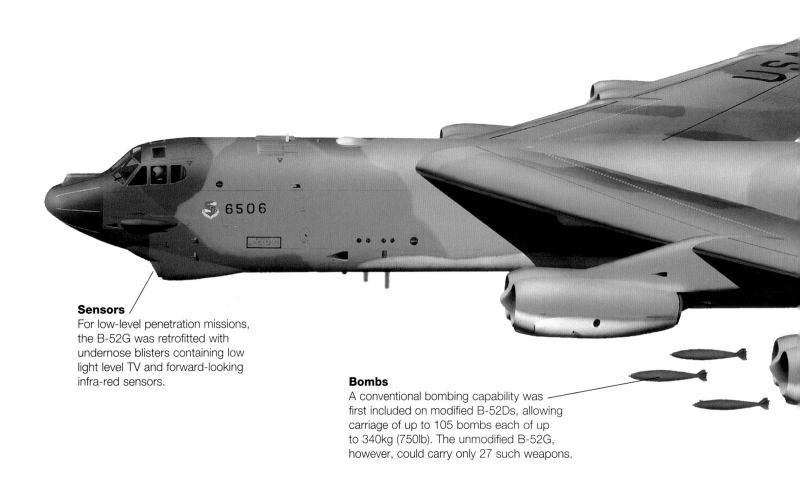

Sensors
For low-level penetration missions, the B-52G was retrofitted with undernose blisters containing low light level TV and forward-looking infra-red sensors.

Bombs
A conventional bombing capability was first included on modified B-52Ds, allowing carriage of up to 105 bombs each of up to 340kg (750lb). The unmodified B-52G, however, could carry only 27 such weapons.

the Boeing design promised superior performance to its Convair rival, and won the day. First to fly was the prototype XB-52, in April 1952. With a basic design inspired by Boeing's B-47 Stratojet medium bomber, the new aircraft featured a slender, high-mounted wing, with eight engines carried in clustered pairs below and ahead of the leading edge. The 'bicycle' undercarriage was inherited from the Stratojet. Initially, tandem seating was provided for the pilots. The same configuration was adopted for the second prototype, the YB-52.

The initial production B-52A first flew in 1954, and three examples were completed for test and development work by the manufacturer. As a result, the first model to enter service with the USAF was the B-52B in 1955. Essentially similar to the B-52A, the B-model added a navigation and bombing system. A total of 50 B-52Bs were completed, and of these 27 were converted to reconnaissance standard as the RB-52B.

A major improvement in performance was heralded by the B-52C that also added various new items

This B-52G served with the 72nd Strategic Wing (Provisional) at Andersen AFB, Guam, in 1972. The first missions over Vietnam were flown in 1965 and culminated in the ferocious attacks on North Vietnam in late 1972, which saw the loss of 15 B-52s to surface-to-air missiles. This aircraft was typical of those flying Arc Light bombing missions alongside B-52Ds until 1973.

'Wet Wing'
The B-52G featured a 'wet wing' that increased maximum fuel capacity to 181,813 litres (48,030 U.S. gal), including 2650 litres (700 U.S. gal) in each of two external wing tanks.

Tail Gun
The B-52G was the last version to retain the original defensive armament of four Browning machine guns.

Engines
The four pairs of Pratt & Whitney J57-P-43WB turbojets were mounted in four packs of two under the wings. Water injection was provided for take-off.

USAF
76506

Boeing B-52 Stratofortress

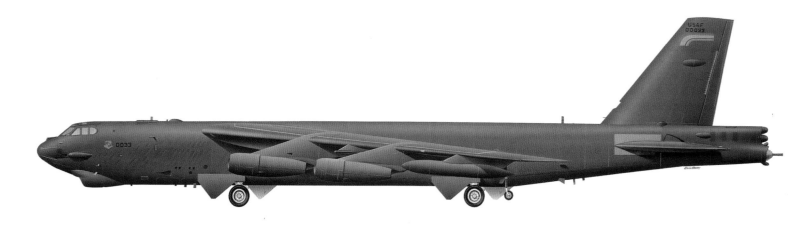

of equipment. A total of 35 were built before it was succeeded by the B-52D, of which 170 were completed. The B-52D differed in the addition of an improved fire-control system to manage the defensive armament of four 12.7mm (0.5in) machine guns in the tail. A total of 100 B-52Es featured a more advanced navigation and weapons delivery system. The B-52F, meanwhile – of which 89 came off the production line – was an effort to counter the increasing weight of the basic design. The F-model therefore featured more powerful J57s, similarly outfitted with water injection to boost take-off power.

The B-52G was envisaged as the final production version, and brought with it the most signifiant

The defintive B-52H, seen in service with the 23rd Bomb Squadron, part of the 5th Bomb Wing at Minot AFB, North Dakota. The unit has flown the B-52 since February 1959.

improvements to date. Airframe modifications were undertaken to reduce weight and improve safety, and integral wing tanks increased range. The tail gunner was also relocated to the crew compartment and the tailfin was now of reduced height. Stores carriage now included radar decoys and standoff missiles. The last of 193 B-52Gs was delivered in 1960 and the model was originally fielded armed with AGM-28 Hound Dog standoff missiles.

A total of 744 B-52s were built with the last, a B-52H, delivered in October 1962. The first of 102 B-52Hs was delivered to Strategic Air Command in May 1961, the new version being powered by an all-new turbofan powerplant, the Pratt & Whitney TF33, providing greater thrust and reduced fuel consumption. The H-model was developed after the cancellation of a planned successor, the North American B-70 Valkyrie. Structural changes were made to permit low-level operations in an effort to defeat enemy surface-to-air missiles. The tail gun armament was also revised, with a single 20mm Gatling cannon replacing the machine guns. Today, survivors can carry up to 20 AGM-86 Air-Launched Cruise Missiles (ALCMs), and the tail gun has been deleted altogether.

Initially nuclear-tipped, the ALCM was later fielded as a conventional cruise missile that has since been used in successive military campaigns, beginning with Operation Desert Storm over Iraq in 1991. Targets during Desert Storm included large troop concentrations,

Specification (B-52H)

Type:	Long-range heavy bomber
Dimensions:	Length: 49.05m (160ft 11in); Wingspan: 56.39m (185ft 0in); Height: 12.40m (40ft 8in)
Weight:	229,068kg (505,000lb) maximum take-off
Powerplant:	8 x 75.62kN (17,000lb) Pratt & Whitney TF33-P-3/103 turbofans
Maximum speed:	1011km/h (628mph)
Range:	14,080km (8800 miles) unrefueled combat range
Service ceiling:	15,151m (50,000ft)
Crew:	5
Armament:	Approximately 31,500kg (70,000lb) of ordnance including bombs, mines and missiles

fixed installations and bunkers. In September 1996, two B-52Hs launched what was then the longest-range combat mission in history, completing a 16,000-mile round trip from Barksdale AFB, Louisiana, in 34 hours. Targets were Iraqi power stations and communications facilities as part of Operation Desert Strike. The B-52 was back in action over Iraq during Operation Iraqi Freedom: in March 2003, B-52Hs launched approximately 100 conventional ALCMs during a single night mission.

As of 2014, the B-52H is the only model in USAF service, and is assigned to Air Force Global Strike Command's 5th Bomb Wing at Minot AFB, North Dakota, the 2nd BW at Barksdale AFB, and Air Force Reserve Command's 307th BW at Barksdale.

Continuous updates have ensured that the B-52 remains a relevant warplane into the twenty-first century. Among items that have been addressed are new avionics, data-link communications, electronic defences and offensive systems, and more powerful, fuel-efficient turbofan engines. Currently, no other U.S. military aircraft can launch such a wide array of weapons.

Built in five sections, the huge wing of the B-52 uses the entire interspar area for fuel carriage. The wing is highly flexible to absorb different loads depending on weights and aerodynamics.

Afghanistan

A B-52H prepares to take on fuel from a tanker during a close-air-support mission over Afghanistan. The B-52's contribution to Operation Enduring Freedom began in 2001, and the bomber has excelled in the close air support role, thanks to its ability to loiter high above the battlefield for extended periods and deliver precision-guided munitions in support of the troops below. Around

10 B-52s were normally in theatre, and these – together with B-1B Lancers – maintained a constant armed presence during Enduring Freedom, typically flying missions that lasted from 12 to 15 hours. Depending on the mission profile, the B-52 usually carried a mixed load of 12 satellite-guided Joint Direct Attack Munitions (JDAMs) and 27 Mk 82 general-purpose bombs or 16 CBU-103/CBU-87 Wind-Corrected Munitions Dispensers (WCMDs) and 27 Mk 82s. The CBU-103 was configured to dispense 202 BLU/97B combined-effects submunitions accurately against soft area targets from high altitude.

Avro Vulcan (1952)

Most successful of Britain's three V-bombers, the Vulcan enjoyed an impressively long service career, starting out as a high-level strategic nuclear bomber and later going into combat as a conventional bomber during the Falklands campaign.

The Vulcan was one of the results of the United Kingdom's Specification B.14/46, which called for a bomber capable of striking a target at a range of 2735km (1700 miles) carrying a nuclear weapon weighing 4536kg (10,000lb), and offering a cruising altitude of 12,190m (40,000ft) and a full-load range of 6437km (4000 miles). This specification

Modifications
Five aircraft were adapted for Black Buck bombing raids, receiving additional ECM equipment and provision for Shrike missiles. Also fitted was the Carousel inertial navigation system for flying over water.

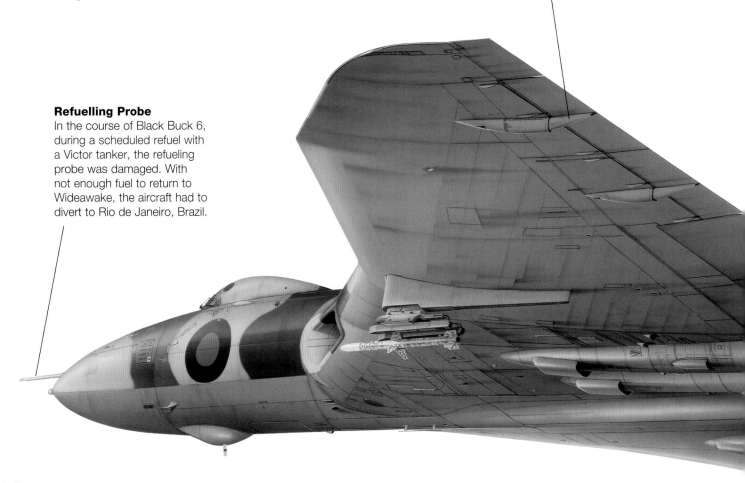

Refuelling Probe
In the course of Black Buck 6, during a scheduled refuel with a Victor tanker, the refueling probe was damaged. With not enough fuel to return to Wideawake, the aircraft had to divert to Rio de Janeiro, Brazil.

Shrike
During Black Buck 6, XM597 launched two AGM-45 Shrike missiles, which destroyed an Argentine Skyguard anti-aircraft artillery radar stationed in the Falklands.

was later revised to become B.35/46, which led to the development of the three V-bombers: the Avro Vulcan, the Handley Page Victor and the Vickers Valiant.

In its initial prototype guise, the Vulcan employed a wing planform that was an almost perfect triangle. In this distinctive form, the aircraft completed its maiden flight in August 1952, and was flown with Rolls-Royce Avon, Armstrong Siddeley Sapphire and finally Rolls-Royce Conway engines. Since the delta wing marked a new departure, a series of Type 707 one-third scale research aircraft had been completed beforehand to test the concept. It would be another 30 years after its first flight before the delta-winged bomber first saw combat over the South Atlantic, in what were then the longest bombing raids ever staged.

After completion of two prototypes, the Vulcan B.M 1 entered RAF service in February 1957. This version had a modified wing of 330m^2 (3554 sq ft) area with the inboard sections accommodating the four Bristol Olympus 101 engines, each developing 48.93kN (11,000lb) of thrust. Compared to the prototypes, the overall planform of the definitive production aircraft was modified with reduced wing sweep from the root to the mid-point, the result being a kinked leading edge. As production progressed, more powerful Olympus Mk 102 or Mk 104 engines were installed. In 1961, aircraft were modified with electronic countermeasures (ECM) equipment in a modified tailcone, becoming the B.Mk 1A aircraft.

Deliveries of the B.Mk 1 amounted to 45 before production switched to 89 of the much-improved

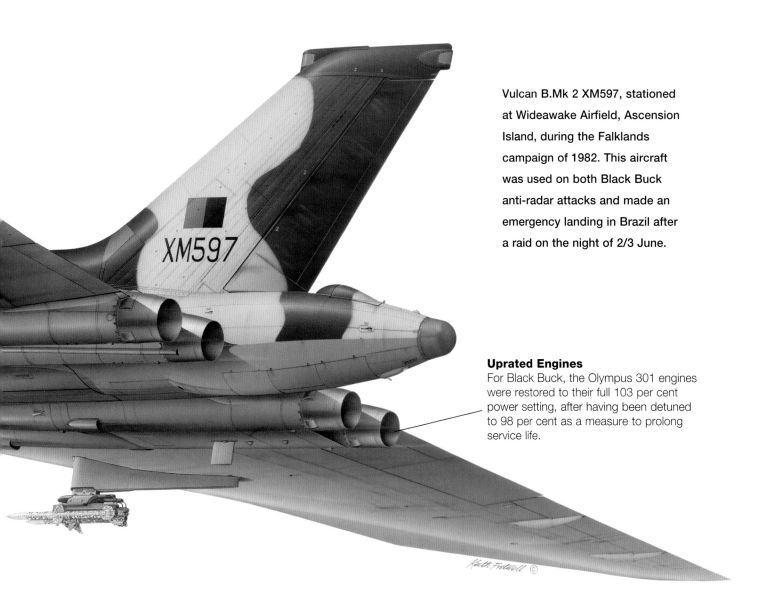

Vulcan B.Mk 2 XM597, stationed at Wideawake Airfield, Ascension Island, during the Falklands campaign of 1982. This aircraft was used on both Black Buck anti-radar attacks and made an emergency landing in Brazil after a raid on the night of 2/3 June.

Uprated Engines
For Black Buck, the Olympus 301 engines were restored to their full 103 per cent power setting, after having been detuned to 98 per cent as a measure to prolong service life.

Avro Vulcan

B.Mk 2 variant. The Mk 2 was entirely re-engineered and its most prominent feature was a much larger but thinner wing, with cranked and cambered leading edge, housing more powerful Olympus engines. Other changes included elevons replacing the B.Mk 1's

Ground crew prepare a Royal Air Force Vulcan Display Team Vulcan B.Mk 2 aircraft for a demonstration during Air Fete '85. A single Vulcan, XH588, remains in airworthy condition as of 2014.

ailerons and elevators, and an inflight refuelling probe. The Vulcan B.Mk 2 entered service in July 1960 and was initially employed in a high-altitude role. The definitive Vulcan B.Mk 2A added the capability to carry a single Blue Steel standoff missile. As the final B.Mk 2 was delivered, almost all the remaining B.Mk 1s had been withdrawn from use.

In 1966 the Blue Steel was also withdrawn from service as the appearance of new surface-to-air missiles prompted a switch to low-level operations, for which a terrain-following radar was added in a nose fairing. At the same time, the ECM fit was appropriately upgraded. In 1962 the B.Mk 2 was re-engined with 88.96kN (20,000lb) Olympus 301 engines. Total production of the B.Mk 2 amounted to 89 aircraft, for a grand total of 134 Vulcans of both marks.

In the early 1980s it became apparent that the Vulcan's fatigue life was running low, as a result of the low-level focus. However, it was decided that the cost

Specification (B.Mk 2)

Type:	Heavy bomber
Dimensions:	Length: 32.16m (105ft 6in) including probe; Wingspan: 33.83m (111ft 0in); Height: 8.28m (27ft 2in)
Weight:	113,400kg (250,000lb) maximum take-off
Powerplant:	4 x 89kN (20,000lb) Bristol Siddeley Olympus 301 turbojets
Maximum speed:	1043km/h (648mph)
Range:	7400km (4600 miles) with bombload
Service ceiling:	18,290m (60,000ft)
Crew:	5
Armament:	Up to 9526kg (21,000lb) of ordnance carried internally

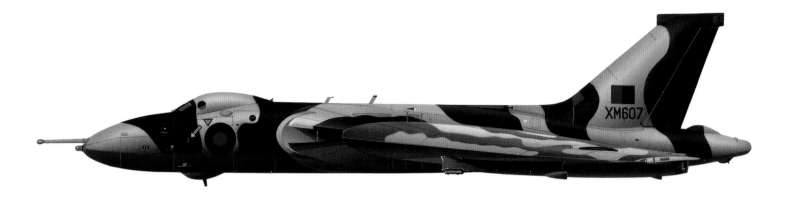

Vulcan B.Mk 2 XM607 was one of the aircraft involved in the first of the Black Buck raids against Port Stanley airfield, flown on 1 May 1982, and armed with 21 1000lb (454kg) bombs.

of extending the service life of the remaining aircraft was too great. It was decided to withdraw the Vulcan force between June 1981 and June 1982.

Falkland Islands Swansong

The Vulcan force was mid-way through being wound down when, in April 1982, Argentine forces invaded the Falklands in the South Atlantic. By now the Vulcan had lost its inflight refuelling capability, and a search was begun for refuelling probes with which to equip the remaining bombers, in order to stage an attack on the Falklands from Ascension Island. Six aircraft were converted as Vulcan K.Mk 2 tankers, with a hose and drogue unit in the rear ECM bay and extra fuel in the bomb bay, while others were equipped for the carriage of conventional bombs, new navigation systems, refuelling probes and underwing pylons for AN/ALQ-101 electronic countermeasures pods and AGM-45 Shrike anti-radar missiles.

In the course of round trips exceeding 12,870km (8000 miles), and under the codename Black Buck, the Vulcans bombed the occupied Port Stanley airfield and related radar installations in the Falklands, putting the runway out of action. The last Vulcans to bow out of service were the K.Mk 2 tankers, finally retired in March 1984.

Maritime Operations

Towards the end of the type's career, nine aircraft were modified for the Strategic Maritime Radar Reconnaissance (MRR role) as Vulcan B.Mk 2MRR aircraft. Conversions were made in 1973 and the aircraft were outfitted with an array of classified electronic, optical and other sensors, as well as additional fuel in the bomb bay. The aircraft were operated by RAF Scampton-based No.27 Squadron from November 1973 to May 1982, assuming the role from Victor B.Mk 2(SR) aircraft of No.543 Squadron that were in turn converted as inflight refuelling tankers. Compared to the standard Vulcan bomber, the B.Mk 2MRR received LORAN-C navigation equipment and the terrain-following radar thimble was removed from the nose. Air-sampling pods could be fitted below the wings for testing the air for contamination, such as dust from nuclear tests.

Lockheed C-130 Hercules (1954)

The most successful Western military transport of the post-war era, the Hercules has enjoyed an unprecedented production run: it has been built in over 70 variants, amounting to a total of more than 2400 aircraft. As well as being the backbone of the U.S. tactical airlift fleet, Hercules have been operated by over 60 nations.

The USAF began looking for a new transport in 1951, drawing upon lessons learnt during the Korean War. The new aircraft was to be capable of hauling large bulky equipment, including artillery pieces and tanks, over long distances. Furthermore, it had to be able to operate from confined spaces, deliver paratroopers and fly on one engine if required. The result proved to be

Cargo Hold
In addition to different loads of troops, the hold could accomodate various items of cargo, including the 155mm (6.1in) howitzer or various types of small truck or helicopter.

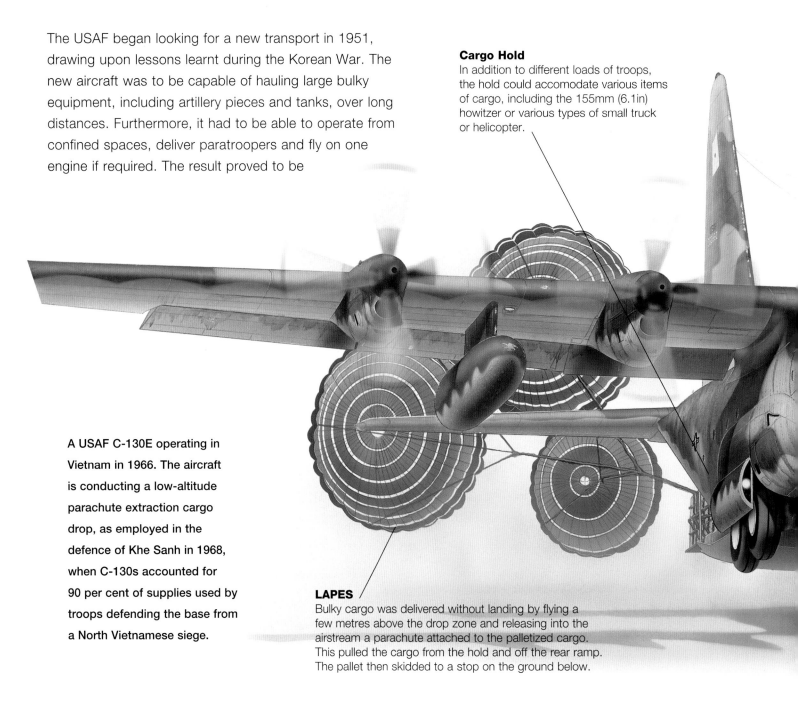

A USAF C-130E operating in Vietnam in 1966. The aircraft is conducting a low-altitude parachute extraction cargo drop, as employed in the defence of Khe Sanh in 1968, when C-130s accounted for 90 per cent of supplies used by troops defending the base from a North Vietnamese siege.

LAPES
Bulky cargo was delivered without landing by flying a few metres above the drop zone and releasing into the airstream a parachute attached to the palletized cargo. This pulled the cargo from the hold and off the rear ramp. The pallet then skidded to a stop on the ground below.

one of the most influential post-war aircraft designs, and a true workhorse that has served all branches of the U.S. military in a variety of roles. Along the way, it has been involved in every conflict and major humanitarian effort in which the U.S. armed forces have participated. Today, it enjoys the longest production run of any aircraft type, Lockheed Martin being responsible for the latest C-130J variants and derivatives.

Schemed by Lockheed's chief engineer Hall Hibbard, the first of prototype YC-130 aircraft made its maiden flight in August 1954. The aircraft was powered by four 2424kW (3250shp) Allison YT56A-1 turboprops driving three-bladed propellers and featured a pressurized fuselage, including the cargo compartment. Other

features necessary or beneficial for the tactical transport role included the high-set wing, integral 'roll-on/roll-off' rear loading ramp and provision for equipment to permit aerial delivery of paratroopers or cargoes, the latter using the low-altitude parachute extraction system (LAPES) method.

The first Hercules for the USAF was the C-130A first flown in April 1955, and of which 231 examples were built at Marietta, Georgia. These would be just the initial examples from a total of 2156 first-generation models. Deliveries to the USAF began in December 1955 and the aircraft was later upgraded with four-bladed Hamilton Standard propellers and nose radar. A total of 230 aircraft were completed as C-130Bs, with the

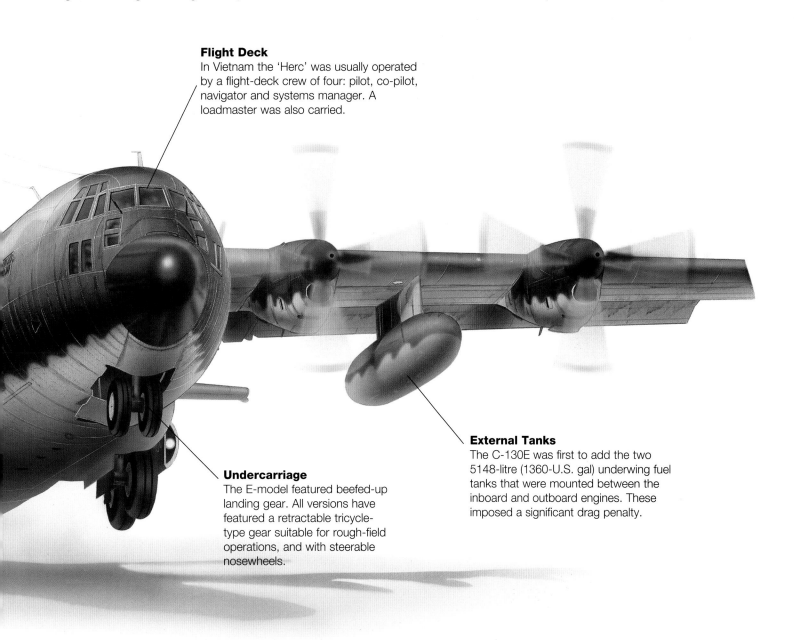

Flight Deck
In Vietnam the 'Herc' was usually operated by a flight-deck crew of four: pilot, co-pilot, navigator and systems manager. A loadmaster was also carried.

Undercarriage
The E-model featured beefed-up landing gear. All versions have featured a retractable tricycle-type gear suitable for rough-field operations, and with steerable nosewheels.

External Tanks
The C-130E was first to add the two 5148-litre (1360-U.S. gal) underwing fuel tanks that were mounted between the inboard and outboard engines. These imposed a significant drag penalty.

Lockheed C-130 Hercules

The C-130K version was built specifically for British use on the basis of the C-130H, and entered RAF service as the Hercules C.Mk 1, seen here on strength with the Hercules Wing at RAF Lyneham in 1990. This is a C.Mk 1P sub-variant with an inflight refuelling probe above the cockpit.

aforementioned modifications included from the outset, as well as improvements to the T56A-1 engines and increased fuel capacity.

In 1961 production switched to the improved C-130, of which 491 were built. These were powered by 3021kW (4050shp) T56A-7s, featured strengthened

wings and landing gear, and offered an increased maximum take-off weight. The 'Echo' was followed by the definitive first-generation Hercules, the C-130H, of which 1809 were built. First flown in November 1964, the C-130 was developed chiefly for the export market and an initial example for the USAF was first delivered in 1975. The H-model incorporated a redesigned and further strengthened wing, new avionics and 3362kW (4508shp) T56A-15 engines. A 'stretched' version of the C-130H appeared as the C-130H-30, increasingly maximum troop capacity from 92 to 128.

In its latest C-130J guise, the Hercules is provided with an all-new powerplant of AE2100 turboprops driving six-bladed Dowty propellers. Other major changes include a two-crew 'glass' cockpit and digital avionics. The C-130J-30 features the same fuselage 'stretch' as the previous-generation C-130H-30.

As an airlifter, the C-130 proved its worth in Vietnam, operating in some of the most remote locations. In its basic form, the C-130 can carry 78 troops, or 92 if a high-density configuration is employed, 64 paratroopers or 74 litter patients. Later in the conflict in Southeast Asia, MC-130 Combat Talons were used to deliver

Specification (C-130H)

Type:	Tactical transport aircraft
Dimensions:	Length: 29.79m (97ft 9in); Wingspan: 40.41m (132ft 7in); Height: 11.66m (38ft 3in)
Weight:	79,380kg (175,000lb) maximum take-off
Powerplant:	4 x 3362kW (4508shp) Allison T56A-15 turboprops
Cruising speed:	556km/h (345mph)
Range:	4002km (2487 miles) with maximum payload of 19,686kg (43,400lb)
Service ceiling:	10,060m (33,000ft)
Crew:	5
Armament:	None

special operations forces and for aerial refuelling. Once fitted with ground-target radar, 20mm (0.79in) Gatling guns, 40mm (1.57in) Bofors gun and, later, a side-firing 105mm (4.1in) howitzer, the Hercules became the AC-130 gunship, which was credited with destroying around 10,000 enemy trucks during the conflict. Fire support developments of the C-130 have continued to appear, among the latest being U.S. Marine Corps KC-130J inflight refuelling tankers armed with missiles for use in Afghanistan. Another role pioneered in Vietnam was combat search and rescue, using the HC-130. A different HC-130 version is employed on long-range maritime rescue missions by the U.S. Coast Guard.

Among special duties for U.S. military Hercules are operations in Antarctica and Greenland that employ the ski-equipped LC-130H, firefighting using a roll-on/roll-off fire retardant delivery system and hurricane hunting using the WC-130J 'Weatherbird'. Electronic warfare derivatives carry the EC-130 designation and today include the EC-130H Compass Call airborne communications jamming platform and the EC-130J Commando Solo, a C-130J modified for use in conducting psychological operations.

Recent Service

A USAF Hercules from the 320th Air Expeditionary Wing takes off from a landing zone in Afghanistan during Operation Enduring Freedom in October 2002. Aside from supporting U.S. military forces around the world, USAF C-130s have seen much recent use in reponse to humanitarian crises, including operations in

Congo, Somalia, Bosnia, Rwanda, Kosovo, Japan and in New Orleans after Hurricane Katrina. As well as delivery and airdrop of supplies, the C-130 can be configured as a flying hospital. In January 2010, C-130s helped haul more than 13,600 short tons of cargo, transport more than 25,800 passengers and transfer 280 patients for medical evaluations from Haiti after a devastating earthquake struck the Caribbean country.

Mikoyan-Gurevich MiG-21 (1955)

Veteran of more conflicts than any other post-war fighter, the MiG-21 has served with around 60 nations and remains in large-scale front-line service to this day. A plethora of variants and upgrades have been fielded as part of a production run that extended to over 11,000, making it the most prolific supersonic fighter.

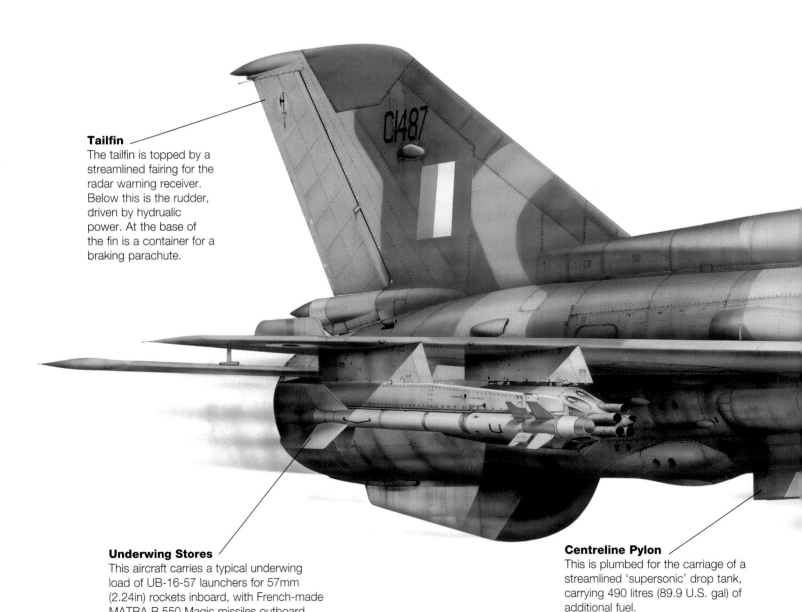

Tailfin
The tailfin is topped by a streamlined fairing for the radar warning receiver. Below this is the rudder, driven by hydrualic power. At the base of the fin is a container for a braking parachute.

Underwing Stores
This aircraft carries a typical underwing load of UB-16-57 launchers for 57mm (2.24in) rockets inboard, with French-made MATRA R.550 Magic missiles outboard.

Centreline Pylon
This is plumbed for the carriage of a streamlined 'supersonic' drop tank, carrying 490 litres (89.9 U.S. gal) of additional fuel.

Small, fast and agile, the MiG-21 was in many ways the antithesis of the increasingly heavy and capable Western fighters that began to be fielded from the early 1960s. The MiG-21, codenamed 'Fishbed' in the West, was originally schemed as a Mach 2-capable bomber interceptor that would be cheap enough to be fielded in significant numbers, making up for its relative lack of sophistication and limited endurance. In the event, the MiG-21 saw widespread combat service, frequently against its Western counterparts, in war zones ranging from the Middle East to Vietnam and Africa.

The original Ye-2 prototype differed from the production aircraft that followed in having a swept, rather than a delta wing, but was a lightweight, simple day fighter. It made its maiden flight in February 1955. Launched into production as the MiG-21F, the initial series-built aircraft were armed with guns only, but quickly gave way to the MiG-21F-13, the first to be built

A MiG-21M of the Indian Air Force's No.7 Squadron 'Battle Axes', stationed at Gwalior in the 1980s. India licence-built 158 examples of the local MiG-21M (Type 88) variant between 1973 and 1981. No.7 Squadron has since re-equipped with the Mirage 2000.

Canopy
Due to the poor rear visibility afforded from the cockpit, the pilot is fitted with a rear-view mirror attached to the canopy. The canopy of the MiG-21M is sideways-opening.

Air Data Probe
A long boom mounted on the nose carries pitot/static heads for the airspeed system as well as pitch/yaw sensor vanes.

in significant quantities, with a narrow-chord vertical tail fin and with gun armament reduced from two to one 30mm (1.18in) cannon. The MiG-21F-13's primary armament was provided in the form of a pair of heat-seeking R-3S (AA-2 'Atoll') air-to-air missiles (AAMs).

Specification (MiG-21bis)

Type:	Fighter-bomber
Dimensions:	Length: 15.0m (49ft 2.5in) with pitot; Wingspan: 7.15m (23ft 5.66in); Height: 4.13m (13ft 6.4in)
Weight:	8725kg (19,325lb) loaded
Powerplant:	1 x 69.62N (15,650lb) Tumansky R25-300 afterburning turbojet
Maximum speed:	2237km/h (1468mph)
Range:	1210km (751 miles) on internal fuel
Service ceiling:	17,800m (58,400ft)
Crew:	1
Armament:	1 x 23mm (0.9in) cannon and 4 x air-to-air missiles or 2 x 500kg (1102lb) bombs

A Romanian Air Force MiG-21M upgraded to Lancer-A standard. While the Lancer A has been withdrawn, in 2014 Lancer-B/Cs continued to serve with two squadrons at two different bases.

In the MiG-21PF the aircraft was first given an all-weather intercept capability, thanks to an RP-21 Sapfir-21 radar. Other changes included deletion of cannon armament and a modified fuselage with a longer nose and larger intake. The canopy and spine were also altered, adding a distinctive bulge aft of the cockpit allowing an increase in fuel capacity. The powerplant was revised, utilizing the 60.58kN (13,613lb) thrust Tumansky R-11F2S-300 turbojet. The MiG-21PF was improved through the introduction of blown flaps, producing the MiG-21PFS version. A boundary layer system provided increased thrust during the landing approach, for which the powerplant was suitably modified. In the MiG-21PFM the previous PFS model was enhanced through the addition of a new ejection seat under a new two-piece canopy that was now sideways-hinged. An export version of the MiG-21PF series was produced as the MiG-21FL, which featured several downgraded systems, including the radar.

Reconnaissance fighter

The MiG-21R was a MiG-21PFM derivative that was adapted for the reconnaissance mission, with reconnaissance equipment carried in an under-fuselage pod. The MiG-12R brought some important changes to the series, including an enlarged dorsal fuel tank and a four-hardpoint wing able to carry drop tanks to further extend range.

With the introduction of two improved versions of the 'Atoll' AAM, the heat-seeking R-13M and radar-

guided R-3R, the MiG-21 was suitably adapted for their carriage. The new aircraft was the MiG-21S, first flown in 1963. The MiG-21S retained the airframe of the previous MiG-21R, with four underwing pylons. The new weapons were allied with a much improved radar, the RP-22S Sapfir-21. A 23mm (0.9in) cannon was reinstated, now carried in a gondola below the fuselage.

Two-seat 'Fishbeds'

As early as 1959, work began on a two-seat trainer version of the MiG-21, taking into account the need to introduce young pilots to the Soviet Air Force's first Mach-2 fighter. The Ye-6U prototype led to the initial MiG-21U that was based on the MiG-21F-13 day fighter. A second cockpit was installed in a redesigned nose section, with a resultant revision in terms of internal fuel carriage. For combat training, the MiG-21U could carry a pair of R-3S AAMs and a pod on the centreline carrying a 12.7mm (0.5in) machine gun. An improved two-seater derivative appeared in the form of the MiG-21US, which incorporated some of the features of the MiG-21PFM all-weather fighter. Power was provided by an uprated R-11F2S-300 engine and the wing was equipped with blown flaps. The ultimate 'Fishbed' trainer was the MiG-21UM that retained the MiG-21US airframe but added a more powerful R-13-300 engine.

Once exported, the MiG-21S became the MiG-21M, which was the first to add a built-in 23mm cannon and was licence-built in India.

The MiG-21SM and its export equivalent the MiG-21MF were a combination of the MiG-21S airframe with a new engine, the R-13-300 that developed 65.33kN (14,652lb) thrust with afterburning. Both models retained the internal 23mm cannon. The MiG-21SMT model (and the rare MiG-21MT export derivative) featured a much increased internal fuel capacity, accommodated in a greatly enlarged fuselage spine. A new powerplant was provided in the form of the R-13F-300, offering increased thrust. Among the roles of the 'big spine' MiG-21SMT in Soviet service was nuclear-armed fighter-bomber.

The definitive 'Fishbed' version was the MiG-21bis, intended to offer improved performance while dogfighting at low and medium altitudes. The main change was the introduction of the R-25-300 engine, developed from the R-13F-300 but offering a further increase in power. Armament included the 23mm cannon and heat-seeking R-60 (AA-8 'Aphid') AAMs, of which up to four examples could be carried, together with a pair of R-3Rs or R-13Ms. The RP-22S Sapfir-21 was retained but the radar was modified to have an improved look-down capability. The MiG-21bis entered Soviet service in 1972 and also enjoyed a long production run in India.

McDonnell Douglas F-4 Phantom II (1958)

The definitive Western fighter of the Cold War era, the F-4 had it all: performance, advanced avionics and the ability to haul huge quantities of sophisticated weaponry. Originally intended as a carrier fighter for the U.S. Navy, the powerful Phantom remains in front-line service as a fighter-bomber and interceptor.

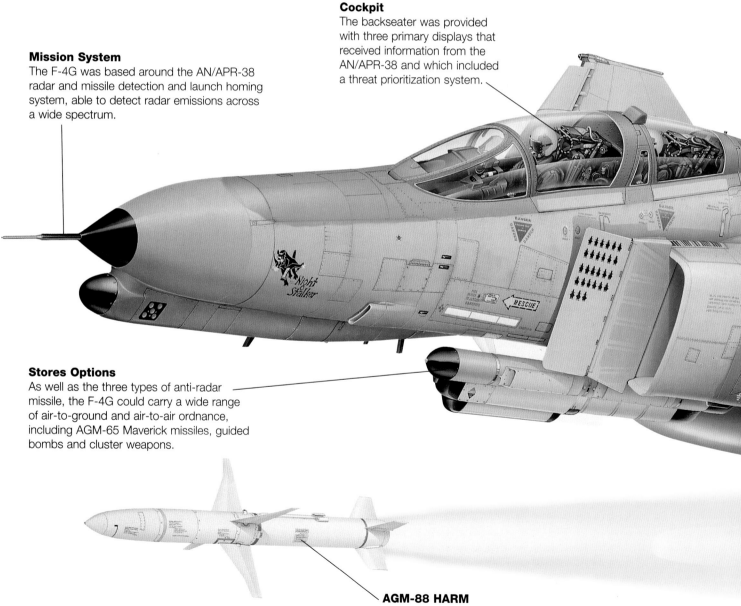

Mission System
The F-4G was based around the AN/APR-38 radar and missile detection and launch homing system, able to detect radar emissions across a wide spectrum.

Cockpit
The backseater was provided with three primary displays that received information from the AN/APR-38 and which included a threat prioritization system.

Stores Options
As well as the three types of anti-radar missile, the F-4G could carry a wide range of air-to-ground and air-to-air ordnance, including AGM-65 Maverick missiles, guided bombs and cluster weapons.

AGM-88 HARM
The HARM homes automatically on hostile radars, providing its receivers are tuned to the correct wavelength. Its high speeds are intended to ensure the radar is destroyed before it can be switched off.

The F-4 began life in the mid-1950s as a private-venture project by the then McDonnell company, and was initially foreseen by the U.S. Navy as a single-seat attack aircraft under the AH-2 designation, since the F8U Crusader was judged adequate for the all-weather fighter role. Plans were then revised, and the Navy elected to receive the F4H interceptor, configured with all-missile armament in the form of four Sparrow III air-to-air missiles (AAMs) semi-recessed under the belly. These weapons would be guided to their target by a powerful Westinghouse AN/APQ-50 radar in the nose, operated by a radar intercept officer in a second rear seat. The first of 23 test aircraft, a YF4H-1, took to the air in May 1958.

The Phantom's superb performance was the result of its powerful twin-turbojets, fed by fully variable air intakes and exhausting via nozzles with a carefully arranged secondary flow. The initial production model for the U.S. Navy was the F4H-1F (re-designated as the F-4A in September 1962), which succeeded in gaining a number of world speed and time-to-height records. Next in line was the F-4B, of which 649 were built. The B-model had a bulged nose containing an AN/APQ-72 radar, and a raised rear seat. First deployed on carriers in August 1962, it became the standard all-weather fighter for the U.S. Navy and Marine Corps. Sub-variants included the F-4G with different radio, and 46 unarmed RF-4B reconnaissance aircraft for the Marines.

This F-4G Wild Weasel of the USAF's 35th Tactical Fighter Wing (Provisional) was based at Sheikh Isa Air Base, Bahrain, in 1991 for duty during Operation Desert Storm. The aircraft was normally assigned to the 52nd TFW based in Germany.

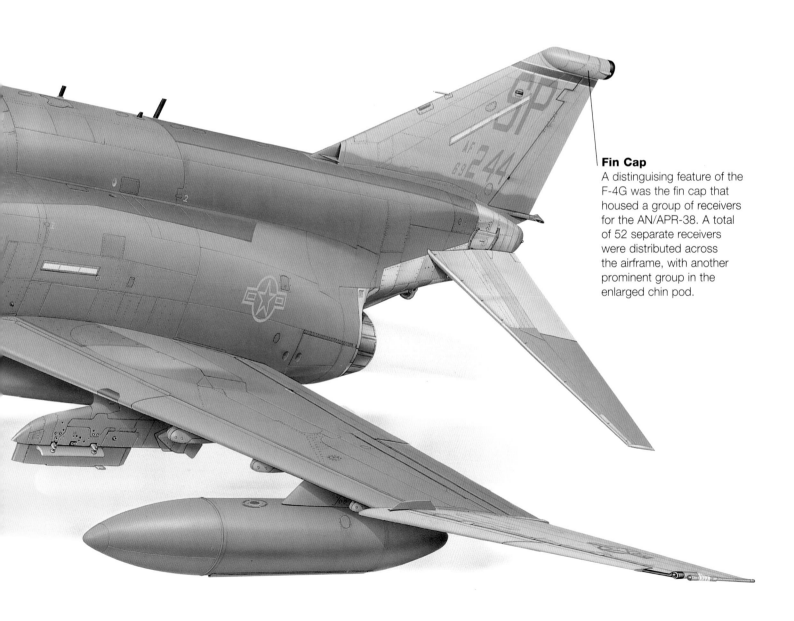

Fin Cap
A distinguising feature of the F-4G was the fin cap that housed a group of receivers for the AN/APR-38. A total of 52 separate receivers were distributed across the airframe, with another prominent group in the enlarged chin pod.

McDonnell Douglas F-4 Phantom II

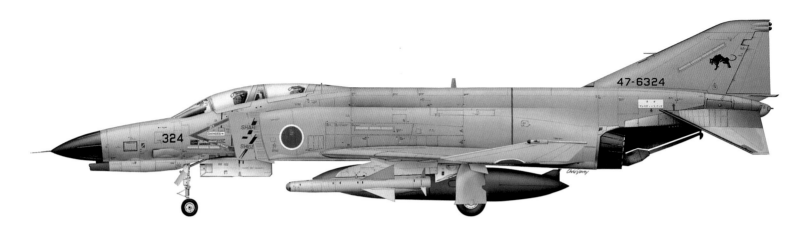

The improved F-4J appeared for the U.S. Navy in 1965 and featured the AN/AWG-10 fire-control system, more powerful engines, an additional fuel tank, slotted tailplane, dropping ailerons, larger wheels and brakes and, subsequently, an electronic countermeasures fairing at the top of the tailfin. A total of 552 F-4Js were built for the Navy and USMC, and in their later life these aircraft were fitted with slatted wings and avionics improvements to produce the F-4S. A similar upgrade to the F-4B produced the F-4N variant.

The USAF first acquired the Phantom in the form of the F-4B, a minimum-change version of the F-4B, with AN/APG-72 radar. This was followed by the F-4D

Three views of an upgraded F-4EJ Kai of the Japan Air Self-Defense Force's 8 Hikotai based at Misawa. The unit had a dual-role ground attack and anti-shipping assignment.

that featured a greater degree of changes for land-based service, and AN/APG-109A radar optimized for ground attack. Drawing upon early experience from the Vietnam War, the USAF fielded the F-4E that included an improved AN/APG-120 radar, increased power, additional internal fuel, and, importantly, an internal 20mm (0.79in) rotary cannon and slatted wing for improved manoeuvrability at high altitude. A total of 1397 F-4Es were completed, making this the most numerous version of the Phantom.

Reconnaissance versions appeared in the form of the RF-4C for the USAF, the aforementioned RF-4B for the Marines and the RF-4E for export. The first RF-4C flew in August 1963 and was followed by a production

Specification (F-4B)

Type:	Carrier-based all-weather fighter
Dimensions:	Length: 17.75m (58ft 3in); Wingspan: 11.71m (38ft 5in); Height: 4.95m (16ft 3in)
Weight:	24,766kg (54,600lb) maximum take-off
Powerplant:	2 x 75.4kN (17,000lb) General Electric J79-GE-8B turbojets
Maximum speed:	2390km/h (1485mph)
Range:	3701km (2300 miles) ferry range
Service ceiling:	18,900m (62,000ft)
Crew:	2
Armament:	4 x AIM-7 Sparrow air-to-air missiles and up to 4 x AIM-9B/D Sidewinder air-to-air missiles, plus up to 7257kg (16,000lb) of attack weapons

For anti-shipping work, the F-4EJ Kai can be equipped with the ASM-2 missile, seen here underwing. This turbojet-powered weapon uses infra-red guidance for terminal accuracy.

run of over 500 aircraft the last of which was handed over to the USAF in 1974. The RF-4C carried most of its specialist equipment in a modified nose section containing cameras and other sensors. The RF-4B confusingly followed the USAF's RF-4C into service, with a first flight in March 1965. A total of 46 RF-4Cs were supplied to the Marines. The RF-4E was initially supplied to West Germany, before enjoying export success with

Wild Weasel

The final dedicated sub-type of Phantom II to enter U.S. service was the Air Force's F-4G, designed to fulfil the Wild Weasel defence suppression mission, detecting and classifying hostile radars before destroying them. A product of the Vietnam War, this hazardous and exacting mission was first flown by specially configured F-100 Super Sabres and F-105 Thunderchiefs, while a total of 35 F-4Cs were similarly converted in 1968–69. Initially known as the Advanced Wild Weasel, the F-4G was specified in 1975 and 116 conversions were made, the type entering service in 1978, including aircraft forward deployed in West Germany. Produced by conversion of F-4Es, the F-4G was equipped with an AN/APR-38 radar homing and warning system, analyzer and jammer and was armed with anti-radar weapons including the AGM-45 Shrike, AGM-78 Standard and the AGM-88 HARM.

sales to Greece, Iran, Israel, Japan and Turkey, as part of a production run that exceeded 160 aircraft.

Export Sales

The Phantom entered British service when the Royal Navy acquired the navalized F-4K for its Fleet Air Arm. Locally designated as the Phantom FG.Mk 1, this version was powered by Rolls-Royce Spey engines and had AWG-11 radar in a hinged nose and an increased-length nose leg. A total of 24 served with the FAA before the RAF acquired 28 more Phantom FGR.Mk 2s, known to the manufacturer as F-4M.

Other key export versions included the F-4F for Germany, later equipped with AIM-120 AMRAAM missiles and with advanced AN/APG-65 radar under the Improved Combat Efficiency (ICE) programme. In Japan, local production by Mitsubishi provided the F-4EJ version, a number of which were subsequently upgraded as the F-4EJ Kai with AN/APG-66J radar and modernized avionics. Israel, one of the most active operators of the type in combat, was responsible for further development of its Phantom fleet, to produce the upgraded Kurnass 2000, which offered an improved ground-attack capability and a modern cockpit and avionics.

The Phantom excelled in combat with the U.S. over Southeast Asia, with Israel in successive wars in the Middle East and with Iran in the war against Iraq. A total of 5057 Phantoms were completed and the type remains in front-line service with export operators Greece, Iran, Japan, South Korea and Turkey as of 2014.

Lockheed SR-71 'Blackbird' (1962)

First revealed in 1964, the aircraft popularly known as the 'Blackbird' remains the world's fastest air-breathing manned vehicle, and during the Cold War years in which it served as a strategic reconnaissance platform for the USAF, the Mach 3+ capable SR-71 was effectively immune to interception.

The existence of the awesome SR-71 was first acknowledged in public in February 1964, when American President Lyndon Johnson revealed that the USAF was operating a new high-speed reconnaissance aircraft, then identified under the A-11 designation. Johnson announced that the aircraft was capable of speeds in excess of 3219km/h (2000mph) and could fly at altitudes over 21,335m (70,000ft). The aircraft's incredible speed and performance ensured it was effectively out of reach of both manned interceptors and the increasingly capable surface-to-air missiles of the kind that had shot down Gary Powers' Lockheed U-2 spyplane over the Soviet Union in May 1960.

The A-11 designation presented to the public at the time was erroneous, and the aircraft later dubbed 'Blackbird' in fact entered service under the designation A-12. This single-seat reconnaissance aircraft first flew in April 1962. A total of 15 were completed and these were operated by USAF and Central Intelligence Agency pilots. As well as two conversions to M-21 drone carrier standard, one of the A-12s was adapted for crew training, adding a second cockpit.

The A-12 also served as the basis for a high-speed interceptor, the YF-12A, that was produced to the extent of three prototypes that were evaluated by the USAF before this program was cancelled.

Windshield
One of the hottest parts of the airframe, the 'knife-edge' windshield was made of special high-termperature resistant glass and plastic laminates.

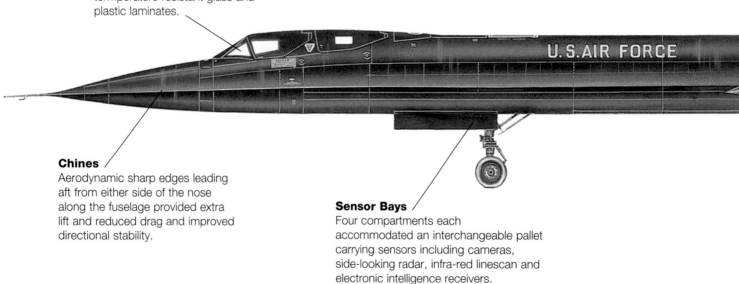

Chines
Aerodynamic sharp edges leading aft from either side of the nose along the fuselage provided extra lift and reduced drag and improved directional stability.

Sensor Bays
Four compartments each accommodated an interchangeable pallet carrying sensors including cameras, side-looking radar, infra-red linescan and electronic intelligence receivers.

Lockheed SR-71 'Blackbird'

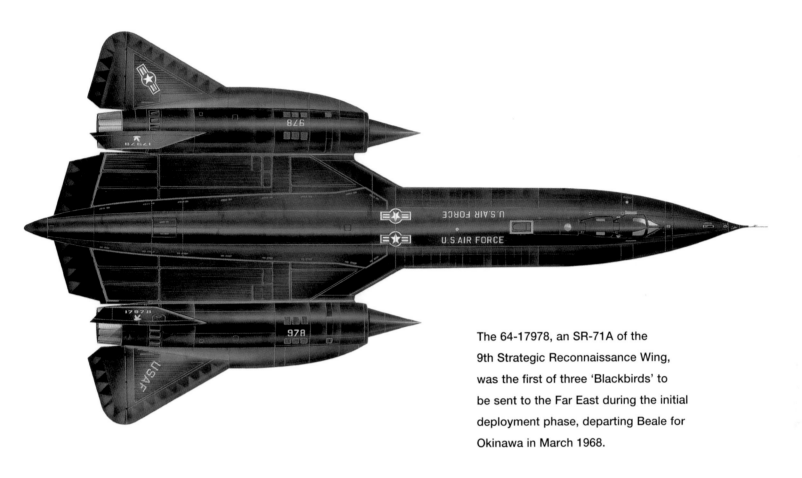

The 64-17978, an SR-71A of the 9th Strategic Reconnaissance Wing, was the first of three 'Blackbirds' to be sent to the Far East during the initial deployment phase, departing Beale for Okinawa in March 1968.

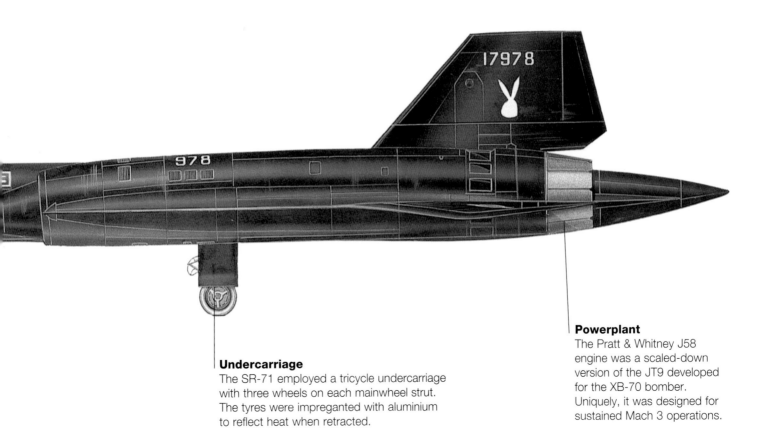

Undercarriage
The SR-71 employed a tricycle undercarriage with three wheels on each mainwheel strut. The tyres were impreganted with aluminium to reflect heat when retracted.

Powerplant
The Pratt & Whitney J58 engine was a scaled-down version of the JT9 developed for the XB-70 bomber. Uniquely, it was designed for sustained Mach 3 operations.

Lockheed SR-71 'Blackbird'

Designed by the famed Clarence 'Kelly' Johnson, the CIA-optimized A-12 was originally to lead to a development for the USAF that would take the form of a two-seat strike/reconnaissance aircraft known as the RS-12. Mock-ups of both the RS-12 and R-12 (single-

In 1997, as tensions surrounding North Korea's nuclear programme intensified, two SR-71As were briefly reactivated before the programme was again terminated a year later.

role reconnaissance) were completed and it was the R-12 that was selected for continued development by the Air Force. The strike version was abandoned on the basis that the USAF would in future receive the North American XB-70 and the General Dynamics F-111 bombers.

The R-12 designation was revised as the SR-71A, and in this form the aircraft entered USAF service with a total of 29 completed. These were complemented by two SR-71B crew trainers equipped with dual controls. One of the two-seaters was lost in an accident, and replaced in turn by a single SR-71C crew trainer that was based on the reused rear fuselage of a YF-12A.

Radical Design

The secret of the SR-71's awe-inspiring performance lay in a number of innovative design features. First, its use of largely titanium construction allowed it to withstand kinetic heating and retain structural integrity at speeds beyond Mach 3. At this speed, certain parts of the

Specification (SR-71A)

Type:	Strategic reconnaissance aircraft
Dimensions:	Length: 32.74m (107ft 5in); Wingspan: 16.94m (55ft 7in); Height: 5.64m (18ft 6in)
Weight:	78,017kg (172,000lb) maximum take-off
Powerplant:	2 x 144.57kN (32,500lb) Pratt & Whitney J58 afterburning turbojets
Maximum speed:	Mach 3.35 at 24,385m (80,000ft)
Range:	5230km (2250 miles) at Mach 3, unrefuelled
Service ceiling:	24,385m (85,000ft)
Crew:	2
Armament:	None

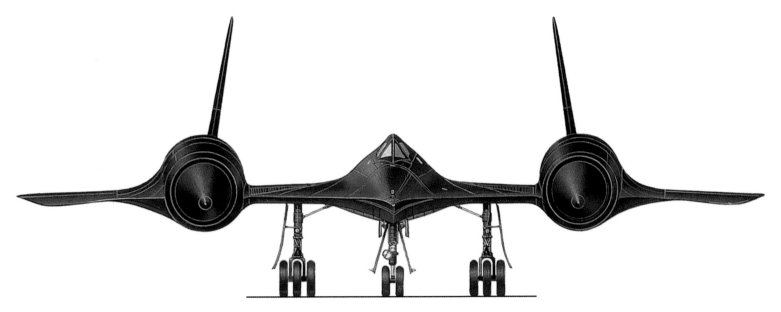

The frontal aspect of the SR-71A was dominated by its huge engine nacelles, blended into the wing leading edge, and the broad chines blending the fuselage into the leading edges.

airframe were heated to temperatures of 3000 degrees Celsius (572 degrees Fahrenheit). In order to cope with the aerodynamic drag found at that speed, Johnson's design employed a slim fuselage and very thin delta wings. Integral lifting surfaces, known as chines, were built into the forward fuselage, preventing the nose from

pitching down at high speed. The SR-71 was propelled towards Mach 3 by two Pratt & Whitney J58 continuous-bleed turbojets. Once the aircraft hit Mach 3, the engines were designed to provide just 18 per cent of total thrust, the remainder being derived from suction in the engine intakes and via special exhaust nozzles at the rear of the multiple-flow nacelles.

As a pilot's aircraft the 'Blackbird' was unforgiving and it demanded total concentration from its crew. One former SR-71A crewmember recalled: 'At 85,000ft [25,908m] and Mach 3, it was almost a religious experience. Nothing had prepared me to fly that fast… My God, even now I get goose bumps remembering.' If an air-to-surface missile launch was detected, the pilot received a warning light on the control panel. At that point, the SR-71A would simply accelerate out of harm's way, leaving the missile to detonate harmlessly. On only one occasion did an SR-71A receive minor damage from a hostile missile.

SR-71A entered USAF service in 1966 and by June 1968 the last A-12s were withdrawn. Flying from their base at Beale Air Force Base, California, and from forward operating locations at Kadena, Okinawa, and RAF Mildenhall in the UK, the 'Blackbird' fleet was active over various war zones, trouble spots and other areas of intelligence interest until the end of the Cold War. In October 1989 the SR-71A fleet was stood down, although consideration was briefly given to reactivation of it in the wake of the 1991 Gulf War. The aircraft was permanently retired by the USAF in 1998.

Drone Carriers

From the initial batch of 15 A-12 reconnaissance aircraft, two examples were converted to become M-21 drone carriers. These served as the 'mother ships' for the D-21 drone, a highly secretive intelligence-gathering vehicle that was launched from the rear of the M-21. Capable of Mach 3.3, the titanium-built D-21 could reach a height of 27,432m (90,000ft) under the power of a ramjet engine. The drone was controlled from an operator's position located aft of the A-12's pilot cockpit. Under the Tagboard programme a total of 30 D-21s were completed and a first launch was undertaken in July 1966. On the fourth launch the drone failed to separate from the A-12 at a speed of Mach 3.2, and then slammed down on to the launch pylon. The result was a pitch-up that could not be recovered from and the A-12 broke up, killing both crew. As a result, the M-21/D-21 programme was cancelled.

General Dynamics F-111
(1964)

A controversial aircraft, the F-111 was subject to a troubled development and suffered high-profile combat losses early on. However, once refined it became almost certainly the most capable precision attack aircraft of its generation and saw combat over Vietnam and later in raids on both Libya and Iraq.

The USAF launched its Tactical Fighter Experimental (TFX) programme in 1960 with the release of a specification. This demanded considerable range, with the effect that the aircraft that eventually emerged as the F-111 was anything but a fighter. Once it entered service, the General Dynamics product was the world's first attack aircraft capable of supersonic speed and with sophisticated avionics that allowed targets to be struck accurately in the course of a single pass and in all weather conditions. Thanks to a generous internal fuel capacity, the F-111 possessed a range greater than any other Tactical Air Command type.

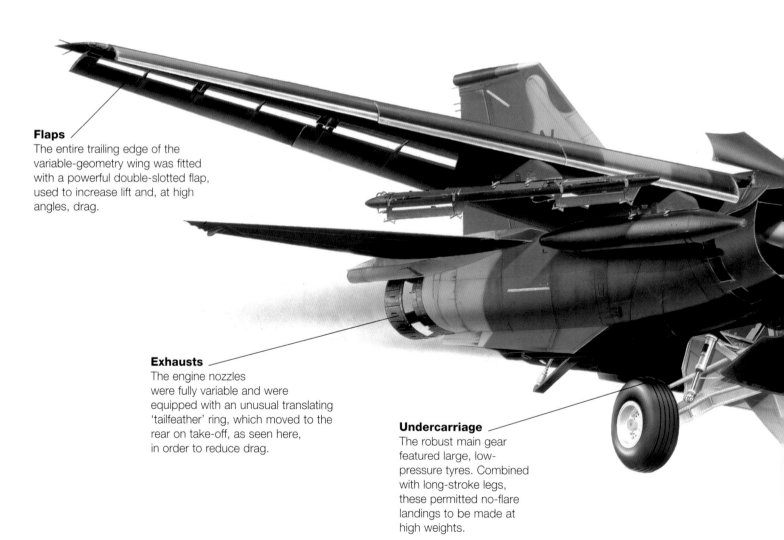

Flaps
The entire trailing edge of the variable-geometry wing was fitted with a powerful double-slotted flap, used to increase lift and, at high angles, drag.

Exhausts
The engine nozzles were fully variable and were equipped with an unusual translating 'tailfeather' ring, which moved to the rear on take-off, as seen here, in order to reduce drag.

Undercarriage
The robust main gear featured large, low-pressure tyres. Combined with long-stroke legs, these permitted no-flare landings to be made at high weights.

After seeing off competition for the TFX bid from a rival Boeing design, the F-111 first flew in December 1964. It became the first production aircraft equipped with a variable-geometry or 'swing' wing, ensuring high supersonic performance, economical cruising speed, long range and relatively short take-off and landing runs at heavy loaded weights. This was combined with augmented turbofan engines and a terrain-following radar. In a notably unusual feature, the two crew were seated side-by-side in a jettisonable escape capsule that could also serve as a life raft or survival shelter. The undercarriage incorporated large wheels and was intended to be robust enough to permit limited

Two views of an F-111F belonging to the commander of the 48th Tactical Fighter Wing and based at RAF Lakenheath, England. This unit deployed some 67 F-111Fs to Taif AB in Saudi Arabia to serve in Desert Storm in 1991, flying around 2500 sorties.

Inflight Refuelling
Above the fuselage was a receptacle for an inflight refuelling 'flying boom'. Provision was not made for the probe and drogue method of aerial refulling.

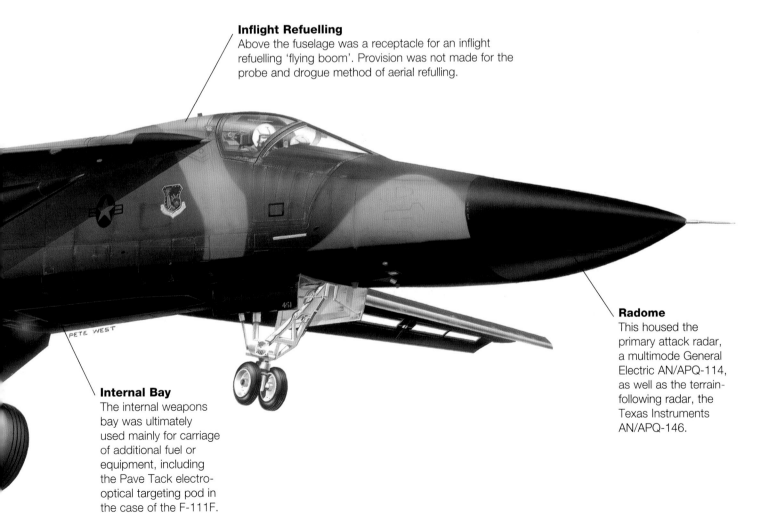

PETE WEST

Internal Bay
The internal weapons bay was ultimately used mainly for carriage of additional fuel or equipment, including the Pave Tack electro-optical targeting pod in the case of the F-111F.

Radome
This housed the primary attack radar, a multimode General Electric AN/APQ-114, as well as the terrain-following radar, the Texas Instruments AN/APQ-146.

General Dynamics F-111

F-111Fs of the 48th TFW were employed almost exlusively to drop laser-guided bombs during Desert Storm, in this case 907kg (2000lb) GBU-24 Paveway IIIs with penetrator warheads.

operations from unprepared strips. A small weapons bay was installed in the lower fuselage, but in practice this was mainly used for fuel carriage, and stores were loaded on pylons under the wings.

Since the U.S. Navy was looking for a fleet air defence fighter to succeed the F-4 Phantom II, the U.S. Department of Defense elected to combine the Navy and Air Force requirements together within the TFX

Specification (F-111F)

Type:	All-weather interdiction and attack aircraft
Dimensions:	Length: 22.40m (73ft 6in); Wingspan: 19.20m (63ft 0in) wings spread; Height: 5.22m (17ft 1.5in)
Weight:	45,359kg (100,000lb) maximum take-off
Powerplant:	2 x 111.65kN (25,100lb) Pratt & Whitney TF30-100 afterburning turbofans
Maximum speed:	2655km/h (1650mph) clean at 12,190m (40,000ft)
Range:	4707km (2925 miles) clean, with maximum internal fuel
Service ceiling:	18,290m (60,000ft)
Crew:	2
Armament:	Up to 14,228kg (31,500lb) of disposable stores carried in a lower-fuselage weapons bay and on six underwing pylons

programme. Although the rival services were not keen on the idea, it was pushed through, leading to the F-111B for the Navy. Under a November 1962 development contract, General Dynamics was to produce a total of 23 aircraft, comprising 18 F-111As for TAC and five F-111Bs that would be developed primarily by Grumman for the Navy. Overweight and under-performing, the F-111B was never going to be satisfactory, and after a series of setbacks the naval version of the TFX was cancelled in July 1968. Although the Navy had planned to order 231 production models, only seven F-111Bs were eventually completed, including the five development aircraft.

Early experience of the initial-production F-111A, of which 141 were built, revealed a number of problems relating to the avionics, engines and intake ducts, leading to modifications. First flown in December 1964, the F-111A entered service with the 474th Tactical Fighter Wing in October 1967. A first deployment to Vietnam followed in March 1968, but three of the six aircraft sent were lost in a matter of weeks. Improvements were incorporated in the second production version, the F-111E that featured improved air intakes and slightly upgraded avionics and was built to the extent of 94 aircraft. There followed 96 of the F-111D version, which featured more advanced, and costly, avionics and was powered by two 87.19kN (19,600lb) TF30-P-9 engines, replacing the 82.29kN (18,500lb) TF30-P-3 units of the previous models. The definitive version for TAC was the F-111F, of which 106 were completed with engines of increased thrust and another avionics update. The F-111F's avionics fit was more modest than that of the F-111D, but was easier to maintain, and this version also included yet more powerful engines in the form of the TF30-P-100, for a much improved thrust-to-weight ratio.

The FB-111A was a strategic bomber that entered service with Strategic Air Command and was equipped with a longer-span wing and strengthened undercarriage to permit operations at increased gross weights. In total, SAC received 76 FB-111As, sufficient to equip two bomb wings. These aircraft had a nuclear strike role and as such could be armed with two internal B43 free-fall variable yield nuclear bombs or AGM-69 Short-Range Attack Missiles (SRAMs), and production for another four SRAMs underwing.

The FB-111's increased-span wing was incorporated on the F-111C variant for the Royal Australian Air Force. The RAAF's F-111s, which also included RF-111C models equipped for reconnaissance, and F-111Gs (reworked former SAC FB-111As) were the last to be retired from service in December 2010.

Last of the F-111 family in USAF service was the EF-111A Raven, a decimated electronic warfare aircraft that was produced by Northrop Grumman through the conversion of 42 F-111As.

F-111s in England

An F-111 of the 20th Tactical Fighter Wing drops unguided bombs on a target range in the UK. Based at RAF Upper Heyford, the 20th TFW was the first of two USAF F-111 wings to arrive in the United Kingdom. The first 20th TFW F-111Es were based at RAF Upper Heyford in September 1970. Six years later, the numbers of 'Aardvarks' in the UK increased significantly when the 48th Tactical Fighter Wing introduced the latest F-111F model to service at RAF Lakenheath. The F-111 force in the UK made headlines in April 1986 after the Operation El Dorado Canyon raid on Libya by the 48th TFW. They launched 18 F-111Fs from Lakenheath, supported by five EF-111As from Upper Heyford for jamming duties. Making use of 28 aerial refuelling tankers, the F-111s were loaded with 907kg (2000lb) LGBs and 227kg (500lb) 'dumb' bombs, and they destroyed five Libyan Il-76 transports, four MiG-23 fighters and two Mi-8 helicopters. One 48th TFW aircraft was lost as it egressed from the area. After Operation Desert Storm, the F-111s departed the UK, with the last F-111Es leaving Upper Heyford in October 1993.

Lockheed C-5 Galaxy
(1968)

For many years the world's biggest military cargo aircraft, the C-5 Galaxy remains the largest and only strategic airlifter in the U.S. Air Force inventory and can carry more cargo farther distances than any other aircraft. Modified to C-5M Super Galaxy standard, the airlifter will remain in service beyond 2040.

Since the C-5 entered operational service in 1970 the airlifter has provided significant support to every major U.S. military operation, including Vietnam, Operation Desert Storm and Operation Enduring Freedom. As well as hauling military cargoes, the C-5 has provided essential humanitarian relief during the response to natural disasters around the world. The C-5 can carry 36 standard pallets and 81 troops simultaneously. The Galaxy is also capable of carrying any air-transportable U.S. Army combat equipment, including such bulky items as the 74-ton mobile scissors bridge. It can also carry outsize and oversize cargo across intercontinental ranges and can take off or land in relatively short distances. Thanks to nose and rear cargo doors, ground crews are able to load and off-load the C-5 simultaneously, thereby reducing cargo transfer times.

Development of the future C-5 Galaxy started in 1963 when the then Military Air Transport Service (MATS) began to look at options for a very large strategic cargo aircraft. Initially schemed under the CX-4 designation,

A C-5B Galaxy of the USAF's 436th Military Airlift Wing in the European One 'lizard' camouflage scheme worn during the 1980s. The B-model was basically similar to the C-5A, but added the various improvements made during that type's service life.

Powerplant
The four General Electric TF39-GE-1C engines are twin-shaft high-bypass turbofans, with a two-stage fan and a 16-stage axial flow compressor. The rear section of the cowling serves as a thrust reverser.

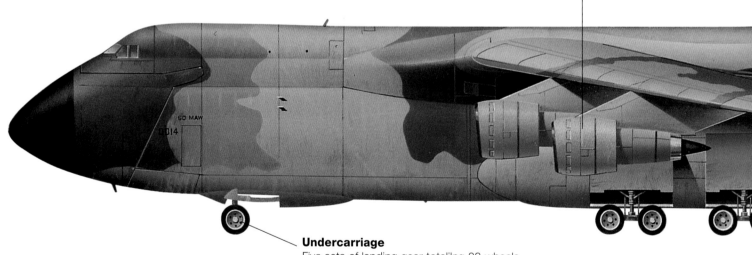

Undercarriage
Five sets of landing gear totalilng 28 wheels distribute weight. A 'kneeling' system permits lowering the parked aircraft to facilitate drive-on/drive-off vehicle loading and adjusts the cargo floor to standard truck-bed height.

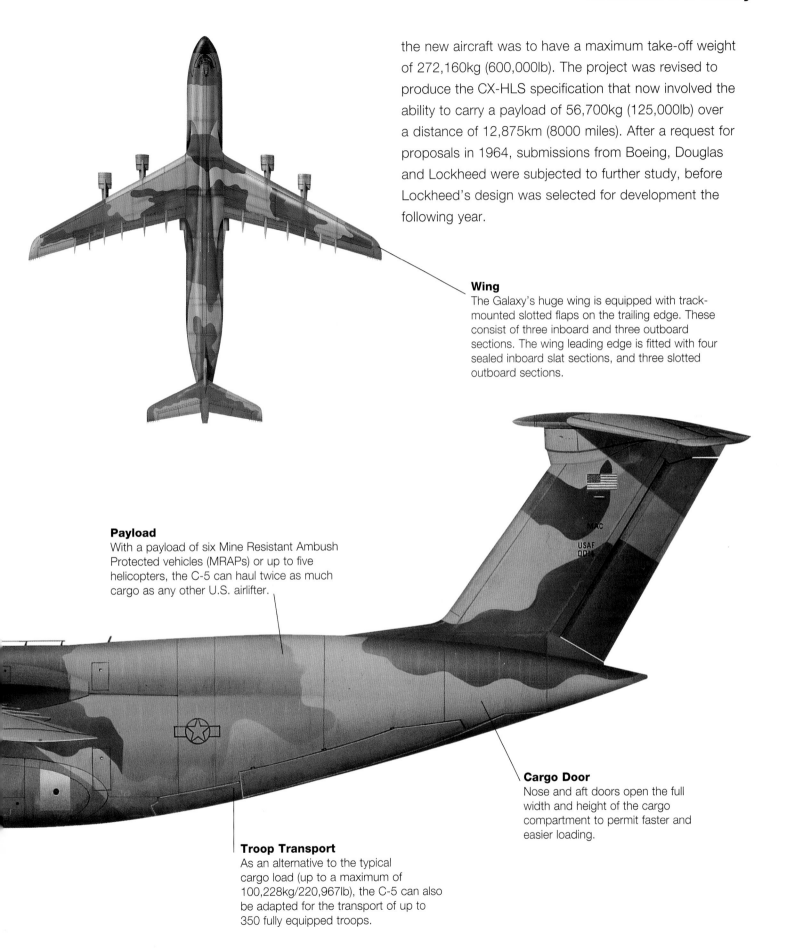

Lockheed C-5 Galaxy

the new aircraft was to have a maximum take-off weight of 272,160kg (600,000lb). The project was revised to produce the CX-HLS specification that now involved the ability to carry a payload of 56,700kg (125,000lb) over a distance of 12,875km (8000 miles). After a request for proposals in 1964, submissions from Boeing, Douglas and Lockheed were subjected to further study, before Lockheed's design was selected for development the following year.

Wing
The Galaxy's huge wing is equipped with track-mounted slotted flaps on the trailing edge. These consist of three inboard and three outboard sections. The wing leading edge is fitted with four sealed inboard slat sections, and three slotted outboard sections.

Payload
With a payload of six Mine Resistant Ambush Protected vehicles (MRAPs) or up to five helicopters, the C-5 can haul twice as much cargo as any other U.S. airlifter.

Cargo Door
Nose and aft doors open the full width and height of the cargo compartment to permit faster and easier loading.

Troop Transport
As an alternative to the typical cargo load (up to a maximum of 100,228kg/220,967lb), the C-5 can also be adapted for the transport of up to 350 fully equipped troops.

Lockheed C-5 Galaxy

A Galaxy dwarfs personnel of the USAF's 445th Airlift Wing as the unit receives the first of 11 C-5s in October 2005. An Air Force Reserve Command wing, the 445th previously operated the Lockheed C-141 StarLifter.

Specification (C-5A)

Type:	Strategic transport aircraft
Dimensions:	Length: 75.54m (247ft 10in); Wingspan: 67.88m (222ft 8.5in); Height: 19.85m (65ft 1.5in)
Weight:	348,810kg (769,000lb) maximum take-off
Powerplant:	4 x 191.27kN (43,000lb) General Electric TF39-GE-1C turbofans
Cruising speed:	890km/h (553mph) at 7620m (25,000ft)
Range:	6035km (3750 miles) with maximum payload of 100,228kg (220,967lb)
Service ceiling:	10,360m (34,000ft)
Crew:	5
Armament:	None

Lockheed began construction of a prototype aircraft in 1966 and this made a first flight in June 1968. The first deliveries to Military Airlift Command (MAC) commenced in June 1970, the first operator being the 437th Airlift Wing at Charleston Air Force Base, South Carolina. Initial plans called for the provision of 115 of the initial-production C-5A model, but the programme was already well over budget and it was decided to restrict the production run to just 81 aircraft, the last of which was delivered in May 1973. The Galaxy saw considerable usage in the final three years of the U.S. conflict in Southeast Asia and thereafter also took part in the resupply of Israel during the October 1973 War in the Middle East.

Once in service, the Galaxy revealed a number of problems, the most serious of which related to the central wing structure that soon proved prone to fatigue. In 1978 Lockheed received a contract to manufacture wings of an almost entirely new design in order to resolve the problem. Two aircraft were trialled with the new wings, before the remaining 77 C-5As were progressively returned to Marietta for refitting, in order to permit the aircraft to complete their originally planned 20,000-hour service life.

In order to meet increasing USAF demand for airlift, production of the C-5 resumed with the improved C-5B model and in March 1989 the last of 50 B-models was added to the 76 C-5As in USAF service. As well as the new wing and other changes introduced to the C-5A in the interim, the C-5B included over 100 system modifications to improve reliability and maintainability.

After a study revealed that 80 per cent of the C-5's airframe service life was remaining, AMC began a programme of modernization in 1998. The C-5 Avionics Modernization Program oversaw improvements to communications, navigation and surveillance/air traffic management compliance. The upgrade also added new safety equipment and a new autopilot.

Super Galaxy

Another part of the C-5 modernization effort is the Reliability Enhancement and Re-engining Program (RERP). Under RERP, 52 C-5s (including one C-5A, two C-5Cs and four C-5Bs) are scheduled to receive General Electric CF6-80C2 engines by 2017. The new powerplant provides a 22 per cent increase in thrust, a 30 per cent reduction in take-off roll and a 58 per cent faster climb rate. With its new engine and other system upgrades, the RERP-modified C-5s become C-5Ms, known to the current manufacturer Lockheed Martin as the Super Galaxy.

In 2004 and 2011, Congress authorized the retirement of a total of 46 C-5As, followed by an additional 27 retirements that were authorized in 2013. Depending on congressional approval, by 2017 the total C-5 USAF fleet should number 52, all of which will be the latest C-5M versions.

They are stationed at Dover AFB, Delaware; Travis AFB, California; Lackland AFB, Texas; Martinsburg Air National Guard Base, West Virginia and Westover Air Reserve Base, Massachussetts.

Air Mobility Command

Using a specially built ramp, airmen load a U.S. Army helicopter training simulator on to a C-5 at Dover AFB. The C-5 is the largest and most capable asset in Air Mobility Command (AMC) service. Led by a general, the AMC serves as the USAF component of U.S. Transportation Command (TRANSCOM), and is responsible for a single numbered air force, the 18th Air Force/Air Forces Transportation headquartered at Scott AFB, Illinois, and which includes 11 airlift, air mobility and air refuelling wings; two airlift groups, and the 618th Air and Space Operations Center or Tanker Airlift Control Center (TACC), which directs tanker and transport aircraft operations worldwide. AMC provides inter- and intra-theater airlift, aero-medical evacuation and tanker support for all branches of the U.S. military. Nearly 133,700 active-duty, ANG and AFRC personnel are assigned to the command, which provides rapid, global mobility and sustainment for U.S. forces. Additionally, it provides humanitarian support at home and around the world.

Tupolev Tu-22M (1969)

The appearance of the Tu-22M bomber came as a shock to NATO, and Western navies in particular soon had to find countermeasures to this powerful strike aircraft, the wartime tasks of which would have included missions against carrier battle groups and convoys supporting any conflict on the European continent.

Today, the Tu-22M is in a class of its own: a large, supersonic, continental-range bomber. Entering production in 1969, the aircraft codenamed 'Backfire' in the West had no design affiliation with the Tu-22 from the same design bureau. By the time production ended in 1993, a total of more than 500 Tu-22Ms of all versions had been built, and the type remains in service with the Russian Air Force. Under a design team led by Andrei Tupolev, work on

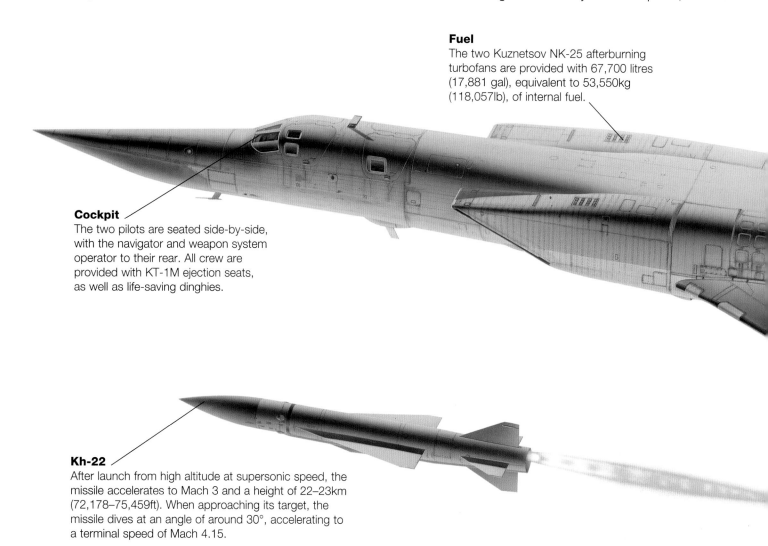

Fuel
The two Kuznetsov NK-25 afterburning turbofans are provided with 67,700 litres (17,881 gal), equivalent to 53,550kg (118,057lb), of internal fuel.

Cockpit
The two pilots are seated side-by-side, with the navigator and weapon system operator to their rear. All crew are provided with KT-1M ejection seats, as well as life-saving dinghies.

Kh-22
After launch from high altitude at supersonic speed, the missile accelerates to Mach 3 and a height of 22–23km (72,178–75,459ft). When approaching its target, the missile dives at an angle of around 30°, accelerating to a terminal speed of Mach 4.15.

the future Tu-22M began in November 1967. Among the specifications for the new bomber were a maximum speed of up to 2500km/h (1553mph) and a range of 7000km (4349 miles) while flying subsonic with a single Kh-22 missile.

There was no 'Backfire' prototype as such, and instead a pre-series batch of eight Tu-22M0 aircraft were completed, the first of these taking to the air for a maiden flight in August 1969. However, the bomber proved much slower than expected, and its range also left much to be desired. Improvements had been made by July 1971, when the Tu-22M1 was introduced, now with variable-geometry, in the form of movable outer wing panels. Range and speed

were improved somewhat and the Tu-22M1 was built in small numbers for evaluation and training.

The first model to enter quantity production was the Tu-22M2 of 1973, offering a speed of 1700km/h (1056mph) and a range of 5100km (3169 miles). The various mission systems were also improved. A total of 211 Tu-22M2s 'Backfire-Bs' were completed by the time production of

A Tu-22M3 of the 924th Naval Missile Carrier Regiment, part of the Russian Navy's Northern Fleet based at Olenya in 1998. Aircraft from this unit were later taken over by the Air Force's 840th Heavy Bomber Aviation Regiment based at Soltsy.

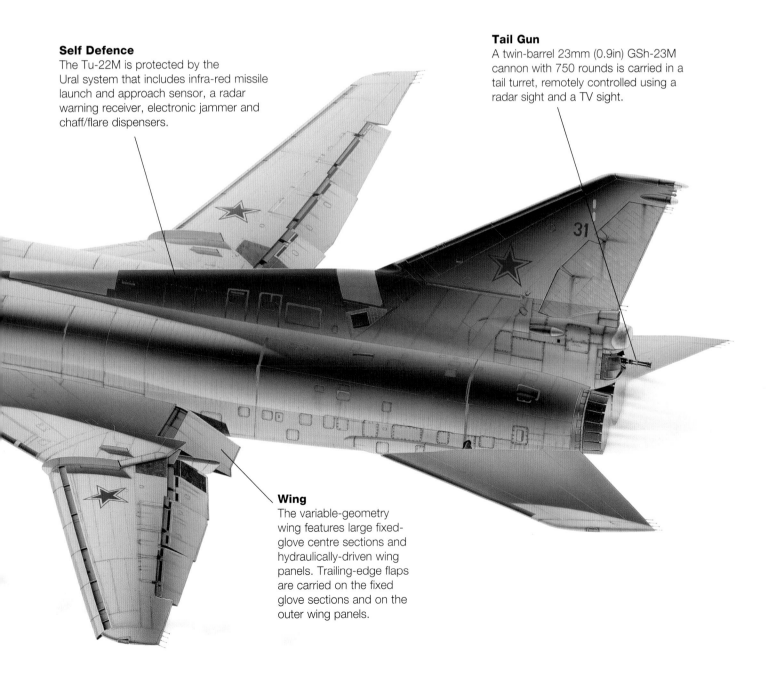

Self Defence
The Tu-22M is protected by the Ural system that includes infra-red missile launch and approach sensor, a radar warning receiver, electronic jammer and chaff/flare dispensers.

Tail Gun
A twin-barrel 23mm (0.9in) GSh-23M cannon with 750 rounds is carried in a tail turret, remotely controlled using a radar sight and a TV sight.

Wing
The variable-geometry wing features large fixed-glove centre sections and hydraulically-driven wing panels. Trailing-edge flaps are carried on the fixed glove sections and on the outer wing panels.

Tupolev Tu-22M

this variant ended in 1983. Despite its capabilities, the Tu-22M2 still failed to meet anything like the original specifications demanded by the military, and in an effort to improve performance the aircraft was re-engined with NK-25 powerplants each of which developed 245kN (55,116lb) thrust with afterburning – an increase of more than 25 per cent. The new engines demanded a fuselage redesign, including new wedge-type air intakes. The result was the definitive Tu-22M3 'Backfire-C'. This model was faster, being capable of a 'dash' speed of 2300km/h

Specification

Type:	Medium-range bomber and maritime strike aircraft
Dimensions:	Length: 42.46m (139ft 4in); Wingspan: 34.28m (112ft 6in) wings spread; Height: 11.05m (36ft 3in)
Weight:	124,000kg (273,373lb) maximum take-off
Powerplant:	2 x 245.18kN (51,115lb) Kuznetsov NK-25 afterburning turbofans
Maximum speed:	2000km/h (1243mph) at high altitude
Range:	2200km (1367 miles) radius of action with 1 x Kh-22 at high altitude, part-supersonic
Service ceiling:	14,000m (45,930ft)
Crew:	4
Armament:	Maximum 24,000kg (52,910lb) of stores including up to three Kh-22 missiles, 1 x twin-barrel 23mm (0.9in) cannon in tail turret

A Tu-22M-3 armed with a Kh-22 missile underwing. This delta-wing missile is made of welded titanium and steel alloys, and powered by a twin-chamber liquid-fuel rocket motor.

(1429mph). It also possessed improved range, including a combat radius of 2200km (1367 miles) when employing a high-profile flight, part of which was flown supersonic.

After a first flight in June 1977 the Tu-22M3 entered production, and a total of 268 examples were completed up to 1993. The final new-build production version was the Tu-22MR reconnaissance aircraft, around a dozen of which were manufactured between 1989 and 1993. This is equipped with a side-looking radar, electronic surveillance measures system, infra-red scanner and cameras.

Carrier-killer

The Cold War role of the Tu-22M would have included maritime strike against high-priority targets such as NATO aircraft carriers and cruise-missile armed warships in the Mediterranean and the Atlantic. Other missions would have included cutting off Europe from supporting American forces by targeting naval convoys, harbours and airfields.

The Tu-22M first went to war, however, during the Soviet campaign in Afghanistan, dropping free-fall bombs from 1984. During the post-Soviet era, Tu-22M3s conducted bombing missions over Chechnya during 1994–96. The Tu-22M3 returned to battle over Georgia in August 2008 and suffered its first combat loss when one bomber was downed by a Georgian anti-aircraft missile, with the loss of three crew.

As of 2014 the Tu-22M3 version remains in service with seven squadrons at bases in Belaya, Shaykovka and Ryazan. While previously the Tu-22M fleet was divided between the Air Force's Long-Range Aviation arm and the Naval Aviation arm, all aircraft are now consolidated within the Air Force, although they retain a maritime commitment.

Considering the continued importance of the Tu-22M3 to the Russian Air Force bomber arm, the defence ministry elected to pursue a programme to extend the service life of the bomber, pending the availability of an all-new replacement aircraft, under Tupolev's PAK DA programme.

An upgrade effort is proceeding only very slowly under the Tu-22M3M programme. New items of equipment include the Kh-32 cruise missile, a replacement for the Cold War-era Kh-22 (AS-4 'Kitchen') missile. The new weapon offers a considerable increase in stand-off range. In future, upgraded 'Backfires' are also due to receive a new Novella-45 radar.

Since the 'full' upgrade has suffered delays, the Russian Air Force has been forced to adopt a stopgap improvement programme in which the aircraft receives a more modest array of new equipment in the course of its routine overhaul. This upgrade includes a modified avionics suite with new computer, navigation system and cockpit displays. The first Tu-22M3 upgraded to this standard returned to service in 2009.

The Tu-22M is not fitted with ailerons. Instead, control is provided using three sections of spoilers/lift dumpers on the outer wing panels and differential deflection of the elevators.

Weapons Options

The primary weapon for the Tu-22M is the Kh-22 (AS-4 'Kitchen') missile, up to three of which can be carried recessed under the fuselage under the fixed wing glove. Kh-22s are provided in versions for high- or low-altitude launch, nuclear or conventional warheads, and with an active radar seeker for anti-ship work or autonomous guidance for use against fixed targets. Free-fall bombs can be carried on pylons inside the bomb bay as well as on four external multiple racks (two under the engine air intake trunks, as seen here, and two under the wings). As well as free-fall bombs, the Tu-22M can carry mines. In practice, the maximum armament load does not exceed 12,000kg (26,455lb), since loads heavier than this would compromise the fuel carried. In 1989 the Tu-22M3 added new armament in the form of the Kh-15 (AS-16 'Kickback') short-range attack missile, but this was later withdrawn.

Grumman F-14 Tomcat
(1970)

The F-14 entered service as a dedicated carrier-based interceptor, built around a powerful fire-control system and long-range missiles. Following the end of the Cold War, the Tomcat was reborn as a multi-role fighter-bomber, and in this form saw out its career with combat duty over Afghanistan and Iraq.

The F-14 was born from the same specification that led to the abortive F-111B fleet defence fighter, and – like the General Dynamics product – the Tomcat included variable-geometry wings as well as the same powerplant and weapons system. However, the F-14 also made use of aerodynamic innovations tailored to ship-borne operations, including retractable foreplanes in the fixed

AIM-9 Sidewinder
Used for close-in air combat, the AIM-9 is provided with infra-red guidance, conferring a 'fire and forget' capability.

Vulcan Cannon
The General Electric M61A1 Vulcan cannon in the nose is provided with 675 rounds of ammunition and can be selected to fire at 4000 or 6000 rounds per minute.

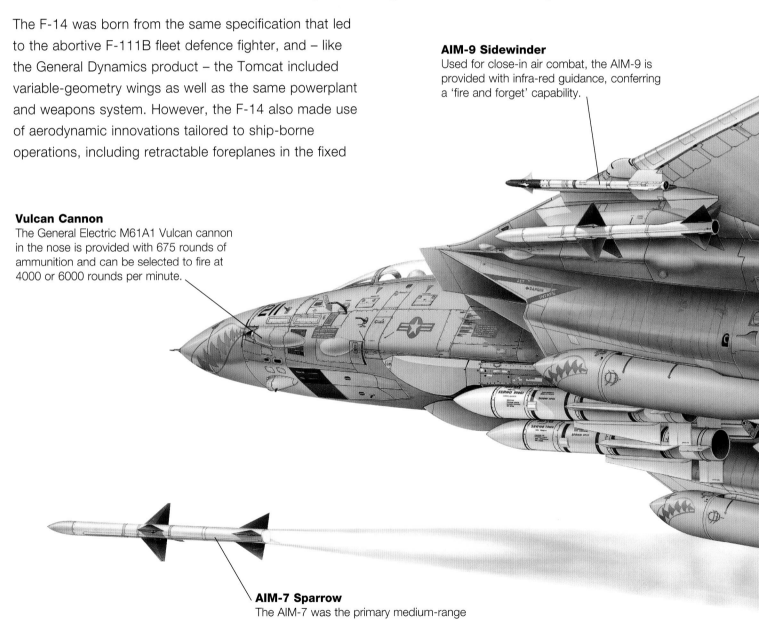

AIM-7 Sparrow
The AIM-7 was the primary medium-range air-to-air weapon for the U.S. Navy F-14. The weapon utilizes semi-active radar homing guidance, tracking the fighter's own radar signals reflected from the target.

portion of the wing leading edges, which served to prevent pitching when the wings were swept back.

The centrepiece of the F-14 was the Hughes AWG-9 radar and fire-control system, allied to 200km (125 mile) range AIM-54 Phoenix air-to-air missiles (AAMs). As well as an internal 20mm (0.79in) rotary cannon, the Tomcat could be armed with short- and medium-range AAMs in the form of the AIM-9 Sidewinder and AIM-7 Sparrow,

respectively. In the 'Bombcat' role that latterly became so important, the F-14 could lift a total of 6577kg (14,500lb) of ordnance, ultimately including laser- and satellite-guided bombs.

The first of a dozen YF-14A development aircraft took to the air in December 1970. The initial F-14A version entered service in 1972 and saw its first combat in U.S. Navy hands in August 1981 when examples shot down a pair

An F-14A of Fighter Squadron (VF) 111 'Sundowners', assigned to the carrier USS *Carl Vinson* (CVN 70), U.S. Navy Pacific Fleet, in the mid-1980s. The unit's 'sharkmouth' motif is worn on the nose and the external fuel tanks, albeit in a toned-down format.

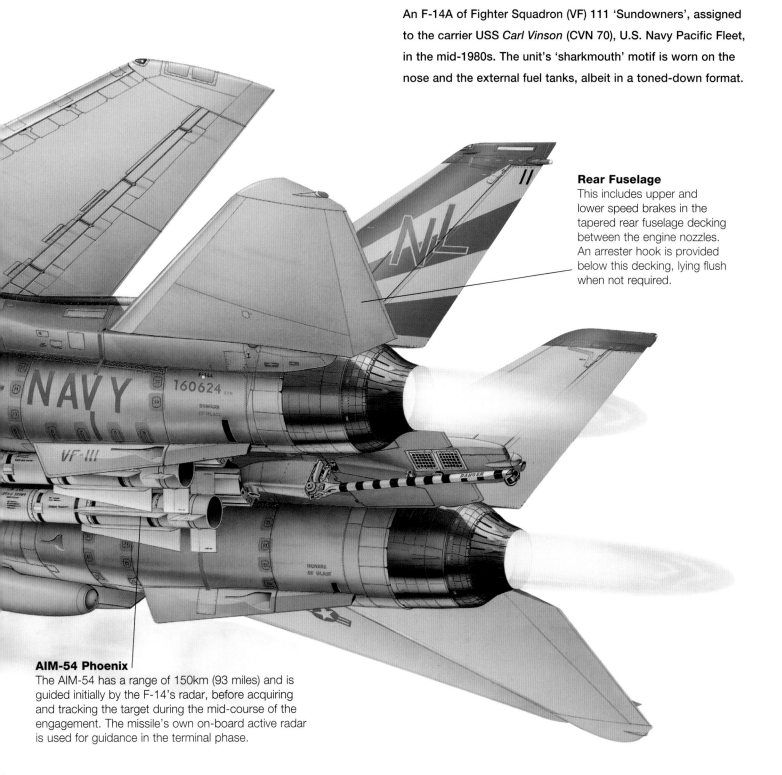

Rear Fuselage
This includes upper and lower speed brakes in the tapered rear fuselage decking between the engine nozzles. An arrester hook is provided below this decking, lying flush when not required.

AIM-54 Phoenix
The AIM-54 has a range of 150km (93 miles) and is guided initially by the F-14's radar, before acquiring and tracking the target during the mid-course of the engagement. The missile's own on-board active radar is used for guidance in the terminal phase.

Grumman F-14 Tomcat

of Libyan Su-22 fighters over the Mediterranean. In another action in January 1989, U.S. Navy Tomcats downed a pair of Libyan MiG-23s over the Gulf of Sidra. Meanwhile, the only export operator, Iran, put its Tomcat fleet to good use during the Iran–Iraq War, in the course of which the type was credited with as many as 64 Iraqi aircraft confirmed destroyed. Even today, the F-14A remains the premier fighter in Islamic Republic of Iran Air Force service.

In addition to 80 aircraft built for Iran, the U.S. Navy took delivery of 556 Tomcats, the first of which was the F-14A that was powered by a pair of Pratt & Whitney TF30

Above: The early days of U.S. Navy Tomcat operations saw units wear flamboyant markings. Typical was this F-14A of VF-1 'Wolfpack', on board USS Enterprise (CVN 65) in the mid-1970s.

Below: The Tomcat's variable-geometry outer wings are equipped with full-span leading edge slats and almost full-span trailing edge flaps. Front-section spoilers provide roll control.

Specification (F-14A)

Type:	Carrier-based interceptor fighter
Dimensions:	Length: 19.10m (62ft 8in); Wingspan: 19.45m (64ft 1.5in) wings spread; Height: 4.88m (16ft 0in)
Weight:	33,724kg (74,348lb) maximum take-off
Powerplant:	2 x 92.97kN (20,900lb) Pratt & Whitney TF30-P-412 afterburning turbofans
Maximum speed:	2485km/h (1544mph) 'clean' at high altitude
Range:	1233km (766 miles) radius of action with 6 x AIM-7s and 4 x AIM-9s
Service ceiling:	more than 15,240m (50,000ft)
Crew:	2
Armament:	1 x 20mm (0.79in) rotary cannon plus up to 6577kg (14,500lb) of external ordnance including 4 or 6 x AIM-54 or AIM-7 AAMs plus 2 x AIM-9 AAMs

turbofans. These initial engines were problematic, and the powerplant issue was addressed with the introduction of the General Electric F110-GE-400 turbofan. The first version with the new engines was the F-14A+, first deployed in 1988. The F-14A+ designation later gave way to F-14B, and this encompassed 32 F-14A rebuilds as well as 38 aircraft that were newly built.

While the F-14B featured a modernized fire-control system, new radios, upgraded radar warning receivers (RWR) and cockpit revisions, the F-14D of 1990 was notably more advanced, with digital avionics that extended to radar processing and cockpit displays. First flown in 1990, the F-14D's revised AWG-9 radar received

the new designation AN/APG-71 and other major changes included the addition of a combined TV/infra-red sensor under the nose, an on-board oxygen-generating system, new ejection seats and updated RWR. A total of 37 new F-14Ds were completed, complemented by 18 F-14A models that were upgraded to F-14D standard.

New Roles

The Tomcat first took on a role in addition to its primary air defence mission with the introduction of the Tactical Air Reconnaissance Pod System (TARPS), and three aircraft so equipped were generally assigned to each squadron.

As mentioned previously, the F-14 always had a residual air-to-ground role, but this was not exploited until late in the type's career. As a 'Bombcat', the F-14 was capable of delivering general-purpose and precision-guided bombs, while simultaneously carrying the AAMs. The F-14 also added the LANTIRN targeting system that allowed delivery of laser-guided bombs and could be used for battle damage assessment.

After service in Operation Desert Storm, in which an F-14 downed an Iraqi Mi-8 helicopter, and air policing missions over the same country in the years that followed, the U.S. Navy Tomcat switched to a primary ground support role, including strike, close air support, reconnaissance and forward air control (airborne), and as such took part in the campaign in Afghanistan beginning in 2001, before returning to the Gulf during Operation Iraqi Freedom that began in 2003.

With the continuing introduction of the Boeing F/A-18E/F Super Hornet, the F-14 was finally withdrawn from U.S. Navy service. The last two squadrons, Fighter Squadron (VF) 31 'Tomcatters' and VF-213 'Black Lions', both flying F-14Ds, officially retired the type in September 2006.

Iranian Survivors

The Islamic Republic of Iran Air Force (IRIAF) is the only operator of the Tomcat in 2014, with three squadrons of F-14As still active. First delivered in 1976, Iran's F-14s achieved much success in the war with Iraq, but ended the conflict with just 34 examples still airworthy. With Tehran frustrated in its attempts to acquire new fighter equipment, the Tomcats have been forced to soldier on, latterly with the aid of local refurbishment and upgrade, local manufacture of components and acquisition of spare parts via third-party sources, thereby avoiding the U.S. arms embargo. Efforts were made to integrate the MIM-23B HAWK surface-to-air missile with the Tomcat, as well as add an air-to-ground capability. More recently, Iran has made attempts to add Russian-made missiles, as well as a reverse-engineered version of the AIM-54. More than 40 examples are still flyable and the IRIAF has a programme under way to modernize its F-14 fleet by 2020.

Fairchild A-10 Thunderbolt II (1972)

Known to those who fly it as the 'Warthog', the A-10 is a tailor-made close support and anti-tank aircraft, employing the unique GAU-8/A Avenger 30mm (1.18in) cannon. Although it has faced opposition from within the U.S. military, the combat-proven Thunderbolt II has always survived to fight another day.

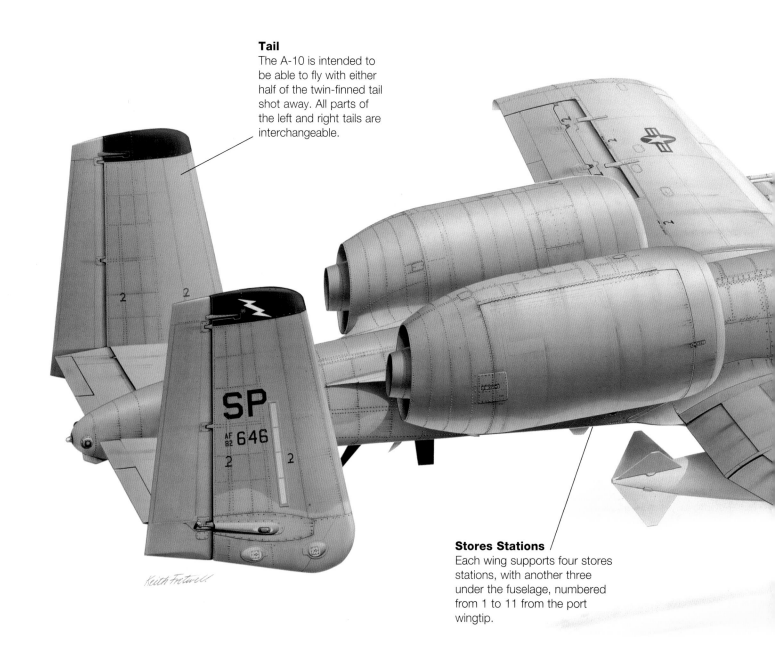

Tail
The A-10 is intended to be able to fly with either half of the twin-finned tail shot away. All parts of the left and right tails are interchangeable.

Stores Stations
Each wing supports four stores stations, with another three under the fuselage, numbered from 1 to 11 from the port wingtip.

In light of Vietnam War experience, the USAF issued the AX specification for a heavily armed new counter-insurgency aircraft in 1967. The aircraft was to be dedicated to close support missions, with a focus on the destruction of enemy tanks and armour. The first of two Fairchild Republic YA-10A service test aircraft took to the air in May 1972 and in January 1973 was selected by the USAF in preference to the Northrop YA-9A after a competitive fly-off. There then followed six pre-production aircraft, one of which was later converted to become a two-seater, as the YA-10B, intended for night/adverse weather operations, although this did not find favour with

the USAF. Instead, the USAF procured a total of 707 of the A.10A production model.

The design of the A-10 took into account the requirements of battlefield survivability and anti-armour firepower. The aircraft was designed around the powerful GAU-8/A Avenger 30mm (1.18in) cannon, a seven-barrel weapon capable of firing at rates of 2100 or 4200 rounds per minute, making it the world's most powerful airborne gun. The twin engines were mounted in widely spaced pods above the rear fuselage in order to minimize the effects of ground fire, while the vertical fins and wing served to shield the exhausts from heat-seeking missiles.

This A-10A of the 510th Fighter Squadron, 52nd Fighter Wing, was based at Spangdahlem AB, Germany, as part of U.S. Air Forces in Europe. During 1993–94, the 510th flew more than 1700 combat sorties from Aviano AB, Italy, in support of Operation Deny Flight over Bosnia.

Ammunition
The Avenger cannon can fire three different rounds: high-explosive incendiary, armour-piercing incendiary and training practice.

AGM-65 Maverick
Two primary seeker heads are available for the Maverick air-to-surface missile as carried by the A-10, comprising TV scene magnification and imaging infra-red (IIR).

Fairchild A-10 Thunderbolt II

The tough airframe included a titanium armoured 'bathtub' for the pilot and cannon ammunition, and multiple other features intended to improve survivability, either through their resistance to battle damage or redundancy. Such items included interchangeable (left or right) flaps, fuselage components, rudders, elevators and main undercarriage. Twin primary hydraulic systems were included, both of which come with manual backup. If required, the pilot could extend the undercarriage using gravity alone. The designers placed an emphasis on ease of maintenance, since it was anticipated that in wartime the A-10 would fly a large number of sorties in rapid succession from austere forward operating locations.

Specification

Type:	Close support aircraft
Dimensions:	Length: 16.26m (53ft 4in); Wingspan: 17.53m (57ft 6in); Height: 4.47m (14ft 8in)
Weight:	22,680kg (50,000lb) maximum take-off
Powerplant:	2 x 40.32kN (9065lb) General Electric TF34-GE-100 high-bypass turbofans
Maximum speed:	706km/h (439mph) 'clean' at sea level
Range:	3949km (2454 miles) with drop tanks
Service ceiling:	13,716m (45,000ft)
Crew:	1
Armament:	1 x 30mm (1.18in) rotary cannon plus up to 258kg (16,000lb) of external ordnance on eight wing and three fuselage pylons

An A-10A of the 706th Tactical Fighter Squadron, 926th Tactical Fighter Group, as it appeared during Operation Desert Storm wearing the 1980s-era European One camouflage scheme.

In its initial form, the A-10 was equipped with avionics including a Pave Penny laser designator pod on a pylon to the right of the forward fuselage and self-protection equipment included jamming pods and a chaff and flare dispenser. In terms of armament, the A-10 is best associated with the Avenger cannon, but its primary weapon was always intended to by the AGM-65 Maverick air-to-surface missile, with TV or laser guidance.

The first operational A-10s were delivered to Davis-Monthan AFB, Arizona in March 1976.

'Warthog' at War

At the end of the Cold War, the USAF considered withdrawing the A-10. In a bid to find a new role, a number of aircraft were redesigned as OA-10As for the forward air control role, equipped with target-marking rockets. The 'Warthog' suddenly received a new lease of life with the 1990 Iraqi invasion of Kuwait, and under the 354th Tactical Fighter Wing (Provisional), 152 OA/A-10s from bases in the U.S. and UK conducted missions with a notable success rate during Operation Desert Storm. As well as two air-to-air victories against Iraqi helicopters, it averaged a kill rate of over 25 tanks a day. By the end of the war, confirmed A-10 tank kills approached 1000 tanks destroyed.

After Desert Storm A-10s were modified to incorporate the Low-Altitude Safety and Targeting Enhancements (LASTE) system that included a Ground Collision Avoidance System (GCAS).

This A-10A carries a typical Desert Storm mixed weapons load of Mk 20 Rockeye cluster bombs, AGM-65D Mavericks, twin Sidewinders and AN/ALQ-119 electronic countermeasures pod.

The A-10 has been employed in every major U.S. military action since, taking in conflicts in the former Yugoslavia, in Afghanistan from October 2001, in Iraq following the U.S.-led invasion in March 2003, in Libya in 2011 and again over Iraq in 2014, this time fighting Islamic State combatants under Operation Inherent Resolve.

The 'Warthog' fleet has also been upgraded accordingly. In 2007 Boeing was contracted for an A-10 wing replacement programme. Avionics updates have added GPS capabilities, improved line-of-sight communications and an infra-red missile warning system.

In the most significant move, A-10As have been converted to the A-10C version beginning in 2007. Centrepiece of the A-10C is the Precision Engagement (PE) package. This adds two multifunction colour displays and an up-front controller in the cockpit.

As of 2014 the Pentagon was planning to retire all of its remaining 386 A-10s immediately, but such moves were blocked by Congress and retirement of the Thunderbolt II fleet was put on hold.

Afghan Missions

An A-10 taxis down the flight line at Bagram Air Base, Afghanistan, after flying a close air support mission. The first major action for the A-10 was flown from this base when the aircraft supported Operation Anaconda in March 2002. Few aircraft have established such a fearsome reputation during anti-insurgent operations in Afghanistan, and the A-10 has won much praise from the troops on the ground. Operations are maintained around the clock, and a typical deployed squadron might fly 10–20 sorties per day. 'Warthogs' loiter in the air waiting for the call to action, or observing the situation below using the Litening III or Sniper pod. In addition to attacking hostile positions, A-10s provide armed escort for rescue helicopters.

Lockheed Martin F-16 Fighting Falcon (1974)

In the last 40 years the F-16 has established itself as the most popular Western fighter in its class, and today serves with 28 nations around the world. The latest production standards and upgrades ensure it will retain its capability well into the twenty-first century, as production continues beyond the 4500-aircraft mark.

The F-16 originated under the Lightweight Fighter (LWF) programme for the USAF, which had the aim of proving the concept of a fighter that would be smaller and cheaper than the F-15. Initially a General Dynamics project, the company flew a first YF-16 demonstrator in February 1974.

After a competitive fly-off against the rival Northrop YF-17, the General Dynamics product was subject to further development, becoming the larger and more capable F-16A Fighting Falcon. This was ordered by the USAF, which required an initial 650, later increased to 1388, soon

The first F-16s arrived in Israel in July 1980. These were newly-built F-16A/B Block 10 Netz (Sparrowhawk) jets and they equipped Nos.117 'First Jet' and 110 'Knights of the North' Squadrons. In 1981 they took part in the raid against the Osirak nuclear reactor in Iraq. An F-16B Netz is seen in the main artwork, with an F-16D Barak illustrated top right.

Radome
In the F-16A this houses a Westinghouse AN/APG-66 coherent pulse-Doppler radar, operating in the I/J bands. The antenna is of the planar array (flate plate) type.

Intake
Unusual for a high-performance jet fighter, the engine intake is simple, with no moving parts. The location ensures the engine is not starved of air even at high angles of attack.

Lockheed Martin F-16 Fighting Falcon

Tailfin
The multi-spar, multi-rib aluminium fin has graphite-epoxy skin and carries a rudder of aluminium honeycomb structure, powered by a servo-actuator. The fin top carries a VHF aerial, anti-collision beacon and directional antennae.

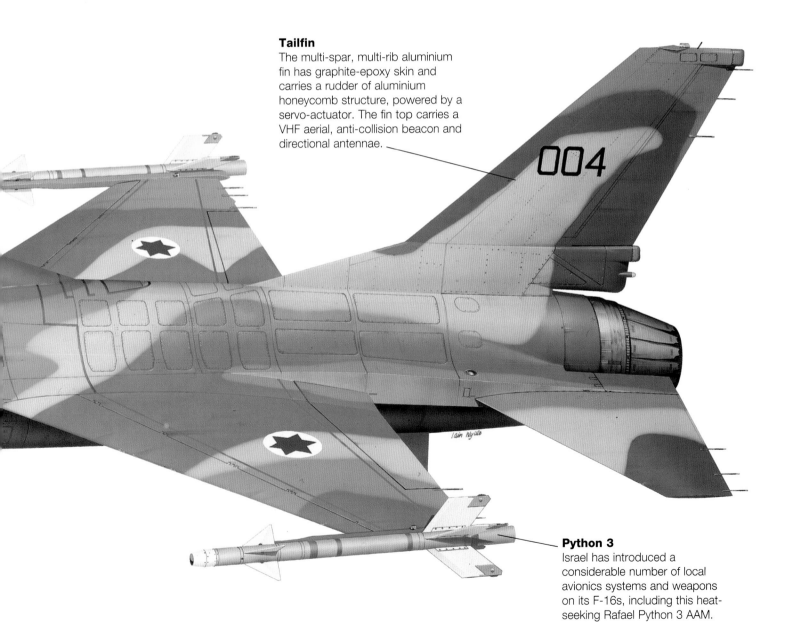

Python 3
Israel has introduced a considerable number of local avionics systems and weapons on its F-16s, including this heat-seeking Rafael Python 3 AAM.

Lockheed Martin F-16 Fighting Falcon

followed by the NATO air forces of Belgium, Denmark, the Netherlands and Norway. So began an export odyssey that continues to this day and which has seen over 4500 examples of the F-16 completed for 28 nations.

While successive variants have progressively added more weight, avionics and capabilities, all Fighting Falcons retain the salient features of the initial production model, including control-configured vehicle (CCV) technology and fly-by-wire flight controls, as well as a generous thrust-to-weight ratio using a single engine fed by a fixed ventral

Specification (F-16C Block 50)

Type:	Multi-role tactical fighter
Dimensions:	Length: 15.03m (49ft 4in); Wingspan: 9.45m (91ft 0in); Height: 5.09m (16ft 8.5in)
Weight:	12,292kg (27,099lb) maximum take-off
Powerplant:	1 x 131.48kN (29,588lb) General Electric F 110-GE-129 afterburning turbofan
Maximum speed:	More than 2125km/h (1321mph) at 12,190m (40,000ft)
Range:	1485km (923 miles) radius of action, with 2 x 907kg (2000lb) bombs and 2 x AIM-9 Sidewinder AAMs
Service ceiling:	more than 15,240m (50,000ft)
Crew:	1
Armament:	1 x 20mm (0.79in) rotary cannon and up to 7072kg (15,591lb) of disposable stores carried on one under-fuselage, six underwing and two wingtip hardpoints

In Israeli service the F-16C and F-16D (seen here) are known as the *Barak* (Lightning). This jet wears No.105 'Scorpion' Squadron markings and carries a GBU-15 glide bomb under its right wing.

intake. The result combines good overall performance with exceptional agility, roll rate, climb and acceleration. The unswept wing features automatically variable camber, and the pilot benefits from a frameless canopy for superior vision, a reclining seat and a sidestick controller in place of the conventional joystick. The throttle, meanwhile, carries controls for the weapons, head-up display (HUD) and radar. In its original F-16 guise, the Fighting Falcon utilized the AN/APG-66 pulse-Doppler radar with look-down/shoot-down capability, but this has given way to successively more advanced models, including the latest active electronically scanned array (AESA) technology in the most advanced versions of the jet.

According to the manufacturer, the F-16 has been completed in 138 different configurations from prototype to the latest production model, the F-16V (V for 'Viper', by which name the aircraft is commonly known). As such, successive changes have taken into account improved cockpit technologies, avionics, sensors and weapons, while at the same time effort has been made to ensure the fighter is more reliable and easier to maintain and support.

Key changes that have been introduced to the aircraft include an increase in range and payload, infra-red sensors and laser targeting devices, and improvements in the field of survivability thanks to more advanced electronic warfare sensors and sophisticated decoys. In order to cope with the increased weight of such additions, the F-16 has received new powerplants to provide increased engine thrust, while extended range has been ensured through the addition of conformal fuel tanks. The cockpit of the latest versions retains the original hands-on throttle and sidestick switch controls, but combines these with large colour displays, night vision goggle (NVG)-compatible lighting, a colour moving map and an increased-area HUD. Other avionics improvements include advanced datalinks, satellite communications and helmet-mounted cueing systems.

Building Blocks

The first sub-variant of the basic F-16A was the combat-capable two-seat F-16B, first flown in 1977 and with reduced fuel capacity. The F-16A and B were built in successive Blocks, numbered 1, 5, 10 and 15, of which the last introduced a major change in the form of an extended horizontal stabilizer. The F-16 ADF conversion had upgraded radar and AIM-7 Sparrow compatibility.

The first major advance came with the F-16C and two-seat F-16D, with an enlarged base leading up to the tailfin and provision for the AIM-120 AMRAAM. The initial Block 25 F-16C/D gave way to the Block 30 and 32 with the General Electric F110-GE-100 or Pratt & Whitney F100-PW-220, respectively. Both options required an enlarged air intake. The Block 30/32 is also capable of deploying AGM-88 HARM missiles. The F-16C/D Block 40/42 retains the same engine options but features avionics changes for improved night/all-weather capability, including LANTIRN navigation and targeting pods, GPS, automatic terrain following and AN/APG-68(V) radar.

In 1991 production switched to the F-16C/D Block 50/52 that is differentiated by the AN/APG-68(V5) radar, NVG-compatible HUD, AN/ALE-47 countermeasures dispenser, AN/ALR-56M radar warning receiver and uprated F110 or F100 engines. Addition of the HARM Targeting System for the Wild Weasel defence suppression role produces the Block 50D/52D. The Block 50 was adopted as an upgrade standard for NATO F-16A/Bs, producing the F-16 MLU (Mid-Life Upgrade). This brings the original cockpit to the Block 50 standard, including wide-angle HUD and NVG compatibility. The MLU aircraft also received AMRAAM capability and have since added further advanced weapons options and avionics upgrades.

Desert Falcon

The latest and most advanced in-service Fighting Falcon version is the Block 60, designated F-16E/F Desert Falcon. Produced for the United Arab Emirates, the F-16E/F introduced an array of sophisticated avionics, based around the Northrop Grumman AN/APG-80 'agile beam' AESA radar, AN/ASQ-32 Internal FLIR and Targeting System (IFTS) and Falcon Edge internal electronic countermeasures system. Conformal fuel tanks are fitted as standard above the inner part of the wing on each side of the fuselage. Precision-strike weapons include the AGM-84H SLAM-ER cruise missile, AGM-154C Joint Stand-Off Weapon (JSOW) and GBU-39/B Small Diameter Bomb (SDB). The Block 60 first flew in December 2003, and the first Desert Falcons were delivered to the UAE in May 2005, going into combat for the first time over Libya during Operation Unified Protector in 2011.

◫ ◫ ◼ Panavia Tornado (1974)

Developed as an all-weather strike aircraft and interdictor, by the mid-1980s the multinational Tornado had established itself as arguably the most important combat aircraft in Western Europe. The warplane also served as the basis for a long-range interceptor and a dedicated defence suppression aircraft.

While multinational collaborative projects are not unusual for 21st-century combat aircraft, the Tornado broke new ground when developed by the tri-national (UK, West Germany and Italy) Panavia from 1968. The aircraft was intended to serve as a long-range, low-level interdictor, with primarily nuclear armament, and featured a combination of variable geometry, fuel-efficient turbofan engines with thrust reversers, a crew of two and a large and varied payload.

For its strike mission, the Tornado IDS (Interdictor Strike) version could call upon its 'swing' wings to loiter efficiently at subsonic speeds, before descending to treetop level for a high speed dash to the target at 1483km/h (921mph).

The three partner nations ordered a total of 644 Tornado IDS aircraft, comprising 220 for the RAF, 212 for the *Luftwaffe*, 112 for the *Marineflieger* (West German Naval Air Arm) and 100 for the Italian Air Force. A first prototype

Refuelling Probe
A detachable retractable inflight refuelling probe can be mounted on the right forward fuselage side, close to the cockpit.

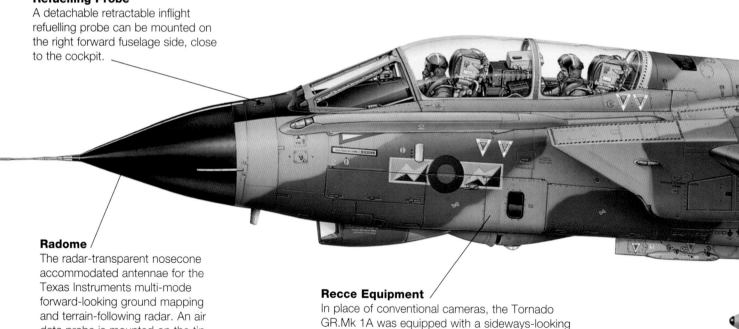

Radome
The radar-transparent nosecone accommodated antennae for the Texas Instruments multi-mode forward-looking ground mapping and terrain-following radar. An air data probe is mounted on the tip of the radome.

Recce Equipment
In place of conventional cameras, the Tornado GR.Mk 1A was equipped with a sideways-looking infra-red system and an infra-red linescanner, providing horizon-to-horizon coverage.

A Tornado GR.Mk 1A of the RAF's No.13 Squadron, based at Marham, Norfolk, in the 1990s. The GR.Mk 1A version retained virtually the full air-to-ground capability, although the twin cannon were deleted to make space for reconaissance equipment.

of the Tornado, then still known as the Multi-Role Combat Aircraft (MRCA) completed its maiden flight in August 1974. A total of six pre-series aircraft were completed.

Deliveries of the Tornado IDS (known in RAF service as the Tornado GR.Mk 1) began in 1979, initially to West Germany. In addition to its primary overland role, the IDS has been adapted to undertake reconnaissance (Tornado GR.Mk 1A in RAF service) and maritime attack missions (Tornado GR.Mk 1B).

Air Defence Variant

With an outstanding RAF requirement for a long-range all-weather interceptor, Panavia developed the Air Defence Version (ADV), which was first flown in October 1979 as the Tornado F.Mk 2. The aircraft accommodated Foxhunter radar and tandem pairs of Sky Flash missiles semi-recessed under a lengthened fuselage. Internal fuel was increased to extend unrefuelled endurance to around four hours 30 minutes, including two hours 30 minutes of patrol at a radius of 602km (374 miles) with full armament.

The interim Tornado F.Mk 2 was soon replaced by the Tornado F.Mk 3, a total of 152 of which were delivered to the RAF beginning in 1986. The F.Mk 3 included hands on throttle and stick controls, radar absorbent material

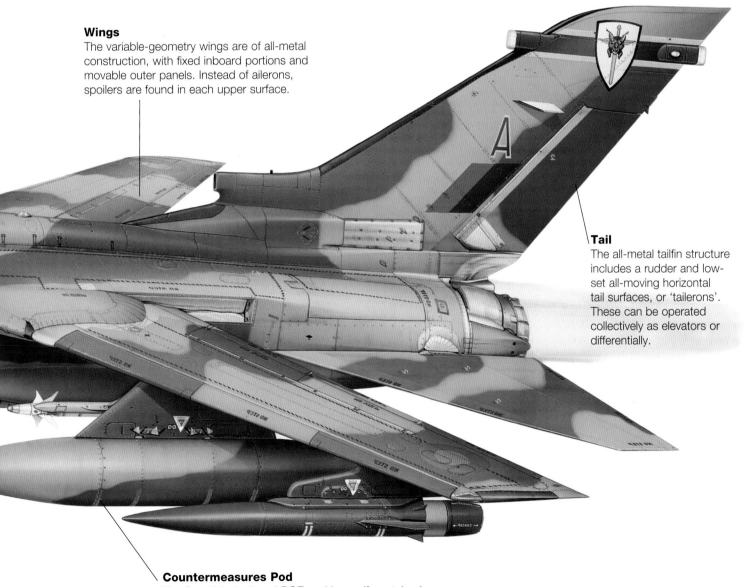

Wings
The variable-geometry wings are of all-metal construction, with fixed inboard portions and movable outer panels. Instead of ailerons, spoilers are found in each upper surface.

Tail
The all-metal tailfin structure includes a rudder and low-set all-moving horizontal tail surfaces, or 'tailerons'. These can be operated collectively as elevators or differentially.

Countermeasures Pod
The Swedish-designed BOZ pod is a self-contained microprocessor-controlled chaff and flare dispenser that augments the Sky Shadow electronic countermeasures pod carried under the opposite wing.

169

Panavia Tornado

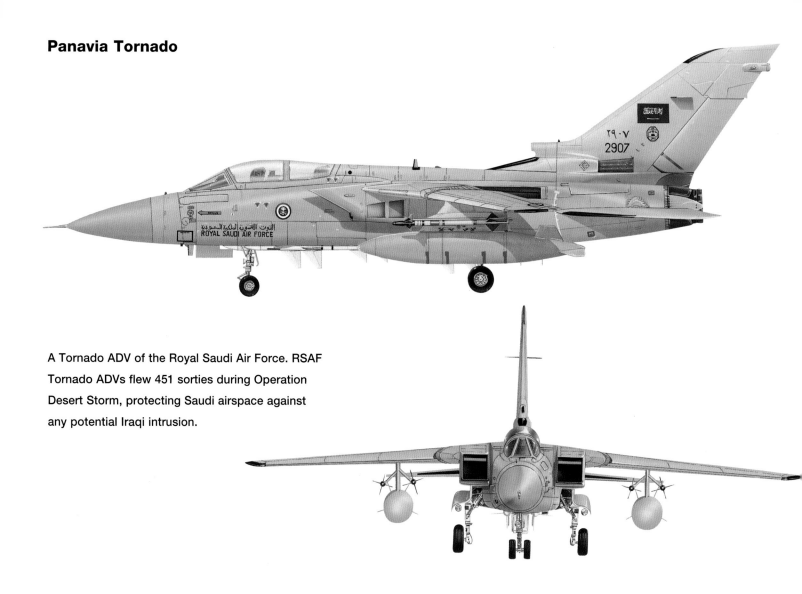

A Tornado ADV of the Royal Saudi Air Force. RSAF
Tornado ADVs flew 451 sorties during Operation
Desert Storm, protecting Saudi airspace against
any potential Iraqi intrusion.

Specification (Tornado GR.Mk 4)

Type:	All-weather interdictor and strike aircraft
Dimensions:	Length: 16.72m (54ft 10.25in); Wingspan: 8.60m (28ft 2.5in) maximum sweep; Height: 5.95m (19ft 6.25in)
Weight:	27,951kg (61,620lb) maximum take-off
Powerplant:	2 x 71.50kN (16,075lb) Turbo-Union RB.199 Mk 103 afterburning turbofans
Maximum speed:	2338km/h (1453mph) at 10,975m (36,000ft)
Range:	1390km (863 miles) combat radius, with a heavy warload on a typical hi-lo-hi mission
Service ceiling:	more than 15,240m (50,000ft)
Crew:	2
Armament:	2 x 27mm (1in) cannon and up to 9000kg (19,841lb) of disposable stores

coating, flare dispensers and subsequently enhanced
computers and datalink capability. Under a Capability
Sustainment Programme the Tornado F.Mk 3 was further
upgraded through the addition of AIM-120 AMRAAM and
ASRAAM missiles, multi-target engagement capability and
improved defensive sub-systems. In its ultimate guise,
the interceptor included a night vision goggles compatible
cockpit with new displays, GPS and secure radios.

In 2001 the RAF began to upgrade its Tornado
GR.Mk 1 fleet, resulting in the definitive GR.Mk 4 that
features new cockpit displays, full compatibility with
navigation and laser designator pods for delivery of
precision-guided munitions, integration of NVGs, an
updated forward-looking infra-red sensor and enhanced
self-defence suite. Subsequently, the RAF GR.Mk 4 has
added advanced weapons including the Storm Shadow
cruise missile and the Brimstone anti-armour missile. A
similar mid-life upgrade has also been undertaken for
the remaining aircraft in German and Italian service. The
Luftwaffe's reduced fleet of Tornado IDS is now armed

with the AGM-88 HARM, GBU-24 Paveway III laser-guided bomb, Taurus stand-off missile, GBU-54 Laser Joint Direct Attack Munition (LJDAM) and the IRIS-T missile for self defence.

The only export customer for the Tornado was Saudi Arabia, which acquired 96 IDS and 24 ADV aircraft. In 2014 only the Saudi IDS remains in service, and these have undergone an upgrade bringing them up to GR.Mk 4 standard. Italy, meanwhile, was another operator of the ADV, taking 24 ex-RAF examples under a lease that began in 1995. The last were returned to the UK in 2004.

The ADV saw combat in Operation Desert Storm, over the former Yugoslavia and in other NATO peacekeeping actions in the hands of all three of its operators: the UK, West Germany and Italy. The IDS first saw action in Desert Storm in 1991 in RAF, Italian and Saudi hands. German Tornados first went into battle over the Balkans before deploying to Afghanistan for reconnaissance duties beginning in 2007. RAF Tornados have borne the brunt of that service's combat operations in the years of the 1991 Gulf War, returning to Iraq and deploying to theatres including Kosovo, Afghanistan and Libya. The Italian Tornado IDS has been used in combat over the Balkans, in Afghanistan and Libya.

The RSAF's Tornado ADVs were equivalent to the RAF's F.Mk 3, and were delivered with the Sky Flash semi-active radar-homing AAM. The Saudi Tornado ADVs were retired in 2007.

Tornado ECR

The West German *Luftwaffe* pioneered the development of the Electronic Combat and Reconnaissance (ECR) version of the Tornado, as a specialist defence suppression aircraft. The heart of the ECR is the internal Emitter Location System (ELS) that enables it to locate and identify hostile radar installations. The ELS is provided with a data library consisting of electronic warfare target profiles, providing an electronic 'order of battle'. Hostile radars can then be

attacked, if required, using AGM-88 High-Speed Anti-Radiation Missiles (HARM). The Tornado ECR was not fitted with on-board cannon. A total of 20 ECR variants are now being updated under Germany's mid-life upgrade programme and will serve exclusively with Aufklärungsgeschwader 51, the *Luftwaffe*'s reconnaissance wing. Italy followed Germany's lead and converted 16 of its aircraft to IT ECR standard with dedicated electronic equipment and HARMs.

Sukhoi Su-27 'Flanker' (1977)

Planned as a Soviet counterweight to the F-15 Eagle, the Su-27 entered service as an air superiority fighter but has demonstrated considerable growth potential, being further developed as a carrier fighter and proving to be an export success.

Sukhoi began work on its T-10 design in 1969 with the aim of creating a highly agile fighter that possessed a very long range, heavy armament and sophisticated sensors. In order to maximize manoeuvrability, the fighter was planned from the start to be unstable, and therefore required a fly-by-wire (FBW) control system. The first prototype of the T-10 took to the air in May 1977 and received the NATO reporting name 'Flanker-A'. However, in its initial form the four original T-10 prototypes displayed a number of serious deficiencies and the

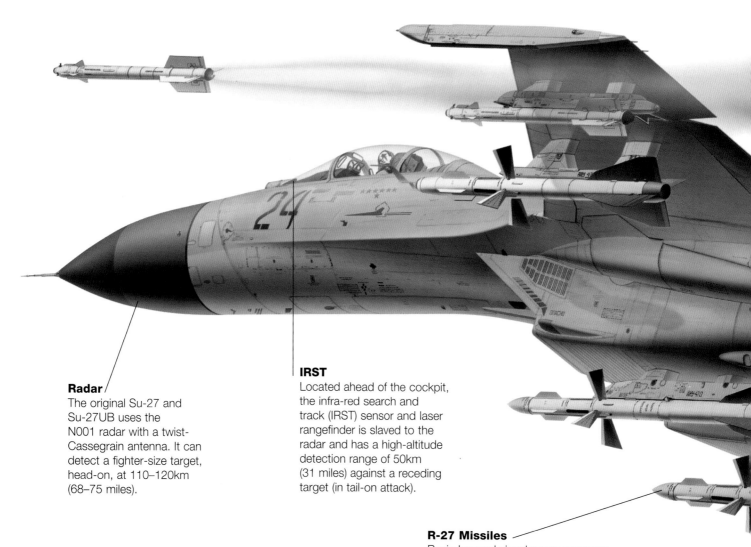

Radar
The original Su-27 and Su-27UB uses the N001 radar with a twist-Cassegrain antenna. It can detect a fighter-size target, head-on, at 110–120km (68–75 miles).

IRST
Located ahead of the cockpit, the infra-red search and track (IRST) sensor and laser rangefinder is slaved to the radar and has a high-altitude detection range of 50km (31 miles) against a receding target (in tail-on attack).

R-27 Missiles
Basic beyond visual range weapons for the Su-27 are the semi-active radar-homing R-27R and infra-red-homing R-27T (AA-10 'Alamo'), and the extended-range R-27ER and R-27ET derivatives.

aircraft required a wholesale redesign, re-emerging as the radically reworked T-10S-1 of 1981.

The T-10S entered series production in 1982, and received the in-service designation Su-27 (NATO 'Flanker-B'). Service entry followed in 1984 and the single-seater was joined by the Su-27UB (NATO 'Flanker-C') fully combat-capable two-seater that first flew in 1985. By the end of the Cold War, a total of just over 400 Su-27s of both versions were in Soviet service.

After the collapse of the USSR, 'Flankers' were passed on to successor states, and Russia began an export

drive for the fighter. First of the export models was the baseline Su-27SK developed for China, basically similar to the 'Flanker-B', but with with additional air-to-ground capabilities. China also received a 'Flanker-C' equivalent, the Su-27UBK. After around 80 Russian-built Su-27SK/UBKs were delivered, China launched licensed production of 95 additional single-seat 'Flankers' (designated as J-11).

Vietnam was the second customer, ordering a first batch of six 'Flankers' (including one two-seater), and a second batch of two Su-27SKs and four Su-27UBKs.

A Su-27 'Flanker-B' of the 582nd Fighter Aviation Regiment, part of the Soviet 4th Air Army based at Chojna, Poland, in 1990. In the same year this unit withdrew its 32 Su-27s from Poland and relocated to Smolensk, Russia, where it disbanded in 1992.

Self Protection
The self-protection suite includes a radar warning receiver (RWR), a two-pod electronic countermeasures (ECM) system and chaff/flare dispensers.

Sukhoi Su-27 'Flanker'

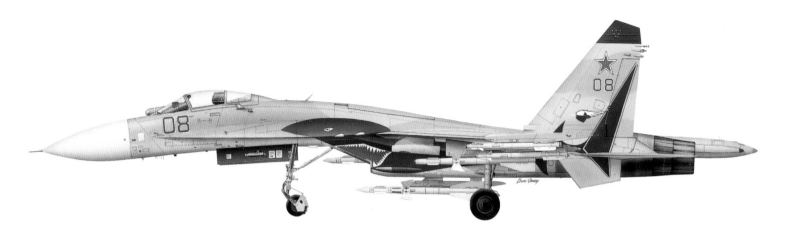

Ethiopia purchased second-hand ex-Russian 'Flanker-B/ Cs', while Indonesian acquired two Su-27SKs and three of the improved Su-27SKM single-seater (the latter equivalent to the Su-27SM described later). 'Flanker-B/C' exports also included ex-Ukrainian aircraft sold to Eritrea and Ethiopia, while Angola received two 'Flankers' from an unknown source, likely Belarus.

The basic 'Flanker' continues to provide the backbone of the Russian Air Force fighter fleet, with 180 examples in service in 2013. These aircraft are undergoing a mid-life upgrade, transforming them into the Su-27SM that is based around a new avionics suite. Delivered to

Above: A specially marked Su-27 'Flanker-B' of the Russian Air Force Training Centre at Lipetsk in the mid-1990s. This unit is tasked with training weapons instructors and developing tactics.

Below: The Su-27 features a prominent leading edge root extension (LERX) that provides additional lift, helping destabilize the heavy radar nose. The starboard wing root contains a 30mm (1.18in) cannon.

Specification (Su-27 'Flanker-B')

Type:	All-weather air superiority fighter
Dimensions:	Length: 21.90m (71ft 10in); Wingspan: 14.70m (48ft 2.75in); Height: 5.93m (19ft 5.5in)
Weight:	33,000kg (72,751lb) maximum take-off
Powerplant:	2 x 122.58kN (27,557lb) Saturn/Lyulka AL-31F afterburning turbofans
Maximum speed:	2280km/h (1417mph) 'clean' at 11,000m (36,090ft)
Range:	3680km (2287 miles) at high altitude
Service ceiling:	17,700m (58,071ft)
Crew:	1
Armament:	1 x 30mm (1.18in) cannon and up to 6000kg (13,228lb) of disposable stores including up to 6 x medium-range and 4 x short-range AAMs

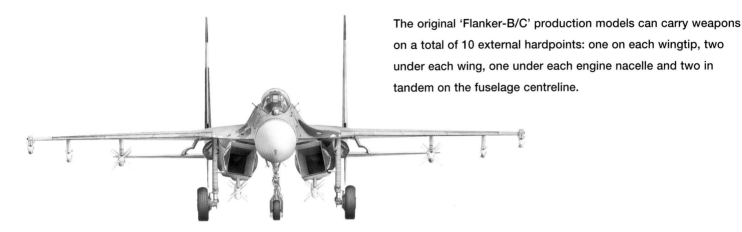

The original 'Flanker-B/C' production models can carry weapons on a total of 10 external hardpoints: one on each wingtip, two under each wing, one under each engine nacelle and two in tandem on the fuselage centreline.

front-line regiments from 2004, the upgraded Su-27SM has been complemented by a small batch of newly built aircraft with improved avionics and mission equipment, designated as the Su-27SM3, which were delivered in 2011. More recently, Russia has procured three more new-build 'Flanker' versions: the two-seat Su-30M2 and Su-30SM, as well as the thrust-vectoring single-seat Su-35S. The Su-30M2 and Su-30SM are both domestic versions of the significantly improved two-seat derivatives of the 'Flanker', which have achieved significant export success.

The multi-role two-seat family was derived from the Su-30 interceptor developed for the USSR and fielded in small numbers. Itself based on the two-seat Su-27UB, the Su-30 added an in-flight refuelling probe and other changes for the long-range mission.

The Su-30 led to the multi-role Su-30MKI developed by the Irkut company for India, which has signed up for 272 aircraft. The Su-30MKI includes advanced avionics suite, including a phased-array multi-mode radar, precision-guided air-to-surface weapons, canard foreplanes, a more sophisticated FBW system and thrust-vectoring engines. The definitive Su-30MKI was preceded by a batch of eight Su-30Ks equipped to a basic configuration.

Essentially similar to the Su-30MKI are the 18 Su-30MKM aircraft (for Malaysia), the 44 Su-30MKA aircraft (for Algeria) and the Russian Su-30SM. Less sophisticated is the Su-30MKK two-seat multi-role 'Flanker' developed for China by the KnAAPO plant. China received 76 aircraft followed by 24 of the Su-30MK2 derivative optimized for anti-shipping. Other customers for the KnAAPO product comprise Venezuela (24 Su-30MK2V), Vietnam (24 Su-30MK2), Indonesia (two Su-30MK and nine Su-30MK2) and (six Su-30MK2). The Russian Air Force's Su-30M2 is also broadly similar.

The definitive single-seat 'Flanker' was conceived in the early 2000s, initially for export. The Su-35 has been ordered by Russia and features a completely new airframe structure, avionics, systems and powerplant. Although not fitted with canards, it includes the super agility of the Su-30MKI family thanks to its 142.2kN (31,900lb) thrust-vectoring Saturn AL-41F1S engines and advanced FBW system. The Su-35S is capable of employing all Russian new-generation air-to-air and air-to-surface guided weapons.

Naval 'Flanker'

Known to Sukhoi as the Su-27K, and to the Russian military as the Su-33, the 'Flanker-D' is a carrier-based air superiority fighter that was first flown in August 1987. Compared to the 'Flanker-B', the Su-33 features an arrester hook, canard foreplanes, a folding tail 'sting', folding wings and tailplane, a strengthened twin nosewheel, modified flight control system, increased-area fin and a retractable flight-refuelling probe. The weapons control system is similar to that of the baseline 'Flanker-B', essentially restricting it to air defence missions. The carrier version entered series production in the early 1990s and in 1993 the first batch of four Su-33s entered service. By 1998 as many as 24 'Flanker-Ds' had been accepted by Russian Naval Aviation and these serve as primary fighter equipment aboard the Russian Navy's sole aircraft carrier *Admiral Kuznetsov*.

Mikoyan MiG-29 'Fulcrum' (1977)

Developed by the USSR in response to increasingly sophisticated Western warplanes, the MiG-29 soon established a formidable reputation as an agile dogfighter. Despite its shortcomings, it has continued to undergo development with efforts to extend its range and the addition of a multi-role capability.

Although it entered Soviet Air Force service as a lightweight counterpart to the heavyweight Su-27 fighter, the MiG-29 traces its roots back to a design for a heavy fighter. This was later scaled down to meet a requirement for a 'frontal' fighter that would primarily serve in a short-range air defence role, but would also offer a secondary ground-attack capability. Detailed design work began in 1974. In order to keep pace with Western fighter development,

Aerodynamics
As part of the high-lift, low-drag design ethos, the MiG-29 employs a widely flared wing leading edge root extension, while the intakes for the widely spaced engines are also optimized for high angle-of-attack capability.

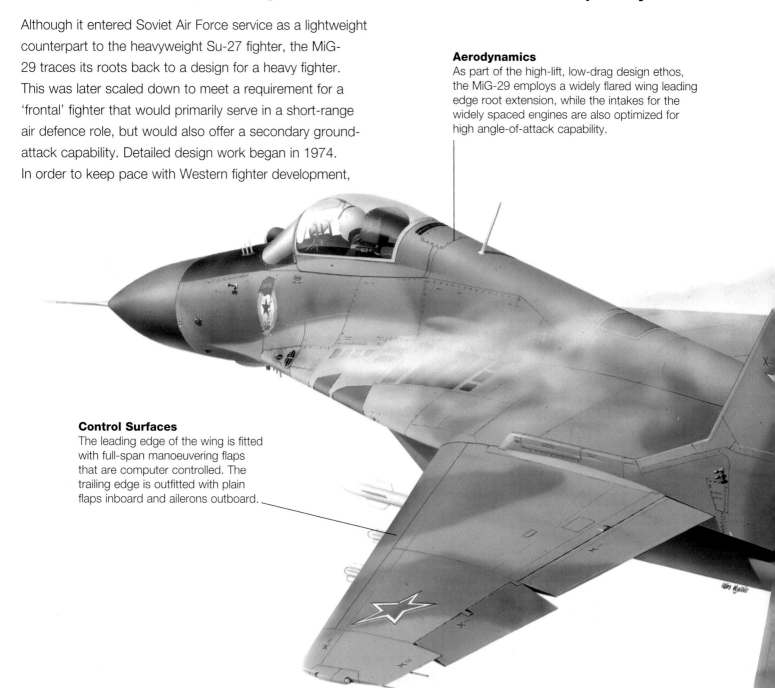

Control Surfaces
The leading edge of the wing is fitted with full-span manoeuvering flaps that are computer controlled. The trailing edge is outfitted with plain flaps inboard and ailerons outboard.

the MiG-29 was to make use of a look-down/shoot-down capability and be able to operate in an electronic countermeasures environment. Other important elements of the design were undercarriage and engine intakes optimized for operations on rough and semi-prepared forward airstrips.

Employing a blended high-lift, low-drag wing and forward fuselage, the MiG-29 was tailored for high angle-of-attack performance, providing superb low-speed and high-Alpha agility. The first of 11 prototypes completed a maiden flight in October 1977. After eight pre-production machines, the initial production version began to be delivered to the Soviet Air Force's Frontal Aviation elements in 1983, and was known to Mikoyan as the 9.12 and to NATO as the 'Fulcrum-A'. In this original form, the primary

mission sensors comprised an N019 pulse-Doppler radar and an infra-red search and track system. The pilot was provided with a helmet-mounted cueing system. The similar 9.12A version was delivered to Warsaw Pact countries and other close allies, while the further downgraded 9.12B was produced for export to non-Warsaw Pact operators.

A two-seat combat trainer was developed and fielded as the 9.51 MiG-29UB 'Fulcrum-B', with radar deleted and a second seat under an elongated canopy. In 1984 Mikoyan flew a first example of the improved 9.13 'Fulcrum-C'

A MiG-29 (9.12) 'Fulcrum-A' of the 237th Composite Aviation Regiment, stationed at Kubinka in the Moscow Military District in the early 1990s. This historic unit still serves as the Air Force's Aviation Equipment Demonstration Centre.

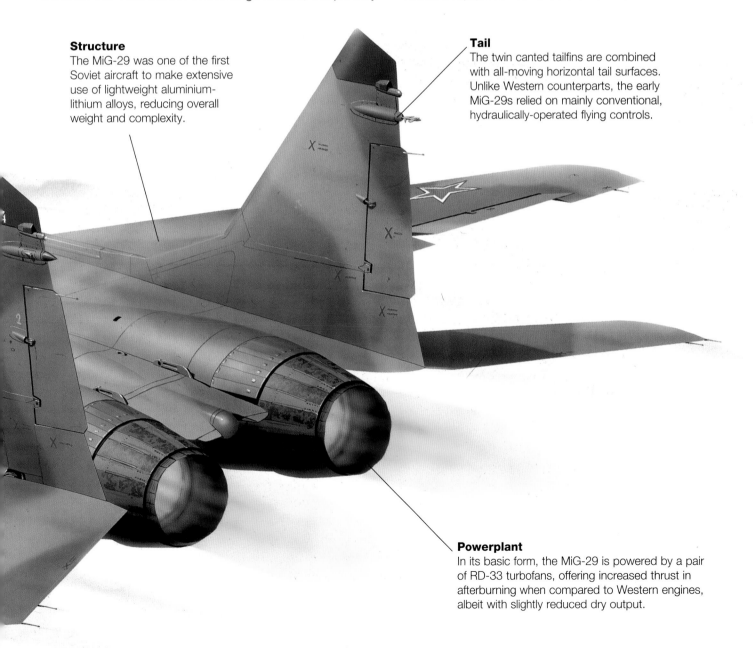

Structure
The MiG-29 was one of the first Soviet aircraft to make extensive use of lightweight aluminium-lithium alloys, reducing overall weight and complexity.

Tail
The twin canted tailfins are combined with all-moving horizontal tail surfaces. Unlike Western counterparts, the early MiG-29s relied on mainly conventional, hydraulically-operated flying controls.

Powerplant
In its basic form, the MiG-29 is powered by a pair of RD-33 turbofans, offering increased thrust in afterburning when compared to Western engines, albeit with slightly reduced dry output.

that retained the basic MiG-29 nomenclature, but which carried additional fuel and avionics in an enlarged spine. A further improved 'Fulcrum-C' was the 9.13S model, the key features of which were a more advanced flight-control system and an improved NO19M radar with multi-target tracking/two-target engagement capability and compatibility with advanced R-77 (AA-12 'Adder') air-to-air missiles. Underwing fuel tanks were also now offered as standard.

After the Cold War, the 9.13 formed the basis of a family of increasingly advanced MiG-29s aimed at the export market, and with enhanced capabilities that included expanded multi-role flexibility and Western communications

Three views of the prototype of the original, abortive MiG-29M armed with advanced weapons including Kh-31 (AS-17 'Krypton') anti-radar missiles and R-77 (AA-12 'Adder') air-to-air missiles.

systems. The first of these upgrade configurations was the baseline MiG-29SE, with the improvements developed for the Soviet MiG-29S, together with the option of Western-style displays and instruments and Western navigation, identification friend or foe (IFF) and radio equipment. The MiG-29SD includes NATO-compatible IFF and

Specification

Type:	Air defence fighter with secondary ground-attack capability
Dimensions:	Length: 17.32m (56ft 10in) including probe; Wingspan: 11.36m (37ft 3.25in); Height: 4.73m (15ft 6.25in)
Weight:	18,500kg (40,785lb) maximum take-off
Powerplant:	2 x 81.39kN (18,298lb) Klimov RD-33 afterburning turbofans
Maximum speed:	2445km/h (1520mph) at high altitude
Range:	1500km (932 miles) with standard fuel
Service ceiling:	19,800m (65,000ft)
Crew:	1
Armament:	1 x 30mm (1.18in) cannon and up to 3000kg (6614lb) of disposable stores carried on six underwing hardpoints

The original MiG-29M launched efforts to create a genuine second-generation 'Fulcrum', including fly-by-wire flight controls, advanced structure, improved powerplant, avionics and weapons systems. The 9.15 yielded five prototypes.

navigation/communications equipment, improved radar, R-77 compatibility and provision for a bolt-on retractable in-flight refuelling probe. The MiG-29SM focuses on enhanced air-to-ground capabilities, and includes a new cockpit display, radar modifications and weapons system improvements allowing the use of TV- and radar-guided bombs and missiles. Most advanced of these upgrades is the MiG-29SMT featuring a 'glass' cockpit, enhanced air-to-ground capabilities and a new, even larger dorsal spine to accommodate extra fuel.

During the 1980s Mikoyan had ambitious plans for a second-generation MiG-29 that would employ an all-new airframe design. This took the form of the land-based 9.15 MiG-29M and the carrier-based 9.31 MiG-29K. However, post-Cold War funding cuts saw these programmes abandoned in the early 1990s.

As the manufacturer's fortunes improved in the twenty-first century, MiG returned to advanced MiG-29 variants, and brought to market a new, unified family of MiG-29 multi-role fighters derived from the 9.15 and 9.31.

The latest variants are based on the navalized MiG-29K and MiG-29KUB (9.41 and 9.47) developed for the Indian Navy. The land-based equivalents are the MiG-29M/M2 variants, and all feature open architecture avionics, Zhuk-ME radar with a slotted planar array, and new RD-33MK engines with full-authority digital engine control (FADEC).

Further enhancements are incorporated in the MiG-35 and two-seat MiG-35D, which boast a multi-mode phased-array radar, a new electro-optical targeting and reconnaissance system, an improved IRST sensor and a new defensive aids system. All of the new versions are also offered with thrust-vectoring engines.

Polish 'Fulcrums'

A NATO member, the Polish Air Force remains an enthusiastic MiG-29 operator. Poland first ordered nine MiG-29As and three MiG-29UBs, the first of which were delivered in 1989. In 1995 Poland decided to purchase 10 surplus MiG-29s (nine MiG-29As and one MiG-29UB) from the Czech Republic. With the withdrawal from service of *Luftwaffe* MiG-29s, 22 former East German aircraft (18 MiG-29Gs and four MiG-29GTs) were offered to Poland for a symbolic Euro. The offer was accepted and in September 2003 the first aircraft arrived in Poland. In

order to operate within NATO, and to extend their service lives, Polish MiGs are being upgraded with a new digital databus with open architecture, a cockpit using imperial units of measurement, a laser inertial platform with embedded GPS and INS, digital video recorder and data transfer system, an up-front control panel, a new UHF/VHF radio, an upgraded IRST sensor and modernized NO19 radar with increased target detection and tracking range.

▮ Dassault Mirage 2000

(1978)

Continuing the tradition of delta-winged Dassault fighters, the Mirage 2000 brought the family up to date and established itself not only as the backbone of the French Air Force but also as a genuine success on the export market. The basic fighter has been adapted for roles including nuclear strike and conventional attack.

While the Mirage 2000 bears superficial resemblance to the dynasty of delta-winged fighters that preceded it, the new fighter combined this configuration with negative longitudinal stability and a fly-by-wire control system, the result being a vast improvement on the previous generation of Dassault warplanes. Retaining a delta wing meant considerable lift, low drag and plenty of internal volume for fuel and avionics, while the computer-based flight controls ensured the aircraft was more agile, handled better at low speed and landed at a more manageable velocity.

The Mirage 2000 can be traced back to an in-house Dassault project, the Mirage 1000 of 1972. In 1975 a planned Dassault Avion de Combat Futur (ACF) was cancelled and a new official specification had to be drafted. This was issued in 1976 and thus began a high-priority programme for a new interceptor fighter to enter service in 1982. Powered by an 83.36kN (18,839lb) thrust

Radar
The Mirage 2000H was delivered with the Thomson-CSF RDM multi-role radar, which provides continuous-wave target illumination for use with Doppler homing missiles.

Super 530 AAM
For air interception, the basic weapon of the Mirage 2000H is the MATRA Super 530D missile, which uses a monopulse continuous-wave Doppler semi-active radar seeker.

SNECMA M53 turbofan, the first prototype made a maiden flight in March 1978. In its initial production form, the Mirage 2000C for the French Air Force featured a broader-chord tailfin and trailing edge root fairings. More importantly, thrust was boosted to 88.26kN (19,842lb) thanks to a new M53-5 engine. First deliveries took place in April 1983.

Complementing the single-seat Mirage 2000C was the two-seat Mirage 2000B conversion trainer, first flown in 1983. With marginally increased length, the Mirage 2000B

suffered a reduction in fuel capacity and had both cannon deleted. A total of 32 Mirage 2000Bs were completed for France, together with 121 Mirage 2000Cs. Although the RDM radar and Super 530F air-to-air missiles were

A Mirage 2000H (known locally as Vajra – Thunderbolt) of No.1 'The Tigers' Squadron, Central Air Command, Indian Air Force, based at Maharajpura Air Force Station, Gwailor, in the 1990s. A former MiG-21 unit, No.1 Squadron was the second IAF Mirage 2000 operator after No.7 Squadron.

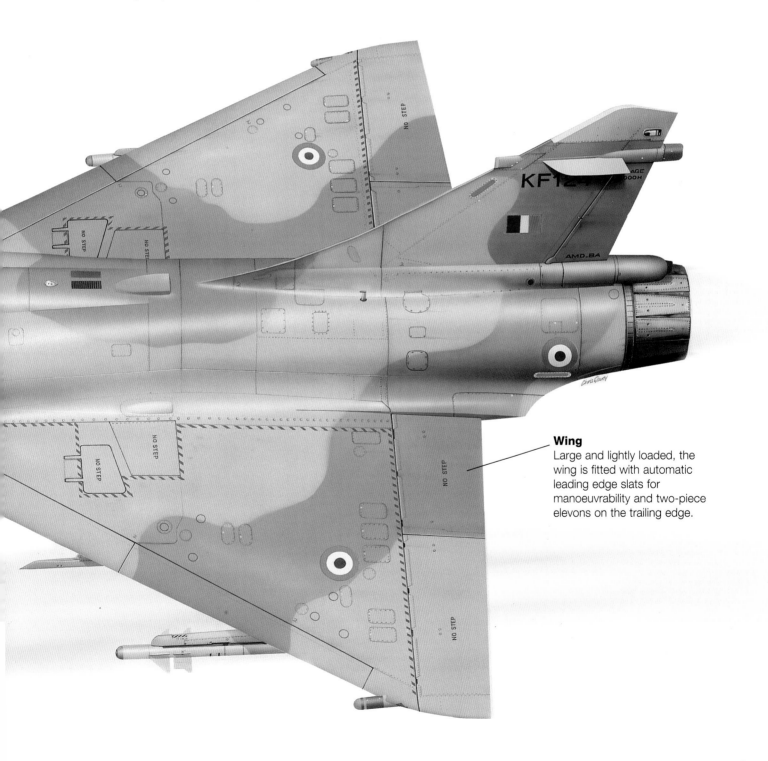

Wing
Large and lightly loaded, the wing is fitted with automatic leading edge slats for manoeuvrability and two-piece elevons on the trailing edge.

Dassault Mirage 2000

originally fitted, both variants were eventually equipped with the RDI radar providing continuous-wave illumination for the Super 530D missile and improved look-down/ shoot-down capability. As production continued, the M53-5 engine was superseded by the 95.12kN (21,384lb) thrust M52-P2.

In 1979 Dassault received a contract to produce two prototypes of a nuclear strike version, which became the Mirage 2000N. Based on the two-seat Mirage 2000B

A Mirage 2000C of the 5e Escadre de Chasse, as it appeared during Operation Daguet, France's contribution to the 1991 Gulf War. The aircraft was one of 14 based in Al Ahsa, Saudi Arabia.

Specification (Mirage 2000-5)

Type:	Multi-role fighter
Dimensions:	Length: 14.36m (47ft 1.25in); Wingspan: 9.13m (29ft 11.5in); Height: 5.20m (17ft 0.75in)
Weight:	15,000kg (33,069lb) maximum take-off
Powerplant:	1 x 98.06kN (22,046lb) SNECMA M53-P20 afterburning turbofan
Maximum speed:	2335km/h (1451mph) at high altitude
Range:	3333km (2071 miles) with drop tanks
Service ceiling:	16,460m (54,000ft)
Crew:	1 or 2
Armament:	2 x 30mm (1.18in) cannon and up to 6300kg (13,889lb) of disposable stores carried on five under-fuselage and four underwing hardpoints

airframe, this features an airframe strengthened for low-level operations, and attack avionics based around the Antilope 5 radar. The primary weapon is the ASMP stand-off nuclear missile. A total of 75 Mirage 2000Ns were built for the French Air Force and the type achieved initial operational capability in 1988.

Post-Cold War, the French Air Force was presented with an increased requirement for conventional strike aircraft, leading to the development of the Mirage 2000D, which is otherwise similar to the Mirage 2000C. First flown in 1991, a total of 75 Mirage 2000Ds were delivered.

The original Mirage 2000B/C became a major export success, the first of which was the Mirage 2000EM/BM for Egypt, with M53-P2 engine and the earlier RDM radar modified for use with the Super 530D intercept missile. India's Mirage 2000H/TH is powered by the M53-5, later replaced by the M53-P2, and also has Super 530D capability. Peru obtained the Mirage 2000P/DP. The United Arab Emirates ordered Mirage 2000EAD multi-role fighters, Mirage 2000RAD reconnaissance aircraft and Mirage 2000DAD combat trainers. The 'first generation' Greek version was the Mirage 2000EG/BG.

The first of the 'second generation' Mirage 2000s was the Mirage 2000-5, designed as an export-optimized multi-role warplane and first flown in 1990. Initially tested as a two-seater, the Dash 5 was subsequently joined by a single-seater. The main feature of the Dash 5 is the Thales RDY multi-mode radar, complemented by a modernized cockpit, improved self-defence suite, the new MICA air-to-air missile and a wide range of guided and unguided air-to-surface ordnance. The first customer was Taiwan (Mirage 2000-5EI and -5DI), followed by Qatar (Mirage 2000-5EDA and -5DDA). The French Air Force, meanwhile, elected to upgrade 37 of its Mirage 2000Cs to a similar standard, thereby producing the Mirage 2000-5F.

The export line was further advanced with the appearance of the Mirage 2000-9, and the essentially similar Mirage 2000-5 Mk 2. Compared to the Dash 5, these introduced the RDY-2 standard radar. The initial customer for the Mk 2 was Greece, followed by the United Arab Emirates (Mirage 2000-9). Both Greece and the UAE also decided to upgrade a number of Mirage 2000s previously delivered to these same advanced standards.

Targeting Pods

While the first air-to-ground version of the Mirage 2000, the Mirage 2000N, was not initially equipped with a targeting pod, this omission was addressed in the conventional-optimized Mirage 2000D. The first targeting pods for this model were the PDL-CT (Pod de Désignation Laser-Caméra Thermique) that provided thermal imaging designation, and the ATLIS day-only system. These were supplemented by the PDL-CTS fitted with the improved Synergie infra-red sensor for a 40 per cent increase in image resolution. Most recently, the Mirage 2000D has added the advanced Damoclès MP laser-designation pod. Meanwhile, Indian Mirage 2000s are fitted with the Israeli Litening laser designation pod. The most advanced Mirage, the UAE's Mirage 2000-9, includes the Damoclès pod (known as Shehab) used in conjunction with a forward-looking infra-red pylon (Nahar).

McDonnell Douglas F/A-18 Hornet (1978)

Replacing the F-4 Phantom II in the fleet air defence role, and the A-7 Corsair II attack aircraft, the Hornet brought the U.S. Navy's carrier air wing into a new era with a genuine multi-role carrier fighter, and the 'legacy' F/A-18 also continues to serve with the U.S. Marine Corps and a number of export operators.

The U.S. Navy originally selected the McDonnell Douglas Hornet under the Air Combat Fighter programme of the mid-1970s, in which the Northrop YF-17 emerged victorious against the General Dynamics YF-16. After the land-based YF-17 had been further developed and navalized, the result was the F/A-18, which would combine fighter and strike/attack roles in a single airframe,

Wingtip Pylon
The wingtip hardpoint is normally reversed to carry a version of the Sidewinder AAMs. Seen here is the AIM-9M, which has now been joined by the advanced AIM-9X.

Cannon
Mounted in the nose is a General Electric M61A1 Vulcan 20mm (0.79in) rotary cannon provided with 570 rounds of ammunition, and firing at a rate of 6000 rounds per minute.

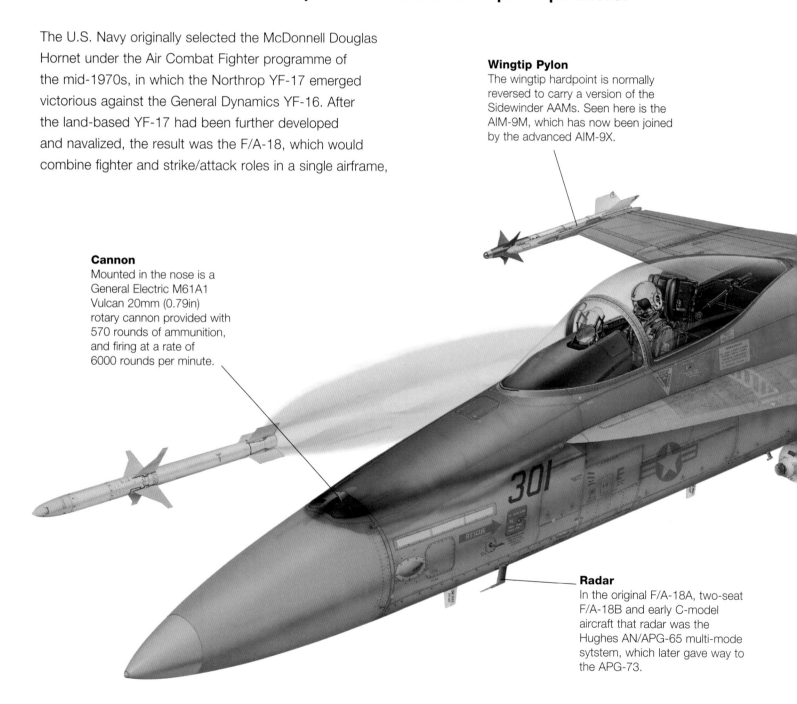

Radar
In the original F/A-18A, two-seat F/A-18B and early C-model aircraft that radar was the Hughes AN/APG-65 multi-mode sytstem, which later gave way to the APG-73.

thanks to the use of a versatile airframe and advanced mission software. Northrop, as design originator, was to have responsibility for future land-based versions of the Hornet, while McDonnell Douglas would take design leadership and a majority workshare on the naval version for the U.S. Navy and Marine Corps. In the event, it was the naval model that also won export orders, although the two companies continued to share the responsibility for development and production. Today, McDonnell Douglas is part of Boeing, while Northrop has become Northrop Grumman. These two firms are now responsible for the

F/A-18E/F Super Hornet, an entirely reworked aircraft, and its EA-18G Growler electronic attack derivative.

The first prototype of what is now referred to as the 'legacy' Hornet (to distinguish it from the Super Hornet) took to the air in November 1978 and was part of a batch of 11 development aircraft, two of which were completed as two-seaters. Production of the initial single-seat F/A-18A yielded 371 aircraft, the first of which were delivered in May 1980. The first fully operational unit was the Marine Corps' squadron VMFA-314, declared operational in January 1983. A first U.S. Navy unit followed suit in August 1983.

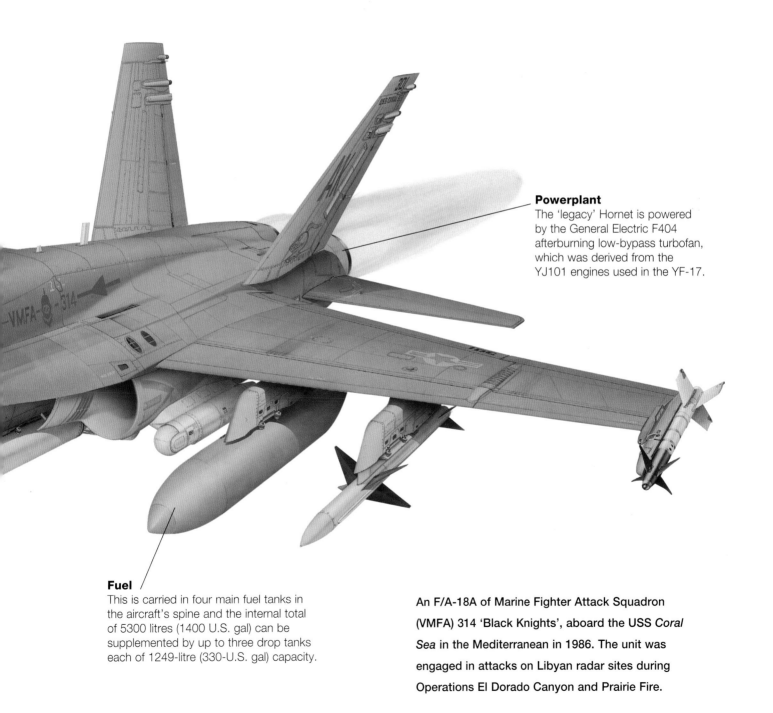

Powerplant
The 'legacy' Hornet is powered by the General Electric F404 afterburning low-bypass turbofan, which was derived from the YJ101 engines used in the YF-17.

Fuel
This is carried in four main fuel tanks in the aircraft's spine and the internal total of 5300 litres (1400 U.S. gal) can be supplemented by up to three drop tanks each of 1249-litre (330-U.S. gal) capacity.

An F/A-18A of Marine Fighter Attack Squadron (VMFA) 314 'Black Knights', aboard the USS *Coral Sea* in the Mediterranean in 1986. The unit was engaged in attacks on Libyan radar sites during Operations El Dorado Canyon and Prairie Fire.

McDonnell Douglas F/A-18 Hornet

The Hornet first saw combat during the 1986 raids on Libya, flying from the carrier USS *Coral Sea*. Since then, the Hornet has been at the heart of U.S. Navy carrier and Marine Corps combat operations.

The F/A-18A gave way to the F/A-18C that became the dominant 'legacy' production variant, a total of 347 being ordered for U.S. Navy and Marine Corps service. First flown in September 1986, the C-model is equipped with the AN/APG-73 synthetic-aperture ground-mapping radar compatible with the AIM-120 AMRAAM and includes enhanced self-protection systems. Other changes include a new NACES ejector seat and small

An F/A-18D of the U.S. Marine Corps' VMFA(AW)-225 armed with 127mm (5in) Zuni unguided rockets underwing, used for target-marking purposes in the forward air controller (airborne) role.

strakes above the wing leading edge root extensions. A night attack capability was added from the 138th F/A-18C, including night vision goggles, full-colour displays, a moving-map function and the AN/AAS-38 forward-looking infra-red pod. The night attack F/A-18C version began to be delivered to operational units in November 1989.

Specification (F/A-18C)

Type:	Carrier-based fighter and strike/attack aircraft
Dimensions:	Length: 17.07m (56ft 0in); Wingspan: 11.43m (37ft 6in) without wingtip missiles; Height: 4.66m (15ft 3.5in)
Weight:	21,888kg (48,253lb) maximum take-off, attack mission
Powerplant:	2 x 78.73kN (17,700lb) General Electric F404-GE-402 afterburning turbofans
Maximum speed:	More than 1915km/h (1190mph) at high altitude
Range:	More than 3336km (2073 miles) ferry with drop tanks
Service ceiling:	15,240m (50,000ft)
Crew:	1
Armament:	1 x 20mm (0.79in) rotary cannon and up to 6200kg (13,700lb) of disposable stores

A two-seat version of the Hornet was developed alongside the F/A-18A, and produced the F/A-18B, which, apart from the addition of a second crew position, was basically unchanged from the A-model. A total of 40 aircraft were completed for the U.S. Navy and Marine Corps.

The F/A-18B has not been employed in an operational role in contrast to the definitive 'legacy' two-seater, the F/A-18D. This is essentially similar to the F/A-18C and after 31 production aircraft had been completed, the D-model also switched to a night attack version, production concluding with delivery of the 109th example. The night attack F/A-18D is primarily employed by the U.S. Marine Corps, with which it replaced the A-6 Intruder.

Export Hornets

Land-based Hornets have been acquired by seven nations, and the first export customer for the type was Canada, which took delivery of 98 single-seat CF-188As and 40 two-seat CF-188Bs between 1982 and 1988.

Australia was next, taking 57 F/A-18As and 18 F/A-18Bs. Spain acquired 60 EF-18As and 12 EF-18Bs. Thereafter, export aircraft were all completed to F/A-18C/D standard, comprising 32 F/A-18Cs and eight F/A-18Ds for Kuwait; 26 F/A-18Cs and eight F/A-18Ds for Switzerland; 57 F-18Cs and seven F-18Ds (initially without attack capability) for Finland and eight F/A-18Ds for Malaysia.

Upgrade of the 'legacy' Hornet was spearheaded by the U.S. Navy, and most export operators followed suit. The AN/ASQ-228 Advanced Targeting Forward-Looking Infra-Red (ATFLIR) pod has replaced the AN/AAS-38 and the range of air-to-ground ordnance has been expanded. The U.S. Navy modified 61 F/A-18As to the A+ configuration, with AN/APG-73 radar and F/A-18C avionics. Of the A+ conversions, 54 have been upgraded to full F/A-18C capability (as F/A-18A++). The F/A-18C+ configuration includes Link 16 datalink, colour cockpit displays, a moving-map display, AN/ALE-47 infra-red countermeasures, NACES and the Joint Helmet-Mounted Cueing System.

Navy Hornets Today

An F/A-18C aircraft assigned to Strike Fighter Squadron (VFA) 136 'Knighthawks' unloads a flare over the Persian Gulf before heading into Afghanistan for a close air support mission. As of October 2013, the U.S. Navy and Marine Corps included a total of 620 F/A-18A/B/C/D Hornets in operational and reserve service and in test roles. An additional quantity of F/A-18Cs were in storage and were planned for avionics upgrades and return to service as F/A-18C+ beginning in 2016.

F/A-18Cs equip 10 active VFA squadrons and one reserve VFA squadron, as well as one Fleet Readiness Squadron, which conducts training. The U.S. Marine Corps provides two to four of its Marine Fighter Attack Squadrons (VMFA) for U.S. Navy Carrier Air Wings (CVWs), and these are equipped with either F/A-18A++ or F/A-18C variants. The Hornet will continue to serve with U.S. Navy CVWs for years to come, gradually giving way to the F/A-18E/F Super Hornet and eventually the F-35 Lightning II Joint Strike Fighter.

McDonnell Douglas AV-8B Harrier II (1978)

With the AV-8B, the U.S. Marine Corps took Britain's first-generation Harrier vertical/short take-off and landing (V/STOL) design and brought this revolutionary aircraft fully up to date. Later aircraft feature radar for a further improvement in capability, and the Harrier II continues to serve aboard U.S. Navy assault vessels.

As a first-generation V/STOL warplane, the Hawker Siddeley Harrier offered only a limited capability. However, the aircraft attracted the attention of the U.S. Marine Corps, which procured it in 1968 as the AV-8A. After gathering experience with the aircraft, the USMC began to pursue

Cockpit
Compared to earlier Harriers, this offered a much-improved field of vision thanks to a single-piece wraparound bubble canopy.

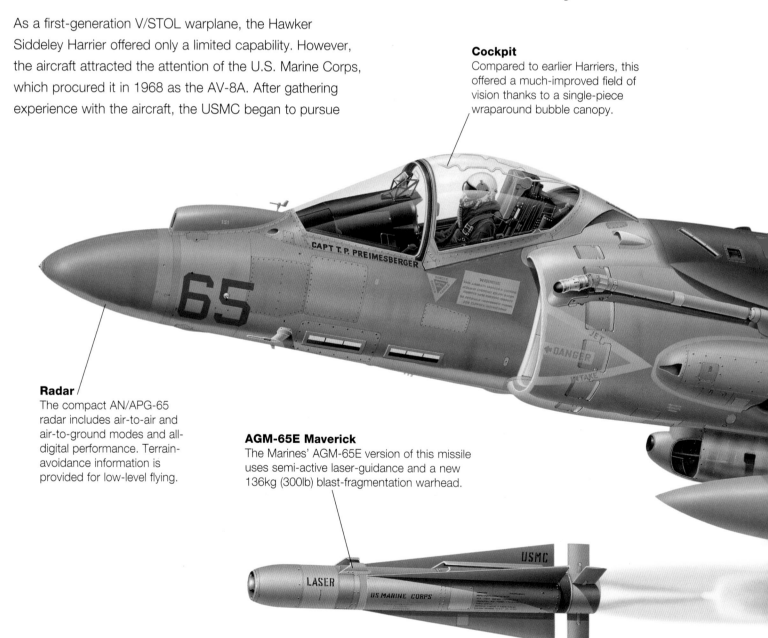

Radar
The compact AN/APG-65 radar includes air-to-air and air-to-ground modes and all-digital performance. Terrain-avoidance information is provided for low-level flying.

AGM-65E Maverick
The Marines' AGM-65E version of this missile uses semi-active laser-guidance and a new 136kg (300lb) blast-fragmentation warhead.

a more advanced development of the basic design, the AV-8B Harrier II. This was a joint project involving McDonnell Douglas (now Boeing) and British Aerospace and aimed to provide the Harrier with improved range and endurance as well as an increased warload.

McDonnell Douglas designed an all-new wing that was both larger (with 14.5 per cent more area and 20 per cent greater span) with a supercritical aerofoil section. Other changes included an airframe that made use of carbon-fibre materials and a new cockpit based around hands on throttle and stick (HOTAS) controls. Various aerodynamic devices were added to improve lift and load-carrying.

A Harrier II+ 'radar bird' of Marine Attack Squadron (VMA) 542, 'Flying Tigers' based at Marine Corps Air Station Cherry Point, North Carolina, in the mid-1990s.

The initial YA-8B service test aircraft, which was a reworked AV-8A, flew in November 1978. Thanks to the new wing, which also possessed a reduced leading edge sweep, the aircraft could now support six hardpoints, and its carbon-fibre structure trimmed weight. Additional weight-saving was provided by more efficient air intakes and carbon-fibre fuselage sections.

Four pre-production AV-8Bs entered USMC testing in November 1981, paving the way for a first production delivery in 1983. The four pre-production aircraft and the first 12 production machines were powered by the F402-RR-404 engine before this was superseded by the 95.42kN (21,450lb) thrust F402-RR-406, equivalent to the Pegasus Mk 105. From the 44th aircraft, a digital engine control unit was fitted. With the 197th aircraft, another new engine was introduced in the form of the F402-RR-408, with an

Refuelling Probe
Normally a standard feature, the bolt-on refuelling probe is retractable and is housed in a streamlined faring when not in use.

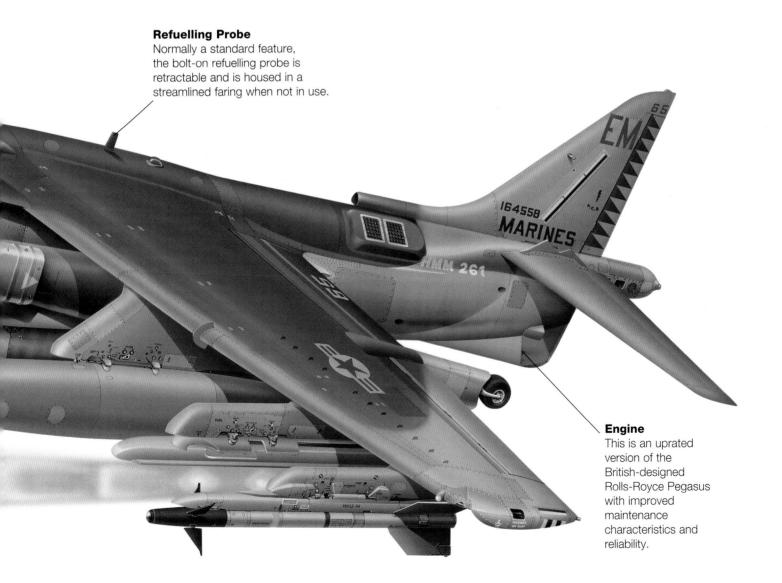

Engine
This is an uprated version of the British-designed Rolls-Royce Pegasus with improved maintenance characteristics and reliability.

McDonnell Douglas AV-8B Harrier II

increase of thrust. In total, production for the USMC extended to 280 aircraft, to which were added six attrition replacements after Operation Desert Storm. The production total included the TAV-8B two-seat training version.

From the 167th airframe, USMC AV-8Bs were delivered to Night Attack standard, which included a forward-looking infra-red (FLIR) sensor, an improved head-up display, a head-down display and a colour moving map. The first Night Attack aircraft was delivered

An AV-8B Night Attack jet of VMA-214 'Black Sheep' as it appeared in 1989. Working up during the 1991 Gulf War, the unit made a first foreign deployment with the AV-8B to Iwakuni, Japan, in October of that year.

Specification (AV-8B)

Type:	Shipborne and land-based V/STOL attack and close support aircraft
Dimensions:	Length: 14.12m (46ft 4in); Wingspan: 9.25m (30ft 4in); Height: 3.55m (11ft 7.75in)
Weight:	14,061kg (31,000lb) maximum short take-off (STO)
Powerplant:	1 x 105.87kN (23,800lb) Rolls-Royce F402-RR-408 vectored-thrust turbofan
Maximum speed:	1065km/h (662mph) at sea level
Range:	1001km (684 miles) on hi-lo-hi attack mission after STO, with 7 x 227kg (500lb) bombs
Service ceiling:	more than 15,240m (50,000ft)
Crew:	1
Armament:	1 x 25mm (0.98in) rotary cannon and up to 6003kg (13,235lb) of disposable stores, after STO

This AV-8B is illustrated carrying a mixed load of two AGM-65E Mavericks, a pair of Mk 20 Rockeye cluster bombs and AIM-9L/M Sidewinders for self defence.

to VMA-214 in September 1989 and the type went on to see operational service during Operation Desert Storm, in the course of which seven aircraft were lost.

When the 205th USMC AV-8B came off the production line it was equipped to Harrier II+ standard, the main feature of which is the addition of an AN/APG-65 radar in a nose radome. First flown in September 1992, the Harrier II+ retains the FLIR sensor above the nose but this is now installed in a broader, squarer housing. The radar allows the Harrier II+ to deploy AIM-120 AMRAAM air-to-air missile, as well as the AGM-84 Harpoon in the anti-shipping role. The USMC planned to receive the last of its 27 aircraft in Harrier II+ configuration, but in the event three of these were diverted to Italy, reducing the total to 24. A first Harrier II+ delivery took place in early 1993 and 73 earlier aircraft were also upgraded to the same standard.

Current Status

USMC AV-8Bs have seen extensive use in Iraq and Afghanistan and the aircraft is now subject to life-extension programmes, addressing the service life of the wing, the vertical tail and some of the subsystems. Life-extension work has focused on the F402-RR-408B powered aircraft, and the TAV-8Bs have also now received the uprated Dash 408B engine.

In a bid to increase the AV-8B's utility in its primary close air support mission, the Litening targeting pod has been integrated and this can be used to pass target coordinates to the aircraft's GPS-guided Joint Direct Attack Munition (JDAM) bombs. A video downlink transmitter allows for real-time streamed video to be sent from the Litening pod to a ground station.

In terms of weapon options, the 227kg (500lb) GBU-38 JDAM has been added to the armoury, while carriage of laser-guided bombs has been boosted through the addition of triple ejector racks. Dual-mode laser/GPS-guided weapons have also been added. In order to fulfil a role detecting improvised explosive devices (IEDs) laid by insurgents in Afghanistan, the AV-8B has also been equipped with the Intrepid Tiger II communications intelligence and jamming pod.

The F-35B Lightning II will start to replace the AV-8B in 2016, and will replace the Harrier II entirely around 2025.

Export Operators

As well as the UK, which received locally built Harrier IIs in a variety of configuration from British Aerospace production, Italy and Spain both purchased the AV-8B from U.S. production. The Spanish Navy acquired the Harrier II to replace the first-generation AV-8S (locally designated VA-1 Matador) aircraft that operated from the carrier *Dédalo*. The 12 EAV-8B (VA.2 Matador) Night Attack aircraft first went to sea operationally aboard the *Dédalo*'s replacement, the *Principe de Asturias*. Most recently, they have served aboard the assault ship *Juan Carlos*. Spain also received one TAV-8B and placed follow-on orders for eight examples of the Harrier II+, and upgraded five earlier jets to this standard. Italy acquired two TAV-8Bs, followed by 16 AV-8B Harrier II+ 'radar birds', which initially served aboard the carrier *Giuseppe Garibaldi*, and more recently aboard the carrier *Cavour*.

Lockheed F-117 Nighthawk (1981)

Lockheed's 'stealth fighter' was developed under conditions of utmost secrecy before being propelled to legendary status on account of its combat role during Operation Desert Storm. The precision attack aircraft fulfilled a niche role with the U.S. Air Force until it was finally retired from service in 2008.

An F-117A operated by the 49th Fighter Wing at Holloman Air Force Base, New Mexico, in 1992. The wing replaced its previous F-15 Eagles with Nighthawks in that year.

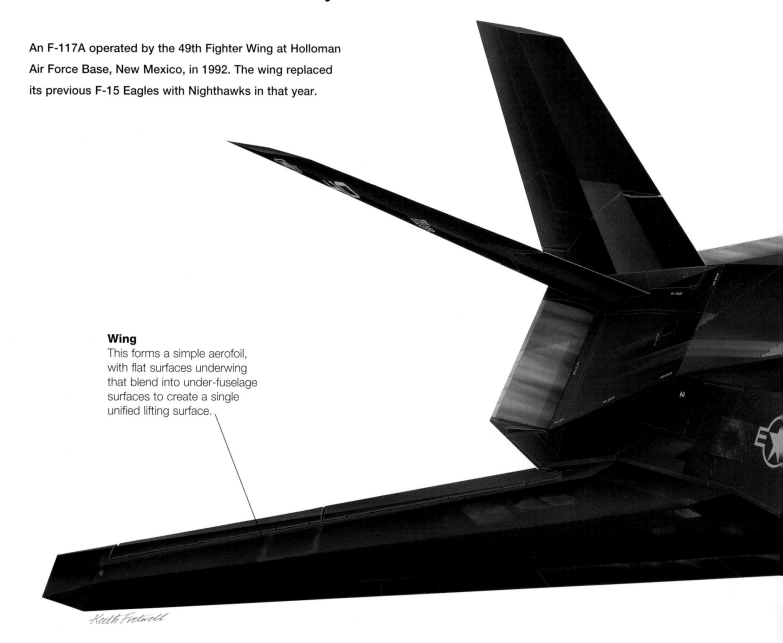

Wing
This forms a simple aerofoil, with flat surfaces underwing that blend into under-fuselage surfaces to create a single unified lifting surface.

Keith Fretwell

The Lockheed F-117A was developed in order to meet a U.S. Air Force request for an aircraft capable of attacking high-value targets without being detected by enemy radar. The design of the aircraft marked a radical departure, making use of advanced materials and technologies to provide radar-evading or 'stealth' qualities. When it first achieved operating capability with the initial unit, the 4450th Tactical Group (renamed as the 37th Tactical Fighter Wing in 1989) in October 1983, the F-117A was the world's first stealth aircraft to enter service.

Initial work on a stealth warplane dated back to 1974 under the guidance of the Defense Advanced Research and Procurement Agency (DARPA), and called for an aircraft that would utilize a combination of radar absorbent materials, radar-reflective internal structure and a 'reflective' external configuration to dramatically reduce its radar cross section (RCS). The primary external feature of the resulting F-117A was its faceted appearance, designed to reflect radar energy in different directions. This design ethos extended to the wing, the aerofoil section of which was formed of two flat

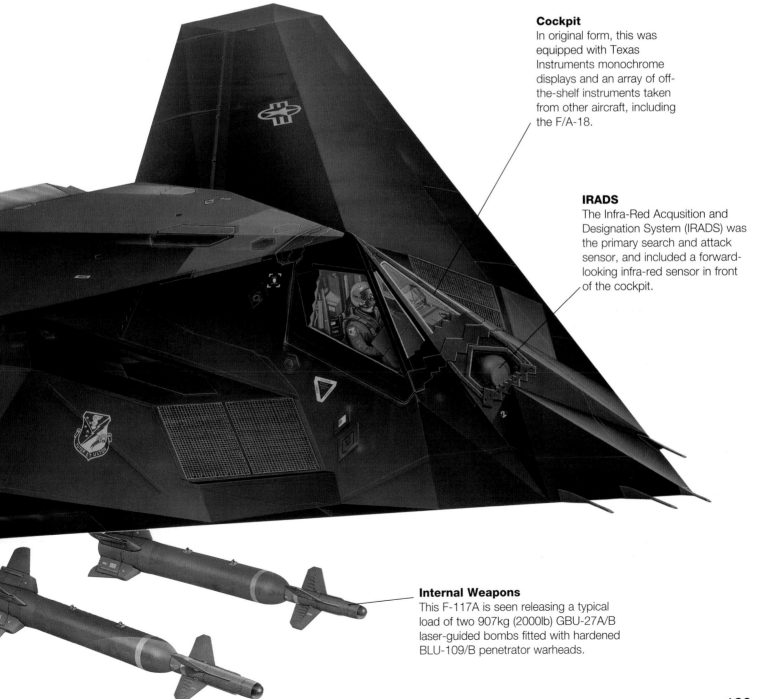

Cockpit
In original form, this was equipped with Texas Instruments monochrome displays and an array of off-the-shelf instruments taken from other aircraft, including the F/A-18.

IRADS
The Infra-Red Acqusition and Designation System (IRADS) was the primary search and attack sensor, and included a forward-looking infra-red sensor in front of the cockpit.

Internal Weapons
This F-117A is seen releasing a typical load of two 907kg (2000lb) GBU-27A/B laser-guided bombs fitted with hardened BLU-109/B penetrator warheads.

Lockheed F-117 Nighthawk

surfaces on the underside and three on the top of the wing. Meanwhile, straight lines were avoided wherever possible, leading to serrated edges on access panels and doors. The pilot's cockpit transparency was coated with gold, again to defeat radar.

In 1976 Lockheed's 'Skunk Works' was contracted to build two sub-scale technology demonstrators to prove the stealth concept. The first example flew in 1977. There followed in 1978 a full-scale development contract, calling for an operational aircraft that would incorporate lessons learned during sub-scale testing. The first of five full-scale development prototypes took to the air in June 1981. Compared to the sub-scale demonstrators, the revised aircraft featured tail surfaces that were canted outward,

Specification

Type:	Stealth attack aircraft
Dimensions:	Length: 20.08m (65ft 11in); Wingspan: 13.20m (43ft 4in); Height: 3.78m (12ft 5in)
Weight:	23,814kg (52,500lb) maximum take-off
Powerplant:	2 x 48.04kN (10,800lb) General Electric F404-GE-F1D2 non-afterburning turbofans
Maximum speed:	about 1040km/h (646mph) at high altitude
Range:	About 862km (535 miles) radius with 1814kg (4000lb) warload
Service ceiling:	11,765m (38,600ft)
Crew:	1
Armament:	Up to 2268kg (5000lb) of disposable stores in two lower-fuselage weapons bays

This F-117A was flown by the commander of the 37th Tactical Fighter Wing. The wing consisted of three units: the 415th TFS, 416 TFS and the 417th Tactical Fighter Training Squadron.

rather than inward. At this time the aircraft was known under the project codename Senior Trend.

Until November 1988, when the F-117A was revealed to the public in the form of a single distorted and grainy photograph, the aircraft had flown in total secrecy and only at night from their base at the Tonopah Test Range, Nevada. The F-117A made an unpublicized combat debut during Operation Just Cause over Panama in December 1989, when two F-117As from the 37th TFW struck a Panamanian Defense Force barracks.

The F-117A was at the forefront of Coalition attack missions during Operation Desert Storm in 1991. During the conflict, the 37th TFW deployed two squadrons, the 415th and the 416th TFS, and 36 aircraft to Khamis Mushait Air Base in Saudi Arabia. F-117A operations began on the first night of the war – 17 January 1991 – when three waves of F-117As were launched, becoming the first Coalition aircraft to cross into Iraqi airspace. In the course of Desert Storm, the F-117As completed 1271 sorties, achieving an 80 per cent mission success rate, and suffered no losses or battle damage. Although the Nighthawks flew only two per cent of the total combat sorties against Iraq in 1991, they were credited with striking 40 per cent of the most highly defended, strategic targets.

Later Career

In 1992 the Nighthawk fleet moved to Holloman Air Force Base in New Mexico, and the unit was renamed as the 49th Fighter Wing. The wing made regular deployments to support operations in the Middle East

A straight line running from nose to wingtip (swept at 67.5 degrees) and similar sweepback on the tailfins served to dissipate radar energy away from its source.

and in the Balkans. During Operation Allied Force over Yugoslavia and Kosovo in 1999, 24 F-117As deployed to Aviano in Italy flew more than 300 sorties. However, the deployment saw the first combat loss of an F-117A, which was shot down by a Serbian surface-to-air missile.

As they had in 1991, a pair of F-117As flew the first missions of Operation Iraqi Freedom in March 2003. During the war, 12 F-117As flew more than 100 sorties and achieved an excellent mission capable rate of 89.3 per cent. By the end of its career, the F-117A's weapons options had been expanded beyond the original options of 907kg (2000lb) GBU-10 Paveway II and GBU-27 Paveway III laser-guided bombs (LGBs) to include the Enhanced (dual-mode) GBU-27, the Joint Direct Attack Munition, 227kg (500lb) GBU-12 LGB and the Wind Corrected Munitions Dispenser (WCMD).

A total of 59 F-117As were built between 1981 and 1990, six of which were lost in non-combat accidents. Once expected to serve until at least 2018, the USAF retired the F-117 fleet in April 2008 after 27 years of service, in order free up funds for modernization.

Stealth Coating

Almost every surface of the F-117 was covered with radar absorbent material (RAM). This provided a critical defence against radar detection, but proved laborious and costly to maintain. After each mission, maintenance specialists had to closely examine the aircraft's special coating to identify if any repairs were needed. If required, the special coatings were reapplied, allowed to cure and then re-inspected. Initially applied as individual sheets, the RAM coating was later available in the form of a spray. Where apertures were present in the airframe, and the RAM was interrupted, the area was covered with a fine-mesh grille, smaller than the wavelengths of most detection radars.

Boeing F-15E Strike Eagle (1986)

While the McDonnell Douglas F-15 Eagle established itself as the West's premier air superiority fighter, with a peerless victory to loss ratio of 104:0, further development led to the F-15E Strike Eagle, an all-weather ground-attack aircraft that retains all the air combat capabilities of the original Eagle.

Once a McDonnell Douglas product, the F-15E Strike Eagle and its derivatives now come under the responsibility of Boeing, which absorbed the previous company. The first flight of the F-15A was in July 1972. In November 1974, the first Eagle was delivered to the 58th Tactical Fighter Training Wing at Luke Air Force Base, Arizona. In January 1976, the first F-15 destined for a combat squadron was delivered to the 1st Tactical Fighter Wing (TFW) at Langley AFB, Virginia.

An F-15E in the markings of the 48th Fighter Wing, based at RAF Lakenheath, England, in 1994. At the time, the unit was active in operations over Bosnia and in enforcing the Iraqi 'no-fly-zone'.

AIM-120 AMRAAM
Carried on the shoulder launch rails, the AMRAAM confers a powerful air-to-air capability, this being a 'fire and forget' missile with active guidance.

Radar
The F-15E was originally fielded with the AN/APG-70 radar, offering a high-resolution synethic aperture mapping mode. The latest USAF upgrade adds the AN/APG-82(V)1 active electronically scanned array (AESA) radar.

Paveway LGB
An important weapon for the F-15E, the Paveway laser-guided bomb series includes weapons of 227kg (500lb), 907kg (2000lb) and 2132kg (4700lb). This is a 227kg GBU-12 weapon.

An improved single-seat F-15C and two-seat F-15D equivalent entered the Air Force inventory in 1979 and were first delivered to Kadena Air Base, Japan. These models were equipped with production Eagle package improvements, including additional internal fuel, provision for carriage of conformal fuel tanks and an increased maximum take-off weight.

When first drafted, the F-15 Eagle was intended to be capable of conducting air superiority or air-to-ground missions with equal efficacy, but the strike role was soon dropped from the original Eagle, and the successive F-15A to D variants that entered service with the USAF have been used exclusively for air-to-air duties. In 1982 McDonnell Douglas began trials of an air-to-ground Eagle, when it modified the second two-seat TF-15A trainer as a privately funded 'Strike Eagle'. At the time, the USAF was looking for a successor to its F-111 and conducted an evaluation of the Strike Eagle against the rival General Dynamics F-16XL, a cranked-wing development of the F-16 Fighting Falcon. The

Wings
The wings are based around an extremely strong torque box of light alloy and titanium, to which are attached wingtip sections, flaps and ailerons of aluminium honeycomb.

Powerplant
The Pratt & Whitney F100 turbofan is a two-stage axial turbofan that offers a very useful thrust-to-weight ratio. The smokeless combustor is provided with air from a 10-stage compressor.

Boeing F-15E Strike Eagle

Strike Eagle was judged the winner and was ordered into production. The first F-15E production machine undertook its maiden flight in December 1986.

The F-15E Strike Eagle began the 'second generation' of F-15s. Equipped with new avionics and with multi-role capabilities, these aircraft remain in production for export operators. In the front cockpit, the USAF's F-15E introduced redesigned controls, a wide-field-of-view head-up display and three CRT displays providing the pilot with navigation, weapons delivery and systems operations data. The rear seat of the aircraft is occupied by the weapons system officer who is provided with four

An F-15E as flown by the commander of the 48th Fighter Wing at RAF Lakenheath. The aircraft is armed for a close support mission, with 14 SUU-30H/B cluster bombs, plus AIM-9s.

multi-purpose terminals for radar, weapons selection and monitoring of enemy tracking systems. Primary sensors comprise the AN/APG-70 radar and the LANTIRN nav/attack system, the latter comprising two separate pods with terrain-following radar linked to the flight control system and a targeting capability for the delivery of laser-guided weapons. The F-15E has subsequently added the more modern Sniper and Litening targeting pods.

The F-15E's original Pratt & Whitney F100-PW-220 turbofans with a digital electronic engine control system were soon replaced by more powerful F100-PW-229s, which were included in production from 1991 and retrofitted in earlier aircraft. The production run for the USAF amounted to 236 aircraft.

The Strike Eagle entered service with the 40th Tactical Training Wing at Luke AFB in 1988, and initial operational deliveries then followed to the 4th TFW at Seymour Johnson AFB, North Carolina. The F-15E made its combat debut during Operation Desert Storm, when its primary mission was to seek and destroy Iraqi 'Scud' mobile ballistic missiles. Since then, the F-15E has been at the forefront of every major U.S. military air campaign.

The first export customer for the Strike Eagle was Saudi Arabia, which initially purchased 72 F-15S aircraft in 1995. These retain the F-15E airframe but lack the conformal fuel tanks and have some items of downgraded equipment. Israel, meanwhile, acquired

Specification (F-15E)

Type:	All-weather strike/attack aircraft
Dimensions:	Length: 19.43m (63ft 9in); Wingspan: 13.05m (42ft 9.75in); Height: 5.63m (18ft 5.5in)
Weight:	36,741kg (81,000lb) maximum take-off
Powerplant:	2 x 106kN (23,830lb) Pratt & Whitney F100-PW-220 afterburning turbofans
Maximum speed:	More than 2655km/h (1650mph) at high altitude
Range:	1271km (790 miles) radius of action, typical mission with maximum warload
Service ceiling:	18,290m (60,000ft)
Crew:	2
Armament:	1 x 20mm (0.79in) rotary cannon plus up to 11,000kg (24,250lb) of external ordnance

The F-15E carries conformal fuel tanks on the sides of the fuselage. Each holds 2737 litres (723 U.S. gal) of fuel, and is fitted with three stub pylons for attaching weapons.

25 F-15I Ra'am (Thunder) versions featuring equipment of local origin.

Boeing has also delivered 40 F-15K Slam Eagles to the Republic of Korea. Developed to meet Korea's FX requirement, the F-15K has General Electric F110-GE-129A engines, AN/APG-63(V)1 active electronically scanned array (AESA) radar, Joint Helmet-Mounted Cueing System (JHMCS), an updated cockpit with seven multi-function displays, the Lockheed Martin Tiger Eyes sensor suite with infra-red search and track (IRST) system and the AGM-84 SLAM-ER missile. Singapore purchased at least 24 F-15SG jets that are broadly similar to the F-15K, but with APG-63(V)3 radar.

Most recently, Saudi Arabia placed an order for a new version, the F-15SA, the most advanced Eagle to date, which features the AN/APG-63(V)3 radar, Joint Helmet-Mounted Cueing System, IRST, Sniper, a BAE Systems defensive suite and new fly-by-wire controls. The Saudis are acquiring 84 new F-15SAs and upgrading up to 70 existing F-15S aircraft to the same standard.

Eagles of Enduring Freedom

An F-15E from the USAF's 4th Fighter Wing flies over Afghanistan in April 2006. The USAF rotates detachments of F-15Es to Southwest Asia from where they conduct close air support missions for troops on the ground engaged in rooting out insurgent sanctuaries and support networks. Over Afghanistan, F-15Es typically carry a mix of 227kg (500lb) GBU-12 laser-guided bombs and 907kg (2000lb) GBU-31 GPS-guided bombs, plus up to 500 rounds of ammunition for their M61A1 20mm (0.79in) cannon. For surveillance and targeting, the Strike Eagles are fitted with the Lockheed Martin Sniper XR targeting pod. Flying from Bagram in Afghanistan, F-15Es combine with F-16s to provide close air support coverage for all of eastern Afghanistan, two squadrons of aircraft putting most of their aircraft into the air each day, and also flying frequent 'show of force' missions involving no ordnance.

Dassault Rafale (1986)

Described by the manufacturer as an 'omni-role' fighter, the Rafale has excelled in action with both the French Air Force and Navy and its undoubted capabilities across the combat spectrum have attracted interest on the export market.

The Rafale traces its origins back to the Avion de Combat Experimentale (ACX) programme that was designed by Dassault in the early 1980s before France's withdrawal from the multinational European Fighter Aircraft (EFA) project in 1985. One of the reasons behind the French leaving the programme was the requirement for a smaller and lighter combat aircraft that could operate from aircraft carriers.

The ACX originally took the form of a technology demonstrator and was first flown in July 1986. The ACX, renamed Rafale A, established the primary design features of the production Rafale, including the basic aerodynamic

Rafale B01 was the two-seat prototype, which completed its initial flight in April 1993. B01 was the first Rafale to fly with the RBE2 multi-mode radar, housed within a recontoured nose.

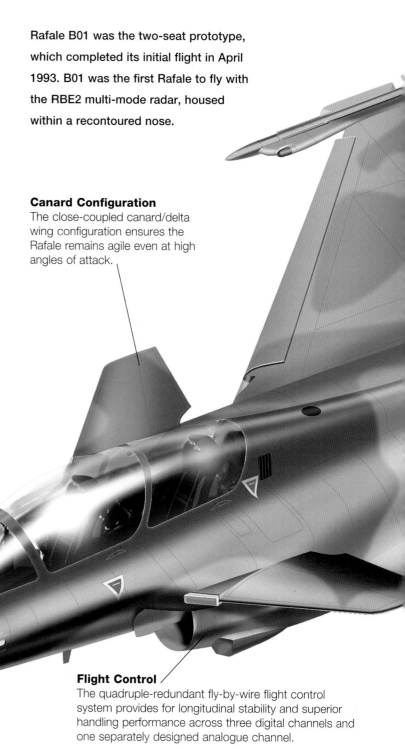

Canard Configuration
The close-coupled canard/delta wing configuration ensures the Rafale remains agile even at high angles of attack.

Refuelling Probe
The refuelling probe is fixed in order to avoid any deployment or retraction problem and is a permanent fixture.

Flight Control
The quadruple-redundant fly-by-wire flight control system provides for longitudinal stability and superior handling performance across three digital channels and one separately designed analogue channel.

configuration, fly-by-wire control system and structure that made extensive use of composites. In its initial form, the Rafale A demonstrator was powered by a pair of 68.6kN (15,422lb) thrust General Electric F404-GE-400 turbofans. After initial flight tests, including carrier touch-and-gos, had been completed with this powerplant, an example of the planned SNECMA M88-2 turbofan was substituted for one of the F404s.

Experience with the Rafale A led to the Rafale C, initially known as the Avion de Combat Tactique (ACT), which first flew in May 1991. A single prototype was completed for the French Air Force's single-seat Rafale C model and it was followed by the first example of the Air Force's two-

Engines
The M88-2 uses advanced technologies including integrally bladed compressor disks ('blisks'), and a low-pollution combustor with smoke-free emissions.

Stealth Treatment
Airframe radar cross section is minimized by using appropriate materials and mould line, including serrated edges to the trailing edge of the wings and canards.

Dassault Rafale

An early Rafale M of the French Navy. The Rafale is the only non-U.S. fighter cleared to operate from the decks of U.S. carriers, using their catapults and their arresting gear.

seat Rafale B, flown in April 1993. In its basic form, the production Rafale includes the RBE2 multi-mode radar that incorporates a passive electronically scanned array (PESA), and a Spectra defensive aids package.

The French Navy's requirement for an Avion de Combat Marine (ACM) led to development of a carrier-based Rafale M that was first flown in December 1991. Compared to the land-based aircraft this version is

Specification (Rafale C)

Type:	Multi-role fighter
Dimensions:	Length: 15.27m (50ft 1.25in); Wingspan: 10.80m (35ft 5.25in); Height: 5.34m (17ft 6.25in)
Weight:	24,500kg (54,012lb) maximum take-off
Powerplant:	2 x 75kN (16,861lb) SNECMA M88-2 afterburning turbofans
Maximum speed:	1913km/h (1189mph) at 11,000m (36,090ft)
Range:	1055km (655 miles), low-level with warload and drop tanks
Service ceiling:	16,765m (60,000ft)
Crew:	1
Armament:	1 x 30mm (1.18in) cannon and up to 9500kg (20,944lb) of disposable stores carried on 14 under-fuselage, underwing and wingtip stations

somewhat heavier, due to its reinforced undercarriage, and provision for catapult take-off and arrested landing.

Improving Standards

The Rafale has been delivered equipped to progressively more advanced Standards. The initial production aircraft, delivered from December 1998, were of the F1 Standard. This was optimized for the air-to-air role and became operational in 2004 with French Navy Rafales that launched from the carrier *Charles de Gaulle* during Operation Enduring Freedom. First of the 'omni-role' Standards, the F2 entered service with the French Air Force and Navy in 2006, the aircraft now able to conduct both air-to-air and air-to-ground missions.

The definitive F3 Standard has the capability to use a further improved RBE2 radar, adding an active electronically scanned array (AESA). The F3 is also equipped with Damoclès laser designation pod and the Pod Reco NG (Pod de Reconnaissance de Nouvelle Génération, or new-generation recce pod). The latter store is capable of providing extremely sharp images at stand-off distances, and all recorded data can be transmitted back to base in real time. F3 adds an anti-ship capability with the AM.39 Exocet missile, buddy-buddy refuelling and a nuclear capability with the ASMP-A cruise missile. A conventional stand-off attack capability is enabled by the SCALP EG cruise missile. This latest Standard was qualified by the French Defence Ministry in 2008.

The French Defence Ministry has ordered 180 Rafales, for a total of 132 aircraft for the French Air Force (63 Rafale Bs and 69 Rafale Cs) and 48 Rafale Ms for the French Navy. India has a requirement for at least 126 Rafales having selected the fighter as winner of its competition to find a new Multi-Role Medium Combat Aircraft (MMRCA).

The French Navy's Flottille 12F converted to the Rafale at Landivisiau, officially re-forming on the Standard F1 in June 2001. The first operational French Air Force Rafale unit was Escadron de Chasse (EC) 1/7 'Provence', stationed at Saint-Dizier air base in northwest France since 2006.

The Rafale went into combat over Afghanistan in 2006, and in 2011 French Air Force and French Navy aircraft engaged in coalition operations over Libya, conducting air superiority, precision strike, deep strike and intelligence, surveillance, target acquisition and reconnaissance (ISTAR) and strike coordination and reconnaissance (SCAR). More recently, French Air Force Rafales have taken a leading role in Mali, helping destroy enemy infrastructure and support friendly troops in contact. The Rafale has also been active against Islamic insurgents in Iraq, flying from its forward base at Al Dhafra in the United Arab Emirates.

AASM Hammer

The AASM (Armement Air-Sol Modulaire, Air-to-Surface modular weapon) is a low-cost, all-weather 'fire-and-forget' weapon. Intended to attack targets at long ranges, the AASM is also known as 'Hammer'. The AASM is powered and can engage targets at high off-boresight angles. Using the AASM, the Rafale does not have to overfly a target to carry out its attack, and can remain safely out of reach. Depending on the target, the aircrew will choose vertical or horizontal impact to cause maximum damage. For long-range engagements, the AASM is equipped with a bolt-on tail unit/range-extension kit that combines a solid rocket motor with flip-out wings. Range exceeds 50km (31 miles) for a high-altitude release, reduced to 15km (9 miles) with a low-level firing. Up to six AASMs can be carried by a single Rafale (underwing, as seen here), and up to six widely separated targets can be destroyed in a single pass.

Northrop B-2 Spirit (1989)

The bat-winged B-2 stealth bomber is the most expensive warplane ever built, with a price tag of around US$900 million per aircraft. Tricky to maintain, the small fleet of Spirits remains one of the most potent weapons in the U.S. arsenal.

In November 1988, the B-2 was first revealed to the public when it was rolled out of its hangar at Air Force Plant 42 at Palmdale, California. The stealth bomber subsequently made its first flight in July 1989.

Prime contractor for the Advanced Technology Bomber (ATB) programme that yielded the B-2 was Northrop (now Northrop Grumman), responsible for overall system design and integration. Reflecting the complex and ground-breaking nature of the programme, other contractors involved included Boeing Military Airplanes, Hughes Radar Systems, General Electric Aircraft Engine and Vought Aircraft. The original aim of the Cold War-era ATB was to field a low-observable bomber capable

of attacking Soviet strategic targets, including mobile intercontinental ballistic missiles. A total of six prototypes were funded. Originally the USAF had a requirement for as many as 132 aircraft, but funding restrictions saw this total trimmed back to just 21 aircraft.

The USAF's 'silver bullet' fleet of operational B-2s is today concentrated at Whiteman Air Force Base, Missouri. The first aircraft, named Spirit of Missouri, was delivered to the base in December 1993. The final Spirit was handed over at Whiteman in July 2000, this being the first prototype (AV-1/Air Vehicle One) appropriately upgraded. The aircraft have been configured in successively more capable Blocks, beginning with

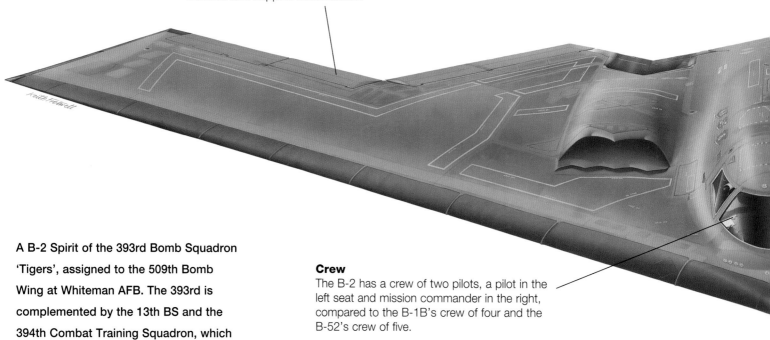

RAM coating
As well as its radar-defeating shape, the B-2 uses radar-absorbing coatings, which require special maintenance and means the aircraft requires a considerable support infrastructure.

A B-2 Spirit of the 393rd Bomb Squadron 'Tigers', assigned to the 509th Bomb Wing at Whiteman AFB. The 393rd is complemented by the 13th BS and the 394th Combat Training Squadron, which also operates Northrop T-38 Talon trainers.

Crew
The B-2 has a crew of two pilots, a pilot in the left seat and mission commander in the right, compared to the B-1B's crew of four and the B-52's crew of five.

Blocks 10 and 20 and culminating in Block 30, which brings fully functional weapons and navigation capabilities.

The B-2's extraordinary appearance is a result of the combined demands of stealth, long range and considerable weapons load. Northrop designers selected the 'flying wing' planform, which combined low-observable characteristics with excellent aerodynamic efficiency and large payload. The use of such a planform makes control and stability a challenge, for which the B-2 is equipped with a quadruplex-redundant digital fly-by-wire system.

The B-2's stealth is derived from a combination of reduced infra-red, acoustic, electromagnetic, visual and radar signatures. Many aspects of the Spirit's low-observability process remain classified. Among those that have been publicized are the bomber's extensive use of composite materials and special coatings. These coatings of radar absorbent material contribute greatly to the maintenance costs and man-hours required to keep the fleet serviceable. Construction of the Spirit makes use of a generous proportion of composites as part of a

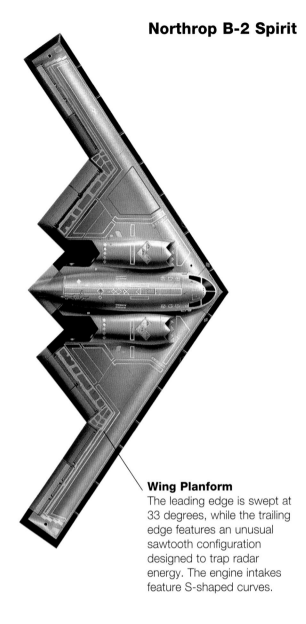

Wing Planform
The leading edge is swept at 33 degrees, while the trailing edge features an unusual sawtooth configuration designed to trap radar energy. The engine intakes feature S-shaped curves.

Engines
The four General Electric F118-GE-110 turbofans exhaust through V-shaped outlets set back and above the trailing edges to shield these from ground-based sensors.

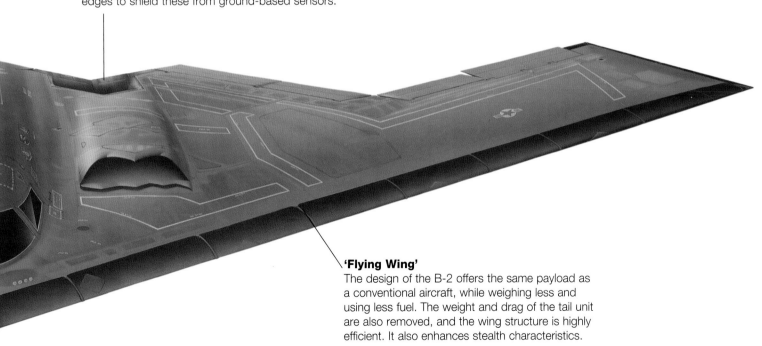

'Flying Wing'
The design of the B-2 offers the same payload as a conventional aircraft, while weighing less and using less fuel. The weight and drag of the tail unit are also removed, and the wing structure is highly efficient. It also enhances stealth characteristics.

Northrop B-2 Spirit

A Spirit breaks away from a tanker after a refueling mission over the Pacific Ocean. Among the roles performed by the B-2 is as part of the USAF's continuous bomber presence, maintained as a deterrent force in the Asia-Pacific region.

Specification

Type:	Long-range strategic bomber
Dimensions:	Length: 21.03m (69ft 0in); Wingspan: 52.43m (172ft 0in); Height: 5.18m (17ft 0in)
Weight:	152,635kg (336,500lb) typical take-off
Powerplant:	4 x 84.52kN (19,000lb) General Electric F118-GE-100 turbofans
Maximum speed:	About 764km/h (475mph) at high altitude
Range:	8334km (5178 miles), hi-lo-hi mission with typical weapons load
Service ceiling:	15,240m (50,000ft)
Crew:	2
Armament:	Up to 18,144kg (40,000lb) of disposable stores carried in two weapons bays in underside of centre section

radar-absorbent honeycomb structure. The engines are designed not to leave contrails, and various other infra-red reduction measures are incorporated. Once in the vicinity of the target, the crew will only use the AN/APQ-181 attack radar momentarily to help prevent detection. Other avionics include a comprehensive and electronic warfare suite.

Alongside the B-1B and B-52H, the B-2 is part of the USAF's manned bomber triad and is capable of delivering both conventional and nuclear munitions. Thanks to its stealth features, the B-2 is able to bring massive firepower to bear anywhere in the world through previously impenetrable defences. Typical wartime missions therefore include attacks on high-value, heavily defended targets. The Spirit has an unrefuelled range of around 9600km (5965 miles).

Spirit at War

The B-2 first saw combat during Operation Allied Force over the former Yugoslavia, where it was responsible for destroying 33 per cent of all Serbian targets in the first eight weeks. These first missions were flown non-stop to Kosovo from the Spirit's home base at Whiteman AFB.

Seen here equipped with a spin recovery parachute for early flight tests, B-2 serial 82-1066 (AV-1) was the first Spirit, delivered to the USAF as the Spirit of America in July 1989.

In support of Operation Enduring Freedom, the B-2 flew some of its longest missions to date from Whiteman to Afghanistan and back. During Operation Iraqi Freedom, B-2s flew 22 sorties from a forward operating location as well as 27 sorties from Whiteman AFB and delivered more than 1.5 million pounds of munitions.

Three B-2s flew missions on the first night of Operation Odyssey Dawn, attacking high-priority Libyan targets in March 2011.

The B-2 attained full operational capability in December 2003. In 2009, the U.S. Air Force's newest command, Air Force Global Strike Command, assumed responsibility for the B-2 from Air Combat Command. The operating unit of the B-2 fleet is the 509th Bomb Wing, which also supplies a single test B-2 to the 412th Test Wing at Edwards AFB, California.

Weapons Options

A B-2 drops 32 inert Joint Direct Attack Munitions (JDAMs) over the Utah Testing and Training Range. In addition to B61 and B83 free-fall nuclear bombs, the Spirit can carry basic and penetrator versions of the 907kg (2000lb) GBU-31 JDAM, and up to 80 of the 227kg (500lb) GBU-38 JDAMs. The Spirit can also accommodate 16 907kg (2000lb) Mk84 general-purpose bombs, the 2041kg (4500lb) GBU-28 laser-guided bomb, the AGM-154 Joint Stand-Off Weapon, 16 Joint Air-to-Surface Stand-off Missiles (JASSMs), and most recently the enormous 13,154kg (29,000lb) GBU-57 Massive Ordnance Penetrator (MOP). The B-2 no longer carries cluster munitions of the 2268kg (5000lb) GBU-37 GPS-Aided Munition (GAM). If required, the B-2 can also carry Mk62 Quickstrike mines.

Lockheed Martin F-22 Raptor (1990)

Widely regarded as the most capable air superiority fighter in service anywhere in the world, the F-22A is capable of both air-to-air and air-to-ground missions, and has been designed to combine stealth, performance, agility and integrated avionics in a single airframe.

The Raptor is described by its operator as representing 'an exponential leap in warfighting capabilities'. The F-22A began life as the Advanced Tactical Fighter (ATF) programme which entered the demonstration and validation phase in 1986. The U.S. Air Force lined up seven companies as contenders for the ATF program,

with Lockheed and Northrop as the primary airframe contractors. Lockheed teamed up with Boeing and General Dynamics, while Northrop's effort was joined by principle contractor McDonnell Douglas. The resulting YF-22 and YF-23 prototypes were built for a fly-off competition, which also involved rival engines from

The U.S. Air Force is the sole operator of the F-22A. Although interest was expressed by Japan, the U.S. Congress never authorized the Raptor for export. After more than eight pre-production models, all 187 aircraft were delivered to the USAF.

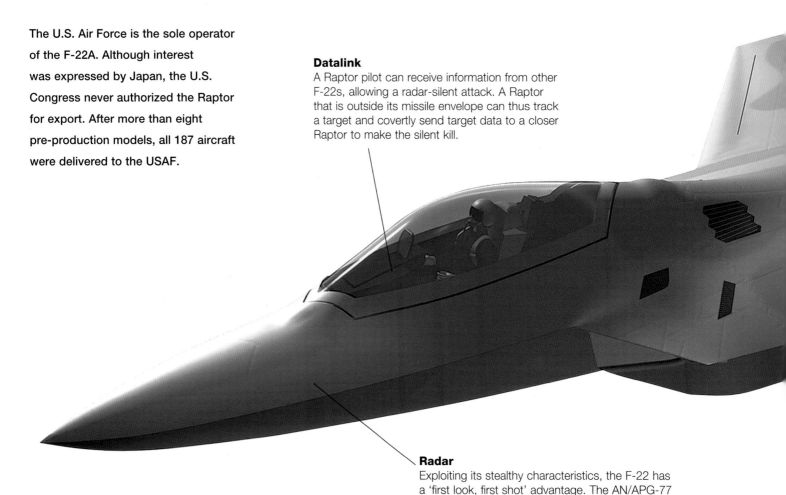

Datalink
A Raptor pilot can receive information from other F-22s, allowing a radar-silent attack. A Raptor that is outside its missile envelope can thus track a target and covertly send target data to a closer Raptor to make the silent kill.

Radar
Exploiting its stealthy characteristics, the F-22 has a 'first look, first shot' advantage. The AN/APG-77 active electronically scanned array (AESA) radar can track targets before going electronically silent.

Pratt & Whitney and General Electric (the YF119 and YF120, respectively). The YF-22 made its first flight in September 1990.

The USAF selected the YF-22 and YF119 as the most promising and launched the engineering and manufacturing development (EMD) phase in 1991. Development contracts were issued to Lockheed/Boeing (airframe) and Pratt & Whitney (engines). EMD included extensive tests of systems and subsystems as well as flight testing with nine aircraft at Edwards Air Force Base, California. A first EMD flight was recorded 1997.

In 2001 the programme received approval to enter low-rate initial production. There followed initial operational and test evaluation by the Air Force Operational Test and Evaluation Centre, which was successfully concluded in 2004. Approval for full-rate production was granted in 2005.

After briefly receiving the F/A-22 designation in recognition of its attack capabilities, the Raptor was renamed as the F-22A in December 2005; at the same time the aircraft achieved initial operational capability with the USAF's 27th Fighter Squadron. At one time, the USAF

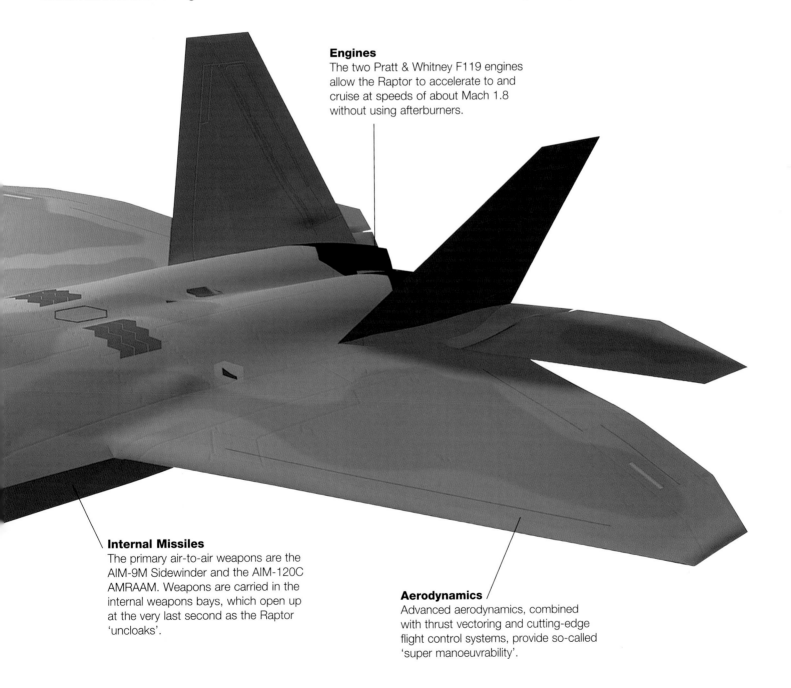

Engines
The two Pratt & Whitney F119 engines allow the Raptor to accelerate to and cruise at speeds of about Mach 1.8 without using afterburners.

Internal Missiles
The primary air-to-air weapons are the AIM-9M Sidewinder and the AIM-120C AMRAAM. Weapons are carried in the internal weapons bays, which open up at the very last second as the Raptor 'uncloaks'.

Aerodynamics
Advanced aerodynamics, combined with thrust vectoring and cutting-edge flight control systems, provide so-called 'super manoeuvrability'.

planned to procure a minimum of 750 ATFs, but the end of the Cold War saw this dramatically scaled back, and finally just 187 aircraft were acquired at a unit cost of $143 million.

The Raptor's prowess in the air-to-air arena is ensured through a combination of sensor capability, integrated avionics, situational awareness and weaponry. Combined with its stealth characteristics and performance, the sensor suite is intended to permit the F-22 pilot to track, identify, engage and kill air-to-air threats before being detected. Primary sensors are the AN/APG-77 active electronically scanned array (AESA) radar and AN/ALR-94 passive receiver system. A high degree of situational awareness is ensured through advanced cockpit design

An F-22A wearing the FF ('First Fighter') tail code of the USAF's 1st Fighter Wing, at Langley Air Force Base, Virginia.

and sensor fusion. In typical air-to-air configuration the Raptor is armed with six AIM-120C AMRAAMs and two AIM-9M Sidewinder missiles.

To ensure its own protection while in flight, the F-22A also relies on low-observable 'stealth' technologies. The aircraft can also call upon its sparkling performance

Specification

Type:	Multi-role air dominance fighter
Dimensions:	Length: 18.9m (62ft 1in); Wingspan: 13.6m (44ft 6in); Height: 5.1m (16ft 8in)
Weight:	38,000kg (83,500lb) maximum take-off
Powerplant:	2 x 155.69kN (35,000lb) Pratt & Whitney F119-PW-100 afterburning turbofans
Maximum speed:	Around 2410km/h (1500mph) at altitude (estimated)
Range:	More than 2977km (1850 miles), ferry with 2 x external wing fuel tanks
Service ceiling:	15,240m (50,000ft)
Crew:	1
Armament:	1 x 20mm (0.79in) rotary cannon, plus 2 x AIM-9 AAMs and 6 x AIM-120 AAMs, or (ground attack) 2 x GBU-32 JDAMs and 2 x AIM-120s

The Raptor's agility allows it to make very tight turns, and exploit post-stall manoeuvring capabilities, flying at sustained angles of attack of more than 60 degrees while retaining some roll control.

to evade air-to-air and surface-to-air threats. Power is provided by a pair of Pratt & Whitney F119-PW-100 turbofan engines, which produce more thrust than any other current fighter engine, the F-22A is able to cruise at supersonic airspeeds without using afterburner – a characteristic known as supercruise. Supercruise also offers the advantage in conserving fuel, providing an increase in endurance and range. The engines are equipped with thrust vectoring, combined with advanced aerodynamics and flight controls, and a high thrust-to-weight ratio to provide excellent agility.

Although it was originally planned as an air dominance fighter, the F-22 has latterly emerged as a powerful attack aircraft. In the air-to-ground configuration the aircraft can carry two 907kg (1000lb) GBU-32 Joint Direct Attack Munitions internally. Work is underway to improve the air-to-ground potential of the Raptor, adding radar modifications and the capability to carry eight Small Diameter Bombs. Whether carrying JDAMs or SDBs, the Raptor can also carry two AIM-120s and two AIM-9s for self defence. In this role the F-22A made its combat debut, striking targets in Syria in September 2014.

Operators

An F-22A of 27th Fighter Squadron (FS), 1st Fighter Wing (FW), the USAF's first Raptor unit. Air Combat Command includes the 1st FW at Langley, Virginia, with the 27th and 94th FS, and the 49th FW at Holloman, New Mexico, with the 7th and 8th FS, the 53rd Wing's 422nd Test and Evaluation Squadron at Eglin, Florida, the 57th Wing's 433rd Weapons Squadron at Nellis, Nevada, and the 325th FW's 43rd FS at Tyndall, Florida. Pacific Air Forces fly the F-22A with the 3rd Wing at Elmendorf-Richardson, Alaska, comprising the 90th and 525th FS. Raptors are also operated by Air National Guard wings at Langley and Hickam, and by two Air Force Reserve Command fighter groups at Holloman. Finally, Air Force Materiel Command includes the 412th Test Wing's 411th Flight Test Squadron at at Edwards, California.

 # Eurofighter Typhoon (1994)

A European collaborative project, like the Panavia Tornado that preceded it, the Eurofighter Typhoon aimed to provide four of the continent's air forces with a highly capable air defence fighter that would be superior in all respects to the latest generation of Soviet warplanes then coming on line.

The Eurofighter consortium was established in June 1986, and involved the same three countries – Germany, Italy and the UK – that had developed and built the Tornado. These three were later joined by Spain and although it had been involved in earlier talks regarding a European Fighter Aircraft (EFA), France elected to pursue its own fighter programme.

Early work on the EFA project defined the basic concepts for the future Eurofighter Typhoon, including

A 30+16 is seen during its service with the German Air Force. This airframe was one of nine that were updated to Block 5 standard and transferred from the *Luftwaffe* to the Austrian Air Force, where they complemented six new-build aircraft.

Cockpit
Pilot workload is reduced through the use of features such as direct voice input (DVI) and hands on throttle and stick (HOTAS) control functions and allows single-pilot operations even in the most demanding missions.

Radar
The Captor-M mechanically scanned radar's wide field of regard offers significant benefits in both air-to-air and air-to-surface engagements, offering considerable power and aperture for enhanced angular coverage.

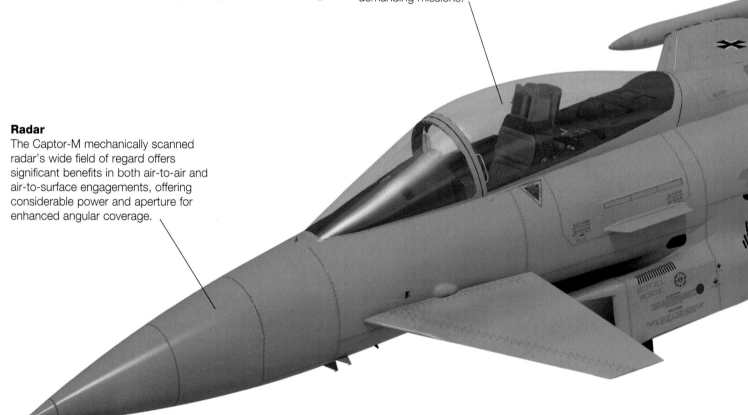

an unstable aerodynamic configuration with canard foreplanes, active digital fly-by-wire controls, extensive use of carbon-fibre composites and other advanced materials, a hands on throttle and stick (HOTAS) cockpit, advanced avionics, multi-function cockpit displays and direct voice command input. Many of these technologies had been tested using a full-scale demonstrator, the

British Aerospace (BAe) EAP (Experimental Aircraft Programme).

Subsequently renamed the Eurofighter 2000, and later still renamed Eurofighter Typhoon, the EFA programme yielded a total of seven development prototypes, of which the first made a maiden flight in March 1994. Of these aircraft, DA.1 and DA.5 were built in Germany, DA.2 and

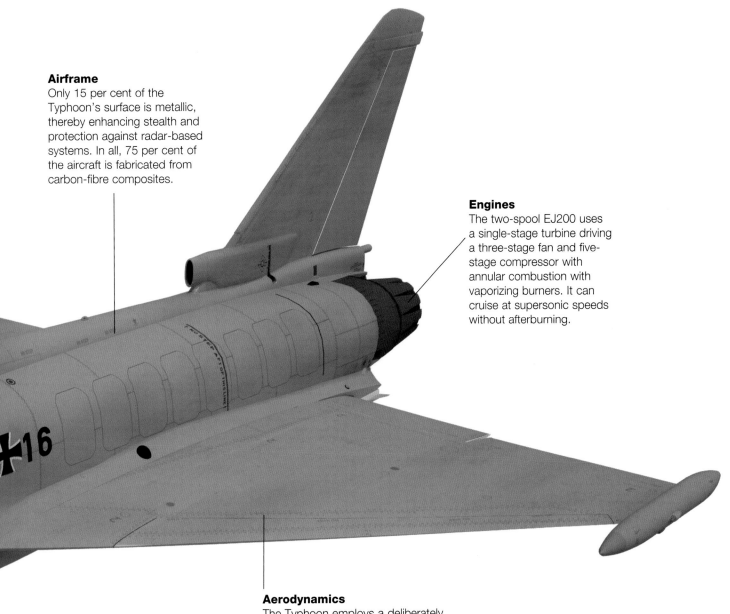

Airframe
Only 15 per cent of the Typhoon's surface is metallic, thereby enhancing stealth and protection against radar-based systems. In all, 75 per cent of the aircraft is fabricated from carbon-fibre composites.

Engines
The two-spool EJ200 uses a single-stage turbine driving a three-stage fan and five-stage compressor with annular combustion with vaporizing burners. It can cruise at supersonic speeds without afterburning.

Aerodynamics
The Typhoon employs a deliberately unstable aerodynamic configuration that delivers superior manoeuvrability at subsonic speeds as well as efficient supersonic capability.

Eurofighter Typhoon

the two-seat DA.4 in the UK, DA.3 and DA.7 in Italy and DA.6 (another two-seater) in Spain.

The first production deliveries of the Typhoon took place in 2003. Eurofighters are being built in three Tranches, or batches. Tranche 1 comprised 148 aircraft: 33 for Germany, 28 for Italy, 19 for Spain and 53 for the UK, plus 15 for Austria, which received some aircraft diverted from Germany. Tranche 2 provided a further 299 aircraft, comprising 79 for Germany, 47 for Italy, 34 for Spain and 67 for the UK, plus 72 for Saudi Arabia (the latter included 24 aircraft diverted from the UK).

Amid reduced defence expenditure and changing requirements, the partner nations split the final Tranche 3

DA.2, serial ZH588, was the first British prototype, and is seen armed with AIM-9L Sidewinder missiles. The aircraft was first flown at Warton in April 1994 and is now at the RAF Museum.

into two parts, 3A and 3B. Tranche 3A comprises 30 aircraft for Germany, 21 for Italy, 21 for Spain and 40 for the UK. Tranche 3B has meanwhile been put on hold. While the Tranches cover production contracts,

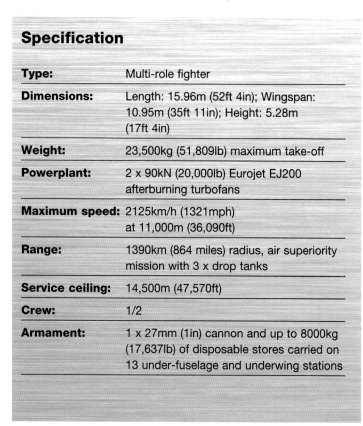

Specification

Type:	Multi-role fighter
Dimensions:	Length: 15.96m (52ft 4in); Wingspan: 10.95m (35ft 11in); Height: 5.28m (17ft 4in)
Weight:	23,500kg (51,809lb) maximum take-off
Powerplant:	2 x 90kN (20,000lb) Eurojet EJ200 afterburning turbofans
Maximum speed:	2125km/h (1321mph) at 11,000m (36,090ft)
Range:	1390km (864 miles) radius, air superiority mission with 3 x drop tanks
Service ceiling:	14,500m (47,570ft)
Crew:	1/2
Armament:	1 x 27mm (1in) cannon and up to 8000kg (17,637lb) of disposable stores carried on 13 under-fuselage and underwing stations

The twin 'chin' engine intakes have a hinged lower lip ('varicowl') to ensure good performance at all speeds and angles of attack. An ogival splitter plate removes boundary layer airflow and feeds the engines with clean, fast-moving air.

additional capabilities are being fielded through Phase Enhancements and Drop programmes.

Drop 1 for the Tranche 1 added human-machine interface improvements, the Link 16 MIDS (Multifunctional Information Distribution System) and Litening targeting pod enhancements. Drop 1 was put to use by the RAF during the Typhoon's combat debut in Operation Ellamy over Libya in 2011. Drop 2 improves situational awareness in the air-to-air role, and enhances the Defensive Aids Sub-System (DASS). Drop 3 brings improvements to the MIDS, DASS and radar.

The Tranche 2 aircraft are the first with a full multi-role capability, although the first remained air-to-air-capable only. Air-to-ground capabilities are being added under the Phase 1 Enhancement (P1E).

Going Multi-role

P1E integrates the Litening III targeting pod, and Paveway IV or GBU-48 Enhanced Paveway II guided bombs. In its ultimate form, P1E adds a full 'swing-role' capability, allowing the Typhoon to undertake air-to-air and air-to-ground roles simultaneously.

The next phase of enhancements will be included under P2E, while will include integration of the Storm Shadow conventional cruise missile, a Brimstone-type anti-armour missile capability, the Meteor beyond visual range air-to-air missile and the CAPTOR E-Scan radar with an active electronically scanned array.

The Tranche 3 aircraft, which began to be delivered in early 2014, are configured from the outset for the E-Scan radar; they also come with provision for the installation of conformal fuel tanks.

As of 2014, the Typhoon is in service with three Tactical Air Wings and one Tactical Flying Group the German Luftwaffe, serving at Neuburg, Laage, Nörvenich and Wittmund. In Italy, Typhoons fly in the air defence role with three wings at Grosseto, Gioia del Collo and Trapani. Spain's Typhoons are also used only for air defence and serve within two wings at Morón and Albacete. In the UK, the RAF Typhoon fleet comprises four squadrons at Coningsby, three squadrons at Lossiemouth and one flight in the Falkland Islands. Austrian Typhoons serve with the Surveillance Wing at Zeltweg. Saudi Arabia, which procued its aircraft under Project Salam, is currently equipping three squadrons at Taif.

CAPTOR Radar

As initially delivered, the Typhoon is equipped with the Captor-M mechanically scanned radar as its primary sensor. A multi-mode unit, this provides an excellent field of regard for a radar of its type. For air-to-air missions, the Captor searches for targets in Range While Search (RWS), Velocity Search (VS) and multiple-target Track While Scan (TWS) modes. Lock-Follow Modes are tailored for long-range tracking and short-range tracking for use in visual identification or gun attacks. Finally, Air Combat Acquisition Modes provide the pilot with a choice of boresight, vertical scan HUD field of view or slaved acquisition. In future, the Typhoon will introduce the Captor-E with an active electronically scanned array (AESA). This will provide a field of regard that is approximately 50 per cent wider than traditional fixed-plate systems.

Lockheed Martin F-35 Lightning II (2006)

The F-35 is a remarkable and ambitious combat programme that combines stealth, sensor fusion and network-enabled operations in a single airframe. It is built in three variants to replace four front-line types with the U.S. Air Force, Navy and Marine Corps, plus a variety of fighters for at least 10 other countries.

An F-35B in the markings of the U.S. Marine Corps. In late 2012 Marine Fighter Attack Squadron (VMFA) 121 'Green Knights' at Marine Corps Air Station Yuma, Arizona, became the first operational Lightning II unit anywhere in the world.

Helmet Sight
Real-time imagery is streamed to the helmet, allowing pilots to 'look through' the aircraft. Pilots thus can see the entire environment surrounding them. The helmet also provides pilots with night vision using an integrated camera.

Radar
AN/APG-81 AESA radar enables the pilot to engage air and ground targets at long range, while also providing outstanding situational awareness for enhanced survivability.

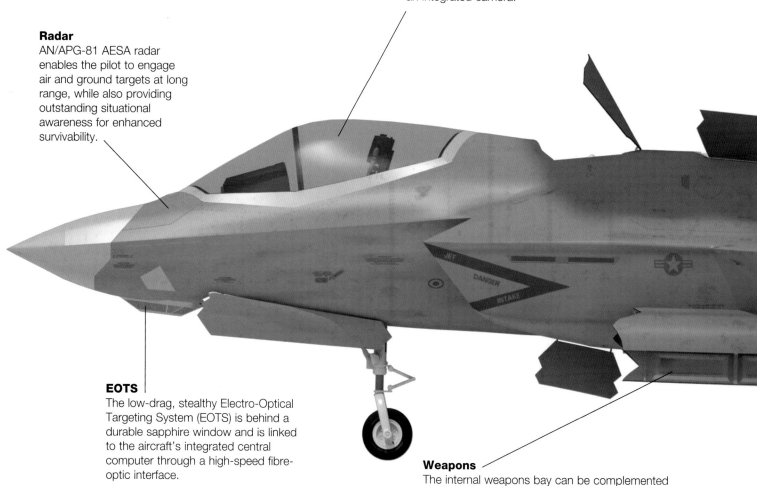

EOTS
The low-drag, stealthy Electro-Optical Targeting System (EOTS) is behind a durable sapphire window and is linked to the aircraft's integrated central computer through a high-speed fibre-optic interface.

Weapons
The internal weapons bay can be complemented by external loads, for example adding four additional JDAMs and two AIM-9X AAMs underwing, complementing two internal JDAMs and two AIM-120s.

Lockheed Martin F-35 Lightning II

Alongside Boeing, Lockheed Martin was selected to participate in the Joint Strike Fighter (JSF) concept demonstration phase in 1997. After prototypes of the Boeing X-32 and Lockheed Martin X-35 had undergone evaluation, the Lockheed Martin design emerged victorious in October 2001. The winning company then joined forces with Northrop Grumman and BAE Systems to begin the production phase.

A first production example of the conventional take-off and landing (CTOL) F-35A was completed at Fort Worth, Texas, in February 2006. Later that year, the F-35 Joint Strike Fighter was named Lightning II. Alongside the F-35A for the U.S. Air Force and most of the foreign operators, Lockheed Martin is building the F-35B short take-off/ vertical landing (STOVL) variant for the U.S. Marine Corps, the UK and Italy, and the F-35C carrier variant (CV) for the U.S. Navy.

DAS
The Distributed Aperture System (DAS) is the only 360-degree, spherical situational awareness system, sending high-resolution real-time imagery to the pilot's helmet from six infra-red cameras mounted around the airframe.

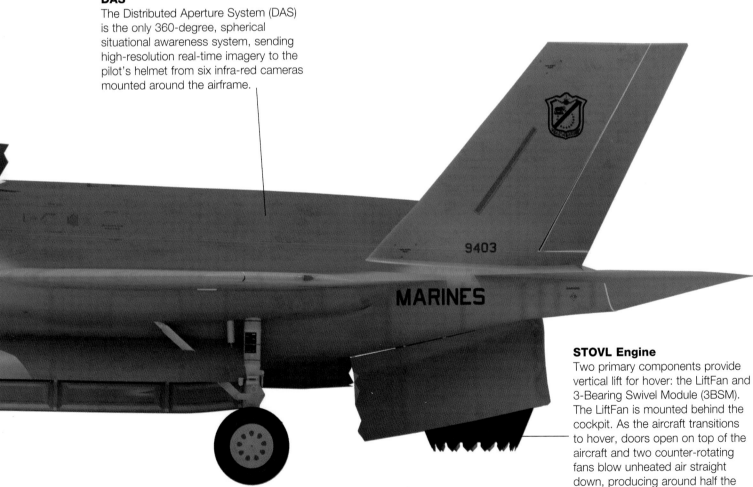

STOVL Engine
Two primary components provide vertical lift for hover: the LiftFan and 3-Bearing Swivel Module (3BSM). The LiftFan is mounted behind the cockpit. As the aircraft transitions to hover, doors open on top of the aircraft and two counter-rotating fans blow unheated air straight down, producing around half the downward thrust needed. The majority of the remaining vertical thrust is provided by the 3BSM at the rear of the aircraft.

Lockheed Martin F-35 Lightning II

Compared to the Harrier, STOVL operations in the F-35B are much simplified for the pilot. Converting from conventional flight to STOVL mode is no more complicated than pushing a button.

The F-35A is the only version to carry an internal cannon – the 25mm (0.98in) GAU-22/A – and will be the most prolific model, replacing the A-10 and F-16 with the USAF and serving with the majority of allied air forces to fly the Lightning II.

The F-35B, which is replacing the AV-8B and F/A-18 with the USMC, is capable of STOVL operation thanks to its shaft-driven Rolls-Royce LiftFan propulsion system and an engine that can swivel 90 degrees when in short take-off/vertical landing mode. The F-35B has a smaller internal weapon bay and reduced internal fuel capacity compared to the F-35A. It is also equipped for the probe and drogue method of aerial refuelling.

The F-35C will replace the 'legacy' F/A-18 with the U.S. Navy and features larger wings and strengthened undercarriage in order to cope with catapult launches and arrested landings. The CV model has folding wingtips and the greatest internal fuel capacity of the three F-35 variants, carrying nearly 9072kg (20,000lb) of internal fuel for longer range. The F-35C also uses probe and drogue refuelling.

At the heart of the Lightning II's capabilities are the various mission systems that include electronic sensors, displays and communications systems that collect and

Specification (F-35A)

Type:	CTOL air dominance and strike fighter
Dimensions:	Length: 15.7m (51ft 5in); Wingspan: 10.7m (35ft 0in); Height: 4.38m (14ft 5in)
Weight:	Around 31,750kg (70,000lb) maximum take-off
Powerplant:	1 x 178kN (40,000lb) Pratt & Whitney F135-PW-100 afterburning turbofan
Maximum speed:	Around 1931km/h (1200mph) with full internal weapons load
Range:	2200km (1367 miles), internal fuel
Service ceiling:	Undisclosed
Crew:	1
Armament:	1 x 25mm (0.98in) rotary cannon, 2 x AIM-120C AAMs, 2 x 907kg (2000lb) GBU-31 JDAMs

share data with the pilot and other friendly aircraft. Individual components include the AN/APG-81 active electronically scanned array (AESA) radar, the AN/AAQ-37 Distributed Aperture System (DAS) providing 360-degree situational awareness, the Electro-Optical Targeting System (EOTS) that combines forward-looking infra-red (FLIR) and infra-red search and track (IRST) functions, the Helmet-Mounted Display System and the Communications, Navigation and Identification (CNI) system. Data from all these sensors are brought together under the sensor fusion concept, providing the pilot with a single integrated picture of the battlefield. Information can also be shared with other pilots and other assets using datalinks, such as the Multifunction Advanced Data Link (MADL).

Low observable, or stealth, features of the F-35 include the integrated airframe design, use of advanced materials, sophisticated countermeasures and provision of an on-board electronic attack capabilities. As well as the F-35's external shape, weapons can be carried internally and mission systems sensors are carefully embedded around the airframe.

The AN/APG-81 is designed to be capable of stand-off jamming for other aircraft – with a claimed 10-times increase in effective radiated power over previous fighters – and the F-35 is expected to use its stealth and survivability to operate in closer proximity to a threat from where it can provide powerful 'stand-in' jamming.

Into Service

In December 2006, the F-35 completed its first flight. In the years that followed, Lockheed Martin completed flight and ground test articles of all three variants. The first production F-35 completed its maiden flight in February 2011 and deliveries began the same year.

The first of a planned 1763 F-35As for the USAF was accepted at Edwards Air Force Base, California, in May 2011. In January 2012 the first two examples of the F-35B variant was delivered to the U.S. Marine Corps' Marine Fighter/Attack Training Squadron (VMFAT) 501 at Eglin Air Force Base, Florida. In total, the USMC plans to acquire 340 F-35Bs and 80 F-35Cs. A first international Lightning II delivery occurred in July 2012, with the initial recipient being the United Kingdom. The F-35B was flown to Eglin AFB for operational test and evaluation, as well as training. The first of a planned 480 F-35Cs was delivered to the U.S. Navy's Strike Fighter Squadron (VFA) 101 at Eglin in June 2013.

Joint Effort

The F-35 makes its initial flight on 15 December 2006 over Fort Worth. The F-35 is in development by the United States and eight other countries: Australia, Canada, Denmark, Italy, the Netherlands, Norway, Turkey and the United Kingdom. Suppliers in all partner countries are producing

F-35 components for all aircraft, not just those for their country. In addition, Israel, Japan and South Korea have selected the F-35A through the Foreign Military Sales (FMS) process. Companies in FMS customer countries compete for industrial participation opportunities of the F-35 program. Of the F-35 partner countries, the UK was the first to receive an aircraft in July 2012, followed by the Netherlands, which took the first of two test aircraft in July 2013 to mark the first F-35A international delivery. A first Australian F-35A arrived at Luke Air Force Base, Arizona, in December 2014, where it will be used for pilot training within the USAF's 56th Fighter Wing.

Index

Page numbers in *italics* refer to illustration captions.

Index

Index